PRISON ON TRIAL

PRISON ON TRIAL

A Critical Assessment

Thomas Mathiesen

SAGE Publications
London · Newbury Park · New Delhi

First published 1990   Reprinted 1992, 1994

 SAGE Publications Ltd
28 Banner Street
London EC1Y 8QE

SAGE Publications Inc
2111 West Hillcrest Drive
Newbury Park, California 91320

SAGE Publications India Pvt Ltd
32, M–Block Market
Greater Kailash – I
New Delhi 110 048

British Library Cataloguing in Publication data
Mathiesen, Thomas
    Prison on trial: a critical assessment
    1. Imprisonment.
    I. Title. II. (Kan fengsel forsuares) – English
    365.

ISBN 0–8039–8224–0
        0–8039–8225–9 Pbk

Library of Congress catalog card number 90–060966

Typeset by The Word Shop, Rossendale, Lancashire

Printed in Great Britain by
Redwood Books, Trowbridge, Wiltshire

Contents

To *Sindre* and *Snorre* – for a better future

Preface

The 1980s have seen a spectacular growth in prison populations in Western Europe and North America. With the exception of a few countries, prison figures have been continuously climbing, and new prisons have continuously been opened to meet the increasing number of prisoners. Entering the 1990s several countries, notably Great Britain and the United States, have witnessed a new and much more central emphasis placed on the prison as a mode of punishment in society.

This development raises more forcefully than ever the question of the defensibility of prison. Does prison in fact have a defence as a major type of punishment and sanction in modern society?

This is the core issue of this book. Throughout penological, sociological and criminological literature, a great deal of evidence exists which illuminates this question. The evidence, however, is scattered and constitutes the semi-secrets of professional researchers in the area. In this book, I try to collect the evidence from a wide range of sources, thus taking stock of the prison as a mode of punishment.

The book is a revised and updated edition of a Norwegian version (Mathiesen, 1987, published by Pax Publishers in Oslo). It has also appeared in Swedish, Danish and German, and will be appearing in Finnish and Italian.

I wish to express my sincere gratitude to members and participants in the Norwegian prison organization KROM – Norwegian Association for Penal Reform, for continuous stimulation and support during the preparation of the Norwegian as well as the English version of the book.

A special thanks goes to Dr Russell Dobash of Stirling University for his great interest and support during the critical initial phase of preparing the English version.

Thomas Mathiesen
Oslo

1

Prison: Does it have a Defence?

The Prison: A System in Growth

'The phenomenon has European dimensions.' Thus wrote Michel Foucault, in 1961, about the sudden and rapid growth of the new institutions of confinement in the 1600s, institutions which brought tens of thousands of people behind walls within a few decades. In his book on the topic, he called the major chapter on the growth of the new institutions 'The great confinement' (Foucault, 1967, Ch. 6).

That title, 'The great confinement', could well be used about the European prison situation of our own time, the late 1900s. And though precise comparisons of numbers and proportions cannot be made, it could be said too that the phenomenon, in the late 1900s, has 'European dimensions'.

In our own time, as in the 1600s, the large, central Western European countries take the lead in a spectacular growth in prison populations. Add to this North America, and the scene of our own time is more complete.

Figure 1.1 shows the increase in prison populations between 1970 and 1985 for four selected large Western countries – the United States, England and Wales, West Germany and Italy. The United States takes the lead, with an increase from about 180 prisoners per 100,000 population in 1970 to a little under 320 in 1985, an increase of about 106 percent over fifteen years. This includes federal, state and local prisons. For the state prisons alone, the increase was even more marked – 156 percent (based on Rutherford, 1986: 49). England and Wales shows an increase from under 80 to close to 100 per 100,000. The figures for England and Wales are all the more serious because figures went *down* during the early 1970s, to a low of a little over 70 in 1974. We shall return to this temporary trend in a moment. Suffice it here to say that it means a major growth in English/Welsh prison populations over a few years. Italy shows an increase from a little over 40 to over 70 per 100,000 during the period. This is close to a doubling of the prison population over a period of fifteen years. Though Italy has shown a decrease after the period (see below), the only country among these four which shows

Figure 1.1   *Average number of prisoners per 100,000 inhabitants for the United States, England/Wales, West Germany and Italy 1970–85*

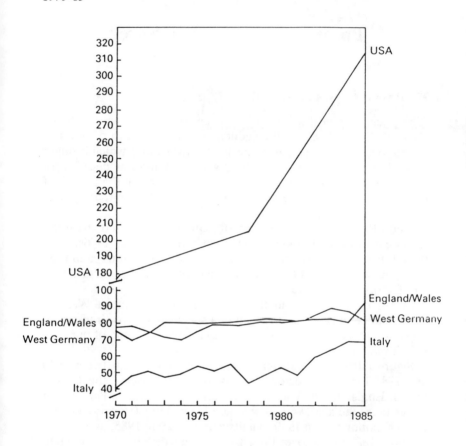

Source for the United States: Rutherford, 1986: 49. Figures only for 1970, 1978 and 1985. The figures comprise federal, state and local prisons. For figures only comprising federal and state prisons, see Austin and Krisberg, 1985: 18.

Source for England/Wales: for 1970–84: *Prison Statistics England and Wales* (1977 and 1984), London: HMSO. For 1985: Sim, 1986: 41.

Source for West Germany: for 1970–84: 'Strafvollzug 1984', Rechtsflege Fachserie 10, Statistisches Bundesamt Wiesbaden. For 1985: information from Statistisches Bundesamt Wiesbaden.

Source for Italy: for 1970–82: *The Prisons in Italy: History, Development, Perspectives* (1985), Ministero di Grazia e Guistizia; Ufficio Studi, Ricerche e Documentazione. For 1983–85: information from Ufficio Studi, Ricerche e Documentazione.

a reversal of the trend during the period is West Germany, with a marked increase up to 1983, but an interesting and major drop after that year.

Why the drop in West Germany? The process started with remand prisoners in 1982, was followed by juvenile prisoners in 1983 and adult sentenced prisoners in 1985 (Feest, 1988). The shift cannot be explained by the unemployment rate (which has increased dramatically rather than decreased). It can only be explained marginally by demographic factors (there are currently smaller birth cohorts, but any major effect of cohort size could only have reached adult criminal courts in 1988 at the earliest). The crime rate cannot explain anything (it has increased, or, for imprisonable offences, only decreased slightly). There have been no major changes in legislation (Feest, 1988: 4–6). The reduction, Feest says, is therefore attributable to changes in the practice of prosecuting authorities and/or judges. He emphasizes the prosecutors in particular, and speculates about whether the long tradition of academic critique of remand, a growing number of ambulatory alternatives with an educative function in relation to prosecutors, and the movement against prison construction channelled through the Greens, may be important background factors explaining increasing restraint on their part. Now, these background factors are partly present in other countries as well. Could their particular activation in the German context follow from Germany's dark political experience in the fairly recent past, an experience not shared (or not to the same extent) by other countries, which warns seriously against an unlimited growth of the use of physical power on the part of the state? We do not know, but sentencing practice at least seems to be a factor, partly keeping figures in check.

But West Germany is the deviant case for the period concerned, not only compared to the other three countries in Figure 1.1, but compared to other large European states. Furthermore, the pressure on the prison systems has also been great in smaller European contries, such as Sweden, Denmark and Norway. Prison administrators have been greatly concerned with the overload in Scandinavian prisons. In Norway, the pressure has not led to a significant increase in the prison population, but to a very sizeable waiting list: you now have to 'queue up' to serve your sentence. The country has about 2000 prisoners at any one time, and – in 1985 – about 6500 on the waiting list. The waiting list increased by 49 percent between 1981 and 1985. Of course, there are priorities in the queue: drug offenders and violent offenders do not have to wait. Yet the list does not include only minor criminals. Thus, in late 1985, about 52 percent of the queue consisted of people who had *not* been convicted for drunken driving (at the time, driving with an alcohol concentration of 0.05 percent automatically implied three weeks or more in prison). Finland is the only Nordic country with a steady decline in its (high) prison figures during the period.

For Western Europe, a condensed general picture of the development can be given. For the member states of the Council of Europe, the prison figures for 1 February 1986 have been calculated with a basis of 100 on 1 February 1983 (Council of Europe, 1986: 27). Only four states showed a decrease from the base of 100 in 1983: Austria to 95, West Germany to 91, Malta to 89 and Sweden to 85. The decline in Sweden was temporary, caused by a change in release practice in 1983 (see pp. 84–6). For all other states where information was provided, a greater or smaller increase could be seen: Belgium to 119, Cyprus to 110, Denmark to 109, France to 122, Greece to 109, Ireland to 145, Iceland to 106, Italy to 120, Luxembourg to 116, the Netherlands to 124, Norway to 103, Portugal to 183, Spain to 104, England/Wales to 105 and Scotland to 108. Altogether, this amounts to fifteen member states. It should be mentioned that three of these, Belgium, Cyprus and Greece, showed a provisional peak in 1984, with a subsequent decline to 1986. However, the main overall tendency is very clear.

Above, we have brought the figures up to 1985 or early 1986. We should note that the overall tendency has continued in the latter part of the 1980s. In absolute numbers, West Germany, Italy, Turkey, Portugal and Malta showed a decrease between 1985 and (approximately) 1987. Denmark and Norway were fairly constant (for Norway, however, note the large queue mentioned earlier). But England and Wales, France, Spain, Belgium, Sweden, Greece, Ireland, Luxemburg and Cyprus showed an increase. Only three states showed a stable decrease from the early part of the 1980s to 1987: West Germany, Turkey and Malta (Council of Europe, 1987: 19–20). The total growth in absolute numbers for member states in the Council of Europe, excluding Austria, Iceland, the Netherlands, Switzerland and Turkey, between 1971 and 1986 is shown in Figure 1.2 (the necessary data for Austria, Iceland, the Netherlands and Switzerland are not available; Turkey is omitted due to special features of the Turkish situation). The overall development for Western Europe has also continued beyond 1986/87: between 1 February 1987 and 1 February 1988, a clear majority of eleven out of nineteen countries within the Council of Europe showed an increase in their prison populations: Iceland (with 13.3 percent), Italy (8.4 percent), Cyprus (8.3 percent), Sweden (7.8 percent), Spain (7.2 percent), Greece (6.1 percent), Luxembourg (5.8 percent), France (4.1 percent), Ireland (3.2 percent), Federal

Republic of Germany (3.1 percent; in contrast to its long-term decline), and the United Kingdom (2.3 percent). In three states, figures were relatively stable: Belgium (0.6 percent), Denmark (−0.2 percent), and Portugal (−1.7 percent). Five countries saw a drop: Turkey (−2.5 percent), the Netherlands (−4.0 percent), Norway (−6.0 percent; note again, however, the large queue), Austria (−6.4 percent) and Malta (−25.3 percent; Council of Europe, 1988: 18). Though it should be noted that detailed comparisons between countries are a hazardous business due to differences in registration practices, the general tendency is clear. For the United States it may be added that by 1989, the state of California had reached 570 prisoners per 100,000 inhabitants (and 255 on death row; information provided at IV International Conference on Penal Abolition, Kazimierz Dolny (Warsaw), May 1989).

Figure 1.2   *Changes in prisoner numbers in Council of Europe member states since 1970 excluding Austria, Iceland, the Netherlands, Switzerland and Turkey*

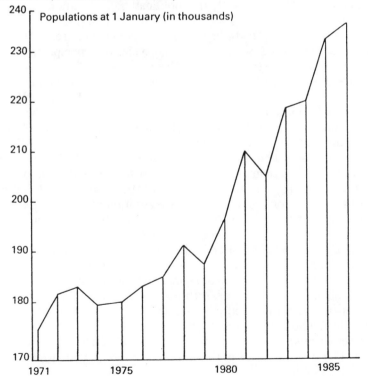

Source: Prison Information Bulletin, Council of Europe, No. 9, June 1987: 18.

The growth becomes all the more significant if it is viewed in a somewhat broader context. Four features should be kept in mind.

First, the growth implies that conscious efforts, made in several Western countries during the 1970s and the early part of the 1980s, to change the course of development of the respective prison systems, were quickly and easily overcome by other forces. The mid-1970s saw a decline and to some extent a reversal of the growth tendency in prison figures. For example, a decline could be seen in several states in the United States, in England and in Sweden. At the same time, conscious efforts were made to channel convicted individuals into alternative measures, and in several countries – such as Sweden and Norway – the political administration in the area of criminal policy was distinctly liberal, with ministers of justice having liberal convictions or inclinations. The early 1980s saw attempts, in Sweden and Denmark, to halt prison increase by, inter alia, changes in release practices and in maximum sentences (for more details, see pp. 84–6 and Chapter 6 below). These efforts and tendencies were rather quickly superseded by later developments in Sweden and Norway, with the political 'fall' of liberal cabinet ministers.

Secondly, if the growth of the prison systems between 1970 and the latter part of the 1980s is seen in a broader time perspective, two major trends appear. Together, the two trends form a general picture. On the one hand, in some countries the growth dates from before 1970. This, for example, is the case for England/Wales, where an important increase took place before 1970, and where the prison population per 100,000 population was about 32 in the 1930s, as opposed to a little less than 80 in 1970 and 96 in 1985. In England/Wales, then, the growth is a part of a long-term trend. On the other hand, in some countries the growth superseded major falls in prison figures before 1970. This is the case for Italy, West Germany and Norway. In Italy, new legislation concerning pardoning was introduced in 1970, bringing prison figures down to the lowest number since records have been kept (1860). In West Germany, the number of short prison sentences was significantly reduced prior to 1970, also bringing prison figures significantly down. In Norway, public drunkenness was decriminalized in 1970, resulting in the release of a large number of alcoholic vagrants, who had spent years in forced labour camps within the prison system, again bringing overall prison figures down. The subsequent increases in prison figures mean that with the possible exception of West Germany, reforms of this kind were more than neutralized by later developments.

One reservation should be made: however overcome by later

developments, some of the reforms, prior to 1970 as well as later, did contain interesting evidence in terms of finer details pointing to the possibility of change in prison policy and figures. We shall return to some of this evidence in the final chapter (Chapter 6).

But as an overall conclusion, it may be said that the present growth has either been part of a long-term trend, or been of such strength that even major reforms prior to 1970 have been cancelled out as far as effect goes.

Thirdly, in several countries the growth has led to appalling prison conditions. The doubling of prison figures in Italy between 1970 and 1985 meant extensive overcrowding. The growth in England/Wales and France, as well as several of the smaller European countries, has brought about the same result. For the United States, conservative and reputable *Time* magazine had this to say about prison conditions as early as 1983 (5 December):

> This spectacular increase has created appalling living conditions for many inmates, who are sleeping in gymnasiums, day rooms, corridors, tents, trailers and other forms of makeshift housing. Until early November, 170 prisoners were sleeping on the floor of a gymnasium at Illinois' Centralia Correctional Center. And Maryland, with one of the country's most grossly crowded systems, is bunking prisoners in basements, recreational areas, temporary buildings and 'anywhere they'll fit', according to an official.

Fourthly, the growth in prison figures has – in varying degrees in many countries – been followed by major building programmes in the prison systems concerned. The building programme in the United States became a public issue in the early 1980s, when, to quote the same cautious source, *Time* informed its readers (5 December 1983) about 'A growing crisis behind bars', and about the fact that 'New prisons cannot be built quickly enough to accommodate all of the new inmates . . . The construction bill alone is enormous: about $4.7 billion in prison and jail construction is planned across the country over the coming decade, including $1.2 billion for 16,500 new cells in California and $700 million for 8,800 in New York'. The sums, in other words, are extremely large. An important development in the United States is the advent of private prisons. The market mechanism, with an emphasis on profit, is currently in the process of penetrating a prison system under pressure. In England/Wales the autumn of 1985 saw the planning of sixteen new prisons, with total costs of about £500 million (1983 value). Twelve thousand new prison places were planned (Sim, 1986: 42). The programme has been characterized as the 'biggest-ever jail-building programme' in England (*The Evening Standard*, 23 November 1983: 5). For the smaller European countries, the building programmes are more modest. But they are usually there, with prison construction for example in Sweden, Norway and Holland.

The growth of the Western prison systems, and the four features mentioned here which expand on the growth, add up to a conclusion. In terms of statistical developments, living conditions, and construction programmes, there are significant differences between Western prison systems – as there are in terms of size, with a range from 45–60 inmates per 100,000 in Holland and the Scandinavian countries through 100 per 100,000 in England/Wales to far more than 300 in the United States. Despite these differences, which should be given their due emphasis, a change appears to be taking place as far as the role of the prison goes: the importance of the prison, as a sanctioning mechanism, seems to be increasing. With some exceptions, the phenomenon seems to be general throughout the West. In some countries, notably the United States and Great Britain, the increase is staggering.

The growth of the prison systems raises a new question: why the growth?

Why the Growth?

The question is complex. It is not easy to give an unequivocal answer. But some explanations may be ruled out, at least as major explanations, and others given credibility. Three possibilities will be briefly reviewed.

The first is that the increase follows from an increased crime rate, notably an increase in registered crime. With the courts as an intervening mechanism, the registered crime rate is presumably automatically reflected in higher prison figures. There are several problems with this explanation. Two may be singled out.

For one thing, we have solid empirical examples showing that the registered crime rate may go up while the prison rate goes down, and vice versa. West Germany today partly provides an example of the former possibility (see p. 3). The 1970s provide a good example of the latter: in many countries – notably in Scandinavia – the crime rate showed a rapid increase during that decade, while prison figures were falling or at least constant.

For another, the crime rate is not unequivocally increasing at present. In the United States, the national crime rate was dropping in the early 1980s, while prison figures were soaring (Moerings, 1986).

An automatic reflection of the general crime rate in prison figures, if it had occurred, could have been interpreted as a consequence of political decisions: it would have implied that the countries concerned simply followed the same criminal policies as earlier. Put differently, even such an automatic reflection would have been a result of political decision making – an often overlooked fact. However, since an automatic reflection hardly exists, even more clearly political interpretations are near at hand.

A second possibility is that a change has been occurring in the pattern of criminalization. New behaviour patterns may have been drawn into the criminal policy orbit and criminalized, or criminalized more harshly. This seems to have happened in several European countries as far as drug offences go. Increased criminalization and harsher legislation/sentencing practice in relation to drug offences has apparently been of great importance in countries like Holland (de Haan, 1986) and Norway (Falck, 1987). For example, Norway recently (1982) changed its classification of drug *use* from misdemeanour to felony (*forseelse* to *forbrytelse*), thus increasing the degree of criminalization. Within a few years, the maximum penalty for drug-related offences in Norway has increased from ten through fifteen to twenty-one years of imprisonment (see also pp. 117–18), a fact which has influenced sentencing practice in a major way. Of course, drug-related offences as such, reflected in the registered crime rate, have also increased. But without the increase in criminalization, and without the above-mentioned spectacular increase in maximum sentences (which is all the more spectacular in view of Scandinavia's relatively low punishment level), the significant increase in the number of long-term drug offenders in prison would certainly not have occurred to the same extent. And that number clogs up the system, and is in a major way responsible for the Norwegian queue.

A third possibility, which does not exclude the second one, is that a general increase in the punishment level has occurred across several, or some, offence types. There is evidence to suggest that this has happened in several countries, partly through legislation, partly through sentencing practice, partly through both. It seems to have happened for example in the United States. Mandatory sentencing legislation, stipulating that offenders convicted of certain crimes, or of a succession of crimes, must go to prison, is part of the pattern. For example, the prison explosion in the state of New York may partly be viewed as a result of a 1978 law requiring judges to imprison all violent-felony offenders. At the same time, minimum prison sentences have been significantly increased in many states. In Norway, the number of long-term unconditional prison sentences, which for that country means one year or more, has increased significantly from 1981 on, as opposed to the shorter sentences, which have stagnated (Bødal, 1984; with supplementary data in Mathiesen, 1987: 36). The number of drug-related offences with long sentences may partly, but probably not wholly, account for this. There seems to be a general tendency, also in Norway, towards a higher punishment level for several offences over and above the drug-related ones.

Of the three explanations given so far, the first – the automatic reflection theory – has been more or less ruled out, whereas the second and the third – new criminalization patterns and a generalized increase in punishment level – have been given credence. As already suggested, different countries probably vary in terms of the latter two explanations. On this level of analysis, it may therefore be said that there is no one 'cause' behind the institutional growth pattern. But on a more generalized level, the two explanations have something in common: whether through new criminalization patterns and/or more or less across-the-board stiffer legislation/sentencing practice, the implication is that a tougher criminal policy, with more active use of prison as a response to criminality, is behind the growth. In one form or another, then, a more severe criminal policy, with more relentless use of prison, seems to be an underlying pattern in a wide range of Western countries.

A New Stage in the Use of Prison?

In several countries the institutional growth pattern is so marked that one wonders whether we are entering a new stage in the use of prison.

When asking this question, we should note immediately that the prediction of institutional development is a hazardous business. The history of institutions is full of examples of predictions that proved to be false. One example is the development of prisons in Norway in the 1800s. As a consequence of the change from corporal punishment to prison towards the end of the 1700s, prison figures showed a spectacular increase during the first part of the 1800s. Responsible authorities, predicting continued increase, were greatly worried, and during the 1840s an extensive building programme was launched. But after the mid-1840s, figures again declined significantly, and continued to do so until 1900. From then on, figures were fairly stable for many decades, in fact during most of this century.

As we shall shortly see, however, the concept of 'stages', and the possibility that we are entering a new stage of penal development, may usefully be introduced without implying that prison figures will continue to rise more or less indefinitely. Irrespective of the difficulties of prediction, a new stage of development in a sociological sense may be hypothesized.

The prior development of Western penal institutions, and the growth of such institutions, may be viewed in terms of two major stages.

The first stage was the 1600s, which we have referred to already. Numerous works have been published on this particular period of institutional history (among them Rusche and Kirchheimer, 1939; Cole, 1939; Sellin, 1944; Foucault, 1967; Wilson, 1969; Olaussen, 1976; Mathiesen, 1977). This was the stage of the first rise of the institutional 'solution' to social problems. Those incarcerated were not just criminals, but a broad range of unemployed beggars and vagrants. And institutionalization did not supplant physical punishment, but was apparently added to it. In the wake of Rusche and Kirchheimer's classic work, which emphasized the importance of variations in the labour market as a causative factor, a great debate has followed concerning the causation of the rise of institutions during the 1600s. We need not enter the debate in detail here; it is well known, and readers not familiar with it are referred to the works mentioned above. For our purposes, two points may briefly be singled out.

First, the institutions which saw such a rapid and spectacular growth in the late 1500s and during the 1600s – so-called hospitals in France, *zuchthäusern* in Germany, *tuichthuisen* in Holland, correctional houses in England, and *tukthus* in the Norwegian periphery 100 years later – were to a large extent *forced labour institutions*. Labour, selected on the basis of market considerations and performed as profitably as possible, constituted a major core of institutional life – knitting in France (Cole, 1939), the rasping of wood in Holland (Sellin, 1944), and so on.

Secondly, however, the emphasis on profitable labour did not necessarily constitute the 'cause' of the rise of institutions. The study of social 'causation' presupposes knowledge of the relevant actors' subjective motivation or definition of the situation. That motivation or subjective experience may be formed by a context of factors, but is in itself a necessary condition for grasping the 'why?' question when it comes to dramatic political changes such as the introduction of institutions on a grand scale throughout a continent. Although there were variations, substantial historical material (summarized in Mathiesen, 1977) suggests that what primarily motivated the French, the British, and even the Dutch mercantilist state builders of the 1600s was the deeply troublesome issue of the vagrants in European cities and towns. After the breakdown of the feudal social order based on disposition over land, Europe in the 1500s and 1600s was overpopulated by large numbers of people – beggars and vagrants in general – a drift in society (for attempts to give figures, see Wilson, 1969: 125; Cole, 1939: 264, 270). The vagrants constituted a deeply disturbing and disruptive element to mercantilist production and trade. The control of the vagrants therefore became an immediate political problem. The numbers were far too large for old-fashioned penal methods alone to be effective, and mass rounding up and subsequent incarceration on a large scale became the solution. Once institutionalized, it is not surprising that the beggars and vagrants were put to work, and to as profitable work as possible. This was entirely in line with mercantilist economic philosophy.

In short, then, the first stage of institutional development had the disciplining of new and highly disturbing groups of people as its motivational background.

The second stage of development occurred during the late 1700s and early 1800s. Again, the phenomenon had European dimensions. This was the time of the differentiation of the criminals, and their placement in actual prisons in the modern sense. And this was the time when the institutional 'solution' actually supplanted physical punishment. Much has been written about the institutions of the 1800s (Rusche and Kirchheimer, 1939, Ch. 8; Foucault, 1977; Melossi and Pavarini, 1981). In terms of ideological content, godly penitence, in the context of radical isolation, was central, at least in Europe. A number of new penitentiaries were built for the purpose. What was the motivational background of this development? The question is clearly complex, but the following hypothesis may be ventured.

By this time, the large European countries were entering a new mode of production, the truly capitalistic mode. A formally free working class was now in the making. But it was an impoverished, destitute working class. Crime was in a very real sense rooted in material poverty. The violent physical penal methods of earlier times could in theory have been used against the crimes of the new class. But physical punishment could not sensibly be related to the new type of discipline – 'the assembly line discipline' – which was now being developed in the economy, and which was demanded in production. It seemed senseless to use spectacular and arbitrary mutilations when people were to be adapted to the pedantic and detailed types of disciplined work now necessary in production. On this motivational background, the new truly disciplinary prisons – the penitentiaries so well described by Foucault – rose as a main method of bringing the impoverished criminals of the new working class in line. Thus, the second stage of institutional development also had the disciplining of new groups – the deviants of the working class in the making – as a main motivational background.

With this as a background, we may return to our original question: are we today entering a third stage of institutional development? Three major developmental points suggest that we are.

First, the major long-term increase in prison populations. Similar increases characterized the two prior stages. As already pointed out, the present increase may level off or even decline at some later date, due to new historical conditions. But as we have illustrated, so in fact did the increases during the 1600s and the 1800s. The concept of 'stage' as used here does not imply that incarceration reaches a new and higher plateau than earlier stages, although this has been suggested as a possibility for some countries (for the United States, see Austin and Krisberg, 1985). The concept of 'stage' only implies that a dramatic and long-term increase takes place.

Secondly, the greatly increased significance of the institutional solution as a component in criminal policy is important. Today that increased significance is reflected in the sizeable or enormous building programmes in a number of countries, and the general expansion of the prison systems in question. Similar increased significance of institutions, including large scale building programmes, characterized the 1600s and the 1800s. Then as now, the institutional solution moved to become a much more centrally located factor in the sanctioning system.

Thirdly, a presumption on the part of responsible authorities is present to the effect that there is an increased need for the disciplining of important population segments and groups. This is reflected in the significantly increased reliance on stiffer legislation involving prison and/or longer prison sentences, partly for new groups such as drug offenders, partly on a more general level. As we have suggested, a presumed increased need for discipline was probably an important motivating factor also in the 1600s and the 1800s. As far as the late 1900s go, we may now briefly expand on this latter point.

As a point of departure, legislators and the courts may be viewed as 'anxiety barometers', that is, institutions which, through their decisions, reflect the anxiety level in society. (The term 'anxiety barometer' is taken from Box and Hale, 1982, 1985, but used independently here.)

Our times are full of disquieting signs. Some of these are close to us and therefore observable, such as, in many Western countries, political protests, conflicts between immigrants and other parts of the population, and stagnation or even dissolution of social services and support systems which a few years ago were thought to be utterly solid. Other worrying signs are reflected through the mass media: for example, increased violence (despite that fact that violent crimes have only increased slowly, and despite the fact that the large majority of them are of the least serious kind), increased drug use (despite the fact that drug use – at least in the Norwegian setting – has stagnated, and despite the fact that heavy use is limited to a few; see Hauge, 1982; Christie and Bruun, 1985), and so on. With their tendency to focus on personified drama, the mass media have a significant magnifying effect on the realities involved in these issues. Together, the actual conflicts and the media-enlarged problems produce a 'legitimacy crisis', that is, minor or major breakdowns in people's confidence in general in the state's attempts at problem solution and people-oriented activity. I would say that 'below' the legitimacy crisis we find the economic crisis: the late capitalistic economic stagnation, in several countries with persistent and extremely high unemployment towards the end of the 1900s. But in people's minds, the crisis appears *as a question of confidence in the state's problem solution in a wide sense.*

There are probably great variations in the extent of the legitimacy crisis in various Western countries. The crisis seems to be widespread and deeply felt in the British context (Hall et al., 1978). It is probably less widespread and not so acute in a society like the Norwegian, with greater confidence in public solutions common to everyone. But the question of confidence is certainly present there too.

The legitimacy crisis is reflected in the decision-making process in legislative bodies and the courts. More precisely, in both of these institutions the legitimacy crisis is perceived *as a new and increased need for discipline in given segments and groups in the population.* Put differently, when the confidence in public and authoritative organs begins to fail, the failure appears, from the point of view of the legislators and the courts, as an increased need for discipline. The definition of the situation on the part of legislators and the courts constitutes a connecting link between external and influential factors such as actual conflicts and media-created problems on the one hand and the growth of the prison system on the other. When legislators and judges experience the situation this way, that experience becomes consequential for penal practice and development (Box and Hale, 1982).

In the preceding discussion, we have viewed the development of the penal system in a sociological context. But the galloping development of the prison solution most certainly also represents a question of values. The question of values is this: do we wish to have this galloping development? Do we want a society which is becoming increasingly reliant on the use of prison as a major method of conflict resolution? The question of values is acutely important.

First, it is important to the increasing number of people – in England one out of a thousand of the population, in the United States between three and four out of a thousand – who are in prison at any one time, and who are subject to isolation, rejection, deprivation and meaninglessness.

Secondly, it is important to the political climate and life of the society. The growth of the prison solution implies a significant change of traditional methods of control. It implies that sheer physical repression is increasingly used in relation to significant parts of the population.

Thirdly, the question of values is important in a wider cultural sense. The use of physical force through prison signals that violence is an adequate method of conflict resolution in society. A significant increase in the use of physical force will strengthen that signal, thus having wide-ranging effects on our norms and on our understanding of our fellow human beings.

This book is written in an attempt to take the question of values seriously. It is written in an attempt to contribute to the levelling off and reversal of the major contemporary trend. It is written in an attempt to contribute to the shrinking – perhaps abolition – of the prison solution.

As I have indicated, the developmental sequence in terms of growth and possible stages may usefully be viewed with a background in broad economic and social forces: the breakdown of the feudal social order towards the 1500s and 1600s, the new mode of production before and during the 1800s, an economically motivated, increasing legitimacy crisis during the late 1900s. These forces create conflicts and issues perceived and treated as issues of discipline. But the implication is not that institutional development is pre-determined, inescapable, and not subject to change through concerted and persistent political action.

My contribution is a modest one: it consists of a collection of arguments. In the chapters that follow, I shall discuss in some considerable detail the usual arguments for the prison solution, used by those advocating that solution. I will confront these arguments with a wide range of empirical evidence and theory, and for each argument I will raise the following question: *Does prison have a defence on these grounds?*

When discussing the various arguments in favour of prison, and when confronting them with theory and evidence, I will not be particularly original. I will rely on my own research, but certainly also heavily on the work of others. So far, however, much of the discussion of these issues has been scattered throughout criminological and sociological literature. Because they are scattered, the various parts of the discussion have little or no bearing on policy, and remain the semi-secrets of criminological and sociological specialists. I see my task as that of bringing the scattered discussion together, thus in a collected and systematic fashion *taking stock* of the prison as a mode of punishment in our society.

When delivering this contribution, and when thus taking stock, I am making an assumption. The assumption is that communicative rationality – where 'rationality' is taken to mean sensible and convincing argumentation rather than efficient methods to reach ends – may have a political effect, and is still a political possibility, in societies like ours.

Certainly, much of sociology and criminology goes against such an assumption. Most significantly, much of what we know about the communication systems of modern society goes against it. Political decision making in our society is very far indeed from anything like a 'seminar'.

Yet I make the assumption, believing that it most certainly should not be left unmade and untried. Added to this, on my part, comes a strong belief in political practice related to argumentation.

Perhaps my belief in communicative rationality in the area of penal policy stems from the fact that I personally live and work in a very small society on the periphery of Europe – where arguments still have a chance. If arguments do have a better chance in such a society than in the large Western countries, perhaps the latter countries may learn something from the former through a book like this.

The Purpose of Punishment and the Organization of the Book

Through the ages, a series of different arguments have been used in support of prison. To a significant degree, the arguments are general in the sense that they are largely not limited only to the prison, but employed in connection with overall state-administered punishment. To a large extent, the arguments have been linked to assertions about the purposes of punishment.

The assertions about punishment and prison may be said to constitute the rationalized, ideologically draped formulations of the alleged new and increased need for discipline discussed earlier. In this book, we will take the assertions about the purposes of punishment seriously, and confront them systematically with empirical evidence and well-grounded theory.

In classical penal theory, the purposes of punishment have usually been divided into two major groups: social defence and retribution. According to the theories of *social defence*, punishment has no value in and of itself. It only has value as a means to protect society against crime. In terms of further refinements, the theories of social defence may vary considerably, but they have protection against crime as a common goal. Because punishment, in this perspective, only has a value in relation to the goal of social defence, the theories are also called 'relative' penal theories.

The penal theories of social defence are usually divided into two main subgroups: the theories of individual and general prevention. By 'individual prevention' we mean the prevention of new criminal acts on the part of the individual who is in fact punished. By 'general prevention' we mean the prevention of criminal acts on the part of individuals not yet punished, or at least not undergoing punishment at the moment. Individual prevention is supposed to be obtained through improvement, deterrence, or incapacitation of the offender. We shall return to these concepts later. General prevention is supposed to be obtained by the deterrent, educative, or habit-forming effect of punishment on others.

According to the theories of *retribution*, 'the purpose of punishment is first of all to fulfil the demands of justice' (Andenæs, 1974: 72, translated from the Norwegian by the present author). Efficacy in terms of prevention is second in importance. As Andenæs goes on to say (1974: 72): 'This has received its most classical expression with *Kant*. According to him, justice must be maintained for its own sake, because "if justice succumbs, the existence of man on earth no longer has any value".' A consistent theory of retribution provides an answer to the question of which acts should be made punishable, as well as to the question of how severe the punishment should be for justice to be satisfied. Because punishment seen in this perspective presumably has a value of its own, the theories of retribution are also called 'absolute' penal theories.

Like the theories of social defence, the theories of retribution are usually divided into two subgroups. On the one hand, proportionality between crime and punishment may be established 'between the external harm incurred and the punishment in question' (Andenæs, 1974: 73). Here the principle of 'an eye for an eye, a tooth for a tooth', the law of talion, reigns. On the other hand, moral guilt rather than the external and often randomly inflicted harm may be the issue. 'In that case, punishment may be seen as a reflection of a more comprehensive moral principle, saying that we should all meet the fate we deserve' (Andenæs, 1974: 73). Here the principle saying that 'as man sows, so shall he reap', the principle of culpability, reigns.

As stated, in this book we will take these basic assertions about the purposes of punishment as our point of departure. Because the book concentrates on the prison, we will speak particularly about prison as punishment. But to some extent it will be necessary also to discuss the assertions about purposes as they relate to punishment in general.

As already suggested, one of the two subgroups of *social defence* takes its point of departure in individual prevention: the question of preventing new criminal acts on the part of the individual who is in fact punished. In turn, individual prevention is supposedly attained through improvement, deterrence or incapacitation. In Chapter 2 we shall take a close look at the first aspect of individual prevention, improvement of the offender. We shall use the word 'rehabilitation' to cover the supposed process. 'Resocialization' is often used more or less as a synonym. We shall discuss historical as well as contemporary material throwing light on the question of whether prison rehabilitates.

After having discussed improvement or rehabilitation as a major type of individual prevention, it might in a way have made sense to go on to a discussion of individual deterrence and incapacitation, thus concluding the discussion of individual prevention. However, we will not follow this sequence. The theory of individual prevention through rehabilitation was severely criticized, and more or less put out of action, during the decades following World War II. As rehabilitation waned, the theories of social defence focusing on general prevention gained strength. Therefore, in Chapter 3 we shall discuss the theories of general prevention. The theories of general prevention – focusing on deterrence, moral education, or habit formation of others – presuppose that the message of punishment is communicated to the larger society. Therefore, we will, inter alia, view general prevention in the light of some aspects of modern communications theory. But other issues related to general prevention will also be discussed.

In Chapter 4 we will return to individual prevention, completing that discussion by a review of issues and literature related to incapacitation and deterrence. As the theories of general prevention have been exposed to debate and criticism, these aspects of individual prevention have been more heavily emphasized. We shall look at empirical studies and related theoretical discussions throwing light on incapacitation through prison, and corresponding studies and information important to the issue of the deterrent effect of prison on those incarcerated.

Chapter 4 on individual incapacitation and deterrence closes the discussion of imprisonment as social defence. In Chapter 5 we shall discuss the theories emphasizing prison as *just retribution*. A series of concrete issues will be reviewed, such as the issue of how the prison sentence is subjectively experienced by those exposed to it.

With Chapters 2 to 5, then, we will have reviewed the major assertions about the purposes of punishment, with particular emphasis on the use of prison. In connection with all of the major assertions, we ask: are the assertions vindicated? Does prison in fact have a defence on these grounds? To anticipate, very largely, the answer is in the negative. The prison is a fiasco, and does not find a defence in the celebrated purposes espoused in penal theory.

Chapter 6 concludes the book with a discussion of what is to be done with the failed prison system.

2
Rehabilitation

The Origin of the Word

The word 'rehabilitation' is frequently used in the context of prisons. Time in prison is supposed to rehabilitate, we say. It may be useful to look briefly at the origin of the word.

'Rehabilitation' is a combined French and Latin word, coming from the French *re*, which means 'return' or 'repetition', and the Latin *habilis*, which means 'competent'. Originally, the word thus denoted 'return to competence'. Today the word denotes in a broad sense the process of bringing something back to functioning order. If we look it up in a dictionary, we find varying shades of meaning such as restoration, reinstatement to former dignity or privilege, reparation of honour. We know these shades of meaning from everyday language. Old houses are rehabilitated in the sense of being restored to their old and venerable form. Living political people are rehabilitated in the sense of being reinstated to their previous dignity or privilege. And if the political person is dead, which is the more usual situation, he or she may be rehabilitated in the sense of being returned to a previous honourable state.

What about the prisoner? The shades of meaning mentioned are also relevant to him or her. The prisoner is to be restored to his or her old form, notably the form before the crime. The prisoner is to be reinstated to his or her old dignity and privileges, before the 'fall'. And the prisoner is supposed to have his or her honour returned.

But there are two significant differences between rehabilitation of houses, living political people and dead political figures, on the one hand, and the prisoners on the other. In the first place: the house is rehabilitated in the sense that damage, wear and tear which the house has been exposed to over time, and for which the house can hardly be held responsible, are repaired and brought back to their original state. The political figure is rehabilitated in the sense that a political or social disparagement for which the political figure was originally held responsible is considered politically or socially invalid and struck from the record. Prisoners, however, are not rehabilitated in the sense that an externally caused damage is later repaired or a disparagement generated by the prisoners themselves is later considered incorrect. Rather, they are rehabilitated in the sense that a damage or a disparagement is overcome while they throughout, even after 'rehabilitation' has taken place, are held fully responsible for having caused a valid and legitimate damage and/or disparagement. This difference, which is fundamental, implies that we actually do not take seriously our ideology emphasizing that crime is conditioned or at least partly conditioned by a context of complex social forces impinging on the individual. Rather, what we take seriously, and what makes the 'return to competence' of the prisoner something very special and very different from that of physical objects, political figures, and so on, is our competing ideology emphasizing that the individual alone is personally responsible for his or her deviance in a way which is never neutralized.

Secondly, the rehabilitation of houses and living and dead politicians takes place through an act of will on the part of responsible authorities. Through a set of actions or a decision, the authorities in question simply carry out the rehabilitation. Prisoners, on the other hand, are not rehabilitated through an act of will, a set of actions or a decision, on the part of some authority. To be sure, if the prisoner returns to what we consider acceptable social life, we are quick to attribute this to a system or a programme established by the authorities. But as a primary point (perhaps especially if return to acceptable social life does not occur), the prisoners themselves are held responsible for the outcome. We conceive of rehabilitation of prisoners as taking place in a process in which the prisoners themselves have the primary – if not the sole – responsibility for a happy ending.

Thus, prisoners are held doubly responsible: they are responsible for the damage and disparagement to which they have been exposed as well as for the 'return to competence'.

These two differences between the rehabilitation of houses, politicians, or what not, on the one hand, and that of prisoners, on the other, are related. Precisely because the issue, in connection with prisoners, is conceived as a damage and a consequent disparagement for which the prisoners themselves are responsible, it follows that it is not primarily up to the authorities to act or decide in a way which restores, but rather primarily up to the prisoners themselves.

Against this background we understand why the authorities in all known societies systematically refrain from establishing a system at release with sufficient resources for social restoration, or with an apparatus symbolizing the restoration of the prisoner's dignity, rights and honour.

It could have been otherwise. The allocation of major resources to be used for social restoration is conceivable. And it would have been possible to combine release with major rituals officially symbolizing to the prisoner and those around him or her that now the time in prison is up, the disparagement is cancelled, dignity and honour is restored. But we only, or almost only, allocate resources to the prisons, and to the building of more of them. And we only have rituals at the entry to the prison, rituals which officially and with pomp and circumstance impose the disparagement and take away dignity and honour.

The Origin of the Ideology

We have looked a little at the origin of the word. The notion of rehabilitation, of bringing the prisoner back to 'competence', may be said to constitute an ideology. Very briefly, by 'ideology' I mean a unified belief system which lends meaning and legitimacy to one's activity. Ideologies are only in varying degrees followed in practice. To the extent that an ideology is not followed in practice, it masks reality: it gives one's activity meaning and legitimacy without actually being carried out as stated.

The ideology of rehabilitation in prison, the ideology which understands the activity in prison as being oriented towards the prisoner's 'return to competence', is as old as the prison itself. With the introduction of the prison, time became the core element: people were placed in prison for given periods of time. And time could presumably be used for rehabilitative purposes.

Let us look in a little more detail at the origin of the ideology as far as prisons go. We find the ideology clearly formulated during the first phase of the history of penal institutions, in the 1600s, before the time of the proper or modern prison (see Chapter 1). Michel Foucault formulates it this way in connection with the French institutions: the French '*Hôpital* does not have the appearance of a mere refuge for those whom age, infirmity, or sickness keep from working; it will have not only the aspect of a forced labor camp, but also that of a moral institution responsible for punishing, for correcting a certain moral "abeyance" which . . . cannot be corrected by the severity of penance alone' (Foucault, 1967: 59). This gave the *Hôpital* a particular moral status. This moral charge invested the directors of the *Hôpital Général* with wide discretionary powers and means of repression, among them 'stakes, irons, prisons, and dungeons' (from the Regulations of *Hôpital Général*, quoted in Foucault, 1967: 59) – methods which, to be sure, are remote from what we today associate with rehabilitation. But nonetheless it was a question of rehabilitation, of 'return to competence' – 'correcting a certain moral "abeyance"'. Labour was apparently seen in this light, though it was certainly also a method of production and income: ' . . . it is in this context that the obligation to work assumes its meaning as both ethical exercise and moral guarantee. . . . The prisoner who could and would work would be released, not so much because he was again useful to society, but because he had again subscribed to the greater ethical pact of human existence' (Foucault, 1967: 59–60).

In particular, the rehabilitation ideology seems to have been given expression in connection with the treatment of youth. In the *Hopital Général* in Paris, a youth section was established by a decree in 1684 – for boys and girls under 25. The decree emphasized that work was to occupy the greater part of the day accompanied by 'the reading of pious books' (quoted in Foucault, 1967: 60). The details in the decree quoted by Foucault clearly show that the work as well as the reading was justified in terms of moral reform. A similar ideology existed in the house of correction in Amsterdam. A state document of 1602, six years after the house had been established, noted that the house received 'young people who had got on the wrong path and are headed for the gallows, so that they can be saved therefrom and kept at honest labor and a trade in the fear of God' (quoted in Sellin, 1944: 41).

The rehabilitation ideology also existed on the periphery of Europe, in countries such as Norway. The prison history of Norway began 100 years later than that of continental Europe, with the construction of four correctional houses (*tukthus*) between 1735 and 1790. In an extremely detailed study of the development of the correctional houses and the so-called slaveries in the northern parts, the historian Kjeld Bugge shows that in contrast to the slaveries at the fortresses, the correctional houses were conceived as 'educational institutions'. This purpose was mentioned in the founding document as well as in various ordinances. As today, this commendable purpose made it possible to develop a euphemistic terminology: the correctional houses were 'benevolent foundations' and the prisoners were 'paupers'. Bugge describes the purpose of the institutions as follows:

> . . . The paupers were to be educated, so that they could be released after a definite or indefinite period of time, and after release be able to support themselves and lease a farm or a house. Men and boys were to be taught a trade and to be supplied with a trade certificate. Women and girls were to be taught spinning, weaving and knitting and the art of running a house, so that they either could be employed in the service of 'decent people' or get married. If married they were even supposed to be

supplied with a dowry. (Bugge, 1969: 127, translated from the Norwegian by the present author)

The author regrets to note, however, that he has not found any example of the paupers being supplied with any dowry.

Perhaps also Norwegian authorities were particularly concerned with young people. It was said about a boy who had been given a six-month sentence in 1756 for having taken to the mountain summer farms 'in order to have his lascivious passions satisfied with the women folk there', that the punishment was a warning 'to young boys who make such ungodly and lecherous running to the summer farms into a kind of trade'. In 1777 the Inspectorate General stated that when youthful and first offenders were sentenced, it was done 'in the hope to bring them to a better way of life in the spirit of discipline and awe' (all quotes from original documents, quoted in Bugge, 1969: 127–8).

In short, though the content of the old house of incarceration in the 1600s to a large extent was forced labour (see Chapter 1), a rehabilitation ideology was built into it. This ideology could grow because the penal sanction now involved the element of time.

Let us look a little more closely at the content of the rehabilitation ideology.

The Content of the Ideology

An historical perspective gives insight also as far as the more precise content goes. It is useful to compare the early development of the ideology with its content today.

In order to do this, I have chosen to look more closely at the early correctional house in Amsterdam. There are several reasons why I chose this particular correctional house. In the first place, it was a very early house, established as early as 1596, prior to the major developments in the 1600s. Secondly, it was in many ways a model for later institutions in Europe. Thirdly, the literature on this particular house is especially rich, and cogently summarized by the American criminologist Thorsten Sellin in a careful study (Sellin, 1944). I therefore concentrate on the correctional house in Amsterdam, but inject comparative remarks concerning today's prisons. By way of conclusion, I shall evaluate in more general terms the development from the 1600s till today.

Two main points will run through the presentation, and surface towards the end of this section of the chapter. First, the main components of the rehabilitation ideology have changed very little between the 1600s and today. To a large extent the rehabilitation ideas are the same today as they were at the time when the prison was invented. Secondly, to the extent that rehabilitation has in fact been attempted, it has to an overwhelming degree not functioned according to plan. In practice rehabilitation, the 'return to competence', has not taken place.

In the following and concluding section of this chapter, I shall try to explain why the main ideological components have been so constant, and why rehabilitation has not followed in practice.

The main components of the rehabilitation ideology in the early Amsterdam house, easily recognized from the ideology of our own times, may be summarized under four broad headings: work, school, moral influence and discipline.

Work

The Amsterdam correctional house was not among the largest European institutions. The cells, originally nine, but later numbering eight, served as workrooms as well as bedrooms. They had plank or mortar floors, each room was entered from the courtyard through heavy doors, the beds had a mattress, a bolster of coarse linen filled with straw, and a feather pillow (Sellin, 1944: 35). In other words, the material standard was high. There were several prisoners to a bed, but this was hardly unusual in the lower classes of Amsterdam at the time.

One entered the house through two doorways, separated by a small yard. The ornamentation of the doorways was symbolic of the work taking place in the house. The first doorway was decorated with a bas-relief showing a man driving teams of lions and tigers, pulling a wagon filled with logs. The man supposedly represented the warden, and the logs symbolized a chief industry in the house. The second doorway was decorated by figures of two half-naked prisoners at work rasping logwood. There was also a medallion in bas-relief depicting a weaver at his loom (Sellin, 1944: 31–3). But the raspers were the more significant: the main industry of the house over time became that of rasping certain types of logwood from Brazil, the rasped wood being used for dyeing purposes. The house was granted a monopoly of the rasping industry, which was heavy work carried out by couples of prisoners with many-bladed saws.

A detailed *ideology of work* followed the construction and development of the house. The purpose of the house should be 'not sore punishment, but the improvement (*beteringe*) and correction of those who do not realize its usefulness to them and would try to avoid it'. The quote is taken from a memorandum on the founding of the house, *Bedenking op de grondvesten vant tuichthuis*, written by one Jan Laurenszoon Spiegel, an influential citizen of Amsterdam (quoted in Sellin, 1944: 27). Spiegel wrote his strongly rehabilitation-oriented memorandum in 1589. More than twenty years before, in 1567, a prison reformer by the name of Dirck Volckertzoon Cornhert had written an essay on the repression of vagrancy, entitled *Boeventucht, ofte middelen tot mindering der schadelycke ledighgangers*, 'The correction of rascals, on the means to reduce the injurious vagrants'. Cornhert's early essay had a strong economic orientation: he forcefully criticized the handling of the vagrants, and emphasized, as alternatives, work in the galleys, in public work projects, and in houses of correction. Since unskilled slaves from Spain were worth between 100 and 200 guilders, the Dutch vagrants, who often had a trade, were more worth alive than dead. They should be put to work if they had committed a crime, this would be to the profit of the country. But Jan Spiegel's memorandum from 1589, more closely linked to the concrete planning of the house, had a milder tone. It emphasized that the treatment should aim to make the prisoners 'healthy, temperate eaters, used to labor, desirous of holding a good job, capable of standing on their own feet, and God-fearing' (Sellin, 1944: 27). Among the most important means to reach this goal was a differentiated work programme. Spiegel 'envisioned an institution with highly diversified industries. He specifically mentioned shoemaking and the manufacture of pocketbooks, gloves, and bags; the making of textiles, such as edgings for collars, cloaks, etc, weaving of fustians and worsteds, linen cloth and tapestry, knitting, etc. He also listed woodwork, cane or reed work, and the making of bone objects. The manufacture of barrels, chairs, lanterns, and wheels was included, as well as cabinetwork, wood carving, stone cutting or carving, carpentry, sawing wood, locksmith(!) and blacksmith work, glass blowing and basketry' (Sellin, 1944: 28). The variety of occupations was supposed to reflect the main industries of the city. Only the most obstinate were to be placed at rasping wood.

This is not the last time in the history of prisons that the idea of a diversified work programme has been launched with great pride and emphasis. In 1956 the Norwegian Prison Reform Commission, which prepared the Norwegian Prison Act of 1958, had the following to say about work:

> Maximum effort should be made to make the work programme of the institution resemble work conditions on the outside, and work should take place under conditions and in surroundings which stimulate work habits and work interests . . . As mentioned already, when choosing type of work for the inmate, his wishes and interests as well as his abilities and skills must be taken into consideration. When deciding work placement,

one must also take into account the individual's particular possibilities to find a job after release . . . For young inmates, and for inmates with long sentences, a more or less systematic work training programme should be carried out as far as possible . . . In addition to the various crafts, mechanized industrial work [should be introduced]. (Komitéen, 1956: 91–2, translated from the Norwegian by the present author)

What, then, happened to Spiegel's proposed diversified work programme in the late 1500s? The idea was enthusiastically received (Sellin, 1944: 29), but never developed to any significant extent (Sellin, 1944: 59). The rasping of wood, originally planned as a method of punishment, became the main industry. Why? Because it was profitable, and because the institution was meant to be self-supporting. In addition, the number of inmates was probably too small and the trade knowledge of the personnel too limited (Sellin, 1944: 59). But the basic importance of profitability may be inferred from the fact that first weaving was tried, but later supplanted by rasping because this activity survived both war and economic competition (Sellin, 1944: 53).

What was kept of Spiegel's programme was an actual wage system. Advanced for its time. But then most of it was a book-keeping transaction, because the inmates were charged the basic wage 'for cost and maintenance' (Sellin, 1944: 58).

The proud ideas of the Norwegian Prison Reform Commission from 1956 have met a similar fate. The work programme of the prisons does not 'resemble work conditions on the outside'. In some modern Norwegian prisons mechanized industry has been introduced, though the question of whether industrial work of this kind suits the composition of the prison population has never been appraised. In many prisons, especially the old ones, the work which is offered is to a large extent meaningless (placing advertisement material in envelopes, folding tobacco packets), or simply non-existent. Fifteen percent of the prisoners are without any employment. There is no wage system, only a system of small allowances.

What remains is that by regulation, prisoners have a duty to work.

School

However, the work programme was not the only component in the rehabilitation ideology of the Amsterdam rasphouse. An *ideology of schooling* was important as an addition to the ideology of work.

Many of the inmates were young, and a school was opened from the beginning, offering instruction in reading and writing. It met daily in winter 'from the time it begins to grow dark' until 7 p.m., including Sundays, and also on Sundays from six to eight in the morning (quotes from Sellin, 1944: 61). The chapel was also the school room, and at the outset a schoolmaster was used for the purpose. A main reason for the instruction was probably that illiteracy prevented the prisoners from being properly catechized (Sellin, 1944: 62).

It is not the last time schooling has been attempted in prison. In 1971 the director of the Norwegian youth prison, which existed at the time, reported on 'the comprehensive educational programme which is being carried out with the assistance of impressive support from the Educational Office of Oslo. A silent pedagogical revolution is presently taking place in the Oslo institution, a programme which has been planned for a long time . . .' (Bødal, 1971; translated from the Norwegian by the present author). At a meeting a little later that year, the then Director of Prisons characterized the co-operation with the educational authorities by saying that 'A new page has been turned!' He overlooked the fact that the page had been turned before, in the early 1600s. During the 1970s and 1980s, educational activity has been introduced in Norwegian prisons. In 1970/71 the school system had a capacity of twenty pupils (with at least 20 hours of education per week). By 1983/84 this capacity had been increased to 453, a little over 20 percent of the total prison population (Langelid, 1986). Put differently, the system lacked such a capacity for close to 80 percent of the population.

What about the implementation of the programmes? In an historical account written in 1663, the Dutch historian Olfert Dapper reports that in the Amsterdam *tuichthuis* the textbooks used included 'the most important and edifying epistles of the Apostles, the proverbs of Solomon, and similar books' (quoted in Sellin, 1944: 62). The books had been printed especially for the correctional house. In principle, schooling of this kind was in accordance with conscientious labour. But conflicts could of course arise between considerations of security and schooling. In such conflicts, schooling lost out. After a time, the practice of using the preacher and schoolmaster as teacher was discontinued, and the work supervisor took his place. And even he appeared to be in trouble when performing his educational tasks: in 1663 Olfert Dapper found that the instruction no longer included any of the raspers, 'since it would be a dangerous matter for the work supervisor to be alone with a mass of such lawless and furious people. These are given for their edification the books to read in their cellrooms, and if they cannot read, to have them read aloud by someone else' (quoted in Sellin, 1944: 62). Towards the end of the 1600s, the school disappeared completely. Sellin suggests that this may have been related to the improvement of the religious education in the community and a removal of young prisoners to other institutions. Yet, illiteracy in the institution must still have been very high, and judging from statements like that of Dapper, the conflict with security considerations was most likely an important contributing factor.

It is not the last time that schooling has lost out in the struggle with prison security. In 1981, the two Norwegian educational researchers Skaalvik and Stenby (see also Langelid, 1986) documented that when there is conflict between the interests of the prison and those of the school, the pedagogical considerations lose out:

> The school has recently made its entry in an established institution. As could be expected, this has taken place on the terms of the established institution. Some of these terms cannot be set aside as long as we are dealing with a prison. Other terms are established without being necessary routines and traditions. Partly, routines and traditions in the prison contribute to preventing the inmates from participating in the school programme. Partly, they impede the implementation of the programme. We have repeatedly found illustrations of pedagogical interests losing out when they have come in conflict with the interests of the prison. (Skaalvik and Stenby, 1981: 380, translated from the Norwegian by the present author)

This is especially serious in view of the fact that interested prisoners regularly experience education as something positive, perhaps the only positive aspect of prison life. In a detailed study of education in prison, the Norwegian researcher Langelid states that the following problem areas are emphasized by teachers. The transfer of prisoners between prisons can take place irrespective of the prisoner's school programme, the transfer from one cell block to another in the prison may imply that the programme is discontinued, disciplinary measures may imply that the prisoner is taken out of the programme for a longer or shorter time, activities outside the prison walls which are a part of the programme are difficult or impossible to implement, planning is made difficult due, among other things, to long periods in pre-trial detention, cramped and partly unsuitable school rooms may impede the programme, and many teachers find co-operation with the prison difficult.

In short, prison security has priority, security 'comes first' (Langelid, 1986: 7). Today as almost 400 years ago.

Moral influence

In addition to a work programme and, as long as it lasted, a school programme, the rehabilitation ideology of old Amsterdam contained a third component: an ideology of *moral influence*. The time in the correctional house was to supply a moral rearmament. In old

Amsterdam, this was especially to take place through religious activity. The *tuichthuis* was at times also called *godshuis*: 'Certainly', Sellin comments, 'every effort was made to give a strong religious cast to the discipline in order to make the prisoners God-fearing people' (Sellin, 1944: 63). The prisoners had to say prayers morning and evening, and before and after each meal. A sermon was preached on Sundays and other religious holidays, in addition to an afternoon service on such days as well. According to Dapper, writing in 1663, at the service the work supervisor 'reads, speaks to, [and] catechizes these youths, and hymns are sung just as in public Calvinistic churches' (quoted in Sellin, 1944: 63). Thus, the activities of the work supervisor were comprehensive. It is interesting to note, however, that the raspers, who after a while comprised the main bulk of the prison population, were excluded from the sermons and services (Sellin, 1944: 63), as they were from the school periods (see above). They were, as we quoted earlier, 'a mass of such lawless and furious people'. Even if it cannot be read directly from these sources, we do get the impression that the programme of moral influence, like the diversified work programme and the school programme, at least partly lost out in a conflict with more basic interests, especially the prison interest in security.

Nor are the attempts at moral influence only history. During the budget debate in the Norwegian Parliament in 1970, the main speaker on the topic of prisons stated: 'Finally . . . I wish to express my satisfaction with the fact that a final appropriation for building a church at Ullersmo Central Prison is in the package . . .' Church services are regarded as important in the 1980s too. But today the notion of moral influence probably has a somewhat different and more general basis: the idea is that prisoners are in a general and diffuse way supposed to be favourably 'influenced' as far as morality goes. In the 1960s and 1970s that favourable moral influence was to take place through 'treatment'.

Discipline
The rehabilitation ideology of the old correctional house thus comprised notions of diversified labour, comprehensive schooling, and moral influence. On all three points, the realities turned out to differ from the ideals. However, a fourth component in the ideology was the notion of *discipline*, and in contrast to the former three components, it seems as if the latter component to a large extent and for a long time was implemented in actual practice. Whether its implementation was actually followed by rehabilitation, a 'return to competence', is another matter.

Life in the *tuichthuis* was filled with order and obedience. In the

Leiden archives a document has been found which contains a proposal for a set of rules for the house. The proposed rules were given a distinctly rehabilitational goal: the author had designed them in order that the inmates 'as they now come to be discharged may never depart from the road of virtue on which they have been directed' (quoted in Sellin, 1944: 64). According to Sellin (1944: 64), the document was submitted to various authorities who in turn handed them to a certain Dr Sebastian Egbertszoon, who on 21 November 1595 submitted a 'Plan of the manner and form of the discipline in the House of Correction' (*Ontwerp vande wyse ende forme des tuchts in den tuchthuyse*). Dr Sebastian's plan was also couched in highly rehabilitational terms – he saw the aim of the house to be that of inculcating all 'Christian and social virtues' (quoted in Sellin, 1944: 64). According to him the treatment should consist of teaching the difference between good and evil and attracting the prisoners towards the good. However, Dr Sebastian did not stop with such general guidelines. He gave a detailed list of specific rules, and of penalties to be used for various infractions (Sellin, 1944: 65):

1 Causing quarrels; lying: bread and water, one day.
2 Cursing; using foul language; refusing to learn; giving food or drink to prisoners under punishment: bread and water, three days.
3 Mild insubordination: bread and water, eight days.
4 Attempting fight; malicious destruction of property, such as clothing, furnishing, etc; refusal to work, first offence: bread and water, fourteen days.
5 Fighting, causing injury: bread and water, two months.
6 More serious insubordination, accompanied by bad words: confinement in dungeon, one month, on bread and water.
7 Refusal to work, second offence: whipping and one month's confinement in dungeon on bread and water.
8 Insubordination, with physical violence: whipping, and confinement in dungeon for six months on bread and water.
9 Deceitful attempt to break out and escape: whipping, and six months' confinement in dungeon in chains.
10 Same offence, but accompanied with violence: same penalty as in (9) and the term of imprisonment doubled.
11 Aiding in escapes: same penalty as in (10).
12 Getting out by deceit alone: doubling of term of imprisonment.
13 Refusal to work, third offence: prisoner to be returned to court for punishment.
N.B.: None of the above penalties should excuse the prisoner from labour.

By 1603 specific rules were adopted for the correctional house, apparently greatly influenced by Dr Sebastian's proposal. Here are some examples (Sellin, 1944: 66):

1 If anyone 'abuses the name of God in curses and oaths or speaks or sings immoral or indecent words, or uses thieves' cant, called "Peddlers' French"', he was 'punished'.
2 Books, letters, or ballads could not be read or sung except those prescribed by the regents. Such material had to be turned over to the supervisor–schoolteacher at inspection. The penalty for a violation of this rule was fixed at loss of meat ration for three weeks.
3 Calling anyone improper names, especially the officers, resulted in the loss of half a day's ration the first time.
4 Knives or sharp instruments, fire-lighting equipment, and tobacco could not be in the possession of a prisoner. Smoking was forbidden. Shears used by the weavers had to be left on the loom.
5 Betting, gambling, or trading was prohibited. If objects were involved, the supervisors could confiscate them and keep them for their own benefit, but if money was involved . . . it should be taken and placed in the 'box', i.e., the collection box into which visitors' fees and other contributions were dropped.
6 Weavers were not allowed to leave their looms or run around and make noises in the shop or beg visitors for gifts.
7 Finally, if anyone failed in the performance of his daily task he was punished and in addition had to 'make up' whatever he had failed to complete.

Point 13 of Dr Sebastian's original plan as well as point 7 above indicates that the emphasis on labour was great.

Milder disciplinary measures are mentioned in connection with the above-mentioned final rules. There were of course also harsher methods. For example, refusal to work resulted in being placed in the 'cellar' on bread and water, as Dr Sebastian had suggested. There were also tougher methods against refusal to work. On 13 November 1618, twenty prisoners were whipped for refusing to work. As in our own time, collective prison work strikes were taken seriously. Other very harsh disciplinary methods existed, among them a 'water cellar' in which the obstreperous continually had to pump water in order not to drown.

How does the story of the disciplinary methods of old Amsterdam compare with today's prisons? Today we do not whip people. Bread and water are out as a method, at least in the Scandinavian prisons. There is no 'water cellar'. And curses and oaths are allowed, though there is great concern among the staff in many prisons over the existence of a prison subculture reflected in argot language ('Peddlers' French'?). But despite the differences, there is very considerable similarity between Dr Sebastian's proposal from 1595, with the ensuing regulations of the early 1600s, and rules, regulations, and attempts to discipline in today's prisons. I said we have no 'water cellar'. But we certainly have a cellar – stripped isolation cells in the bottom of the prison – and that cellar is used frequently in prisons throughout Europe and elsewhere in the world. We have detailed rules that escalate disciplinary punishments with what we consider the seriousness of infractions. Much of what Dr Sebastian wrote, and what the rules of 1603 contained, could be subscribed to by present-day prison directors as methods to be used and problems to be controlled, though they would probably employ somewhat different words. Most importantly, however, and irrespective of differences in details, *the fundamental underlying attitude is to a large extent the same.* And then as now, many of the concrete regulations were and are formulated in such general terms that wide discretionary power over inmates is invested in the prison power structure and personnel.

Conclusions about Past and Present

The time has come for drawing some conclusions. Three main points will be emphasized.

The Main Components are Constant

In the above presentation we have crossed almost four centuries, from about 1600 until about 2000. In Chapter 1 we pointed out that important things also took place in the interim, including the whole development of the second large wave of prison building, around 1800.

Nevertheless, there is a basis for saying that the main components in the rehabilitation ideology have been remarkably constant through the centuries. Work, school, morality and discipline have run through the centuries as main pillars of thinking.

To be sure, the relative emphasis on the four components has varied in time and space. During the first part of the 1600s there was, at least in Holland, apparently an emphasis on all four. In the new European Philadelphia prisons in the late 1700s and early 1800s, there was more selective emphasis on moral influence and discipline, whereas the work and school components were weaker. This may at least be said for the Scandinavian countries, though it should be added that in the North American Auburn prisons there was also a strong emphasis on work. In our own time, the emphasis probably lies primarily on discipline and possibly school, whereas work and moral influence are ideologically weakened. The weakening of the work component has at least taken place in the Scandinavian countries: although work met an enthusiastic response in prison planning during the 1950s and 1960s (especially based on a Swedish model, with large industrial prisons), the enthusiasm is now, towards 1990, much more subdued, though work is still considered a 'good thing'. The weakening of the moral influence component is international, and related to the decline of the so-called 'treatment idea' in the 1970s and 1980s. There are two main reasons why the treatment idea, which was the most important concrete formulation of the moral influence component in the 1950s and 1960s, had to abdicate as the main ideological basis for the use of prison. In the first place, in the 1960s and 1970s, a number of theoretical contributions from the social sciences supported the view that imprisonment 'in the name of treatment' actually implied longer incarceration and a lower degree of legal protection than a regular prison sentence. In 'the name of treatment', time in the institution could be made longer as well as indeterminate (for an early Norwegian critique on these grounds, see Christie, 1962). Secondly, and most importantly, during the same period a large number of empirical studies were produced which showed that regardless of type of treatment programme, and even if the programme was very intensive, the results were largely the same and largely poor. Also methodologically very solid studies, with the careful use of control groups, largely showed this depressing lack of difference. We will return to these studies. The theoretical contributions substantiating that attempts to implement the treatment idea in fact made incarceration longer and more uncertain, would hardly alone have influenced political decision makers. But when combined with the studies demonstrating empirically that 'return to competence' in fact did not follow, they became important: the empirical demonstration of lack of success was in direct conflict with notions which the prison system very explicitly relied on, and which it more or less advertised to the wider public. With the fall of the treatment idea, a number of 'special sanctions' grounded on that idea also fell. In Norway, the borstal or youth prison system, as well as a special system of forced labour for alcoholic petty offenders, were abolished during the 1970s. Similar abolitions took place in other countries during the same period. At a time when the idea of rehabilitation through work is also (at least in the Scandinavian countries) shaky, the system finds its main ideological underpinnings in discipline of the traditional kind, to some extent supplemented (again at least in Scandinavia) by an emphasis on the usefulness of spending the otherwise useless time in prison for an upgrading of the prisoners' elementary or even rudimentary education.

But – and this is the main point here – despite such variations, the prison system rarely if ever finds its arguments *outside* the framework of the four components discussed above. The imagination of the system has to a very pronounced degree lived its life within the framework of work, school, moral influence in a wide sense and discipline.

This implies that the rehabilitational imagination has lived its life within a very traditional, *bourgeois*, frame of reference. Diligent work, good schooling, respectable morality, and strong discipline, are components which may be found individually in many contexts, but which together, and as a collective system of thought, constitute an expression of bourgeois ethics. You could also say that taken together, they constitute the very expression of what Max Weber long ago called 'the Protestant ethic', and which also became the ethic of capitalism (Weber, 1948).

It is, of course, only to be expected that the prisons of a society also express the total morality of the ruling classes in that society.

The System Interests Have Superiority
The fact that the relative emphasis on the four components has varied, that the relative weight within the framework or square of components has changed through time, leads us to the next question: is it possible to find some guiding principle explaining these variations and changes?

This question again is complex, but there is an historical basis for saying that the guiding principle has been the system interests: the component, or components, in the rehabilitation ideology which it has been in the prison system's *own* interest to implement, has, or have been, emphasized, irrespective of the question of rehabilitation of the prisoners.

Combined with discipline, a profitable labour programme was central as a system interest in the *tuichthuis* of old Amsterdam, self-supporting as the house was supposed to be. As we have seen above, the profitable labour programme caused a marked perversion of the work component in the rehabilitation ideology: the idea of a diversified work programme was abandoned, and because it was profitable, the rasping of logwood, originally conceived as a method of punishment, became the main content of the programme.

In present-day Norway, the profitability of labour is not such a central system interest of the prisons, even if representatives of the system try to reduce their deficits through prison labour. The maintenance of discipline, however, still looms large as an interest, together with a certain emphasis on being able to show some rehabilitational rationality through a certain amount of education. In conformity with the priority of discipline, schooling – and even more so moral influence in any qualified sense – must give way when there is conflict, and the work component is implemented only to a very limited extent.

The system interests – the component or components which it is at any time in the prison system's own interest to have implemented – are defined, formulated and communicated to the prison *from the outside*. In the 1600s, the principle of profitable labour was defined and formulated through mercantilist economic activities and policies, and communicated from these activities and policies through the public opinion of the time to the prison. This way, the 'test' of the prison in the interested, evaluating and opinion-formulating public sphere of the time became that of being able to live up to the demand of a profitable work programme. The same held for the principle of discipline, which at that time undoubtedly was also defined and formulated in view of the needs of mercantilist activities and policies. This is clearly suggested by the concrete stipulations contained in regulations, etc (see above).

Today's principle of discipline in Norway, combined with a certain emphasis on school and education, also comes from the outside. Despite the fact that the prison system is expanding, in two ways it is also in a crisis. First, an articulated opinion, expressed through the mass media, exists in the outside public sphere emphasizing that the prisons are unable to maintain internal discipline. Also in Norway, there have been a series of prison strikes, sit-down actions, and riots involving material damage. Allegedly, drugs are pouring into the prisons without the prison authorities being able to stop the flood. In the public sphere, such facts and allegations challenge the ability of the system to maintain minimum internal order. Secondly, the prison system has lost the support of the most significant ideological component of our own time, the treatment ideology. Due to this loss, and because education is increasingly emphasized as the road to success in outside society, the school component is to a certain extent added to that of discipline as a method of legitimizing the prison in the public sphere.

Thus, the demands on the prison system are formulated in the public political sphere, and communicated to the prisons. This is the process through which the system interests of the prison are created.

The next question is how the system interests, received from the outside, are maintained as such inside the walls. This question becomes important when competing ideas, suggestions, proposals, and initiatives appear which have a view towards opening the prison system to fresh starts which run counter to prevailing system interests. How are such initiatives handled and strangled on the inside?

Obviously, the system is organized in such a way that initiatives of this kind may be strangled through sheer power and force from above. It is a semi-military system. But internal power and force in relation to lower-level staff also has its inherent and perhaps paradoxical limitations. If extensively used, or used as the only method, it may actually indirectly threaten the stability of system interests: lower level staff may act in ways which increase the vulnerability of the prison system in the outside public sphere. This happened in Norway in 1988, when the security staff of several large prisons went on an illegal strike. They flatly refused to receive any more prisoners until a number of psychotic prisoners, whom the staff felt they could not handle, were transferred to mental hospitals. The 'reception strike', which, among other things, clogged police cells, created a critical situation for the prison system in the outside public sphere, for a time destabilizing greatly its outside legitimacy.

Because sheer power and force may be counterproductive, other, 'softer' methods are important. I wish to call attention to some of these 'softer' forms. They may be called *neutralization techniques*. They are techniques, used by those responsible for maintaining system interests, which neutralize fresh ideas and initiatives. The techniques vary from the more or less open dismissal of ideas which are in conflict with prevailing system interests to techniques which more subtly and unnoticeably delete them from the agenda. The former techniques are closest to sheer power and force. The discussion is based on observations I made during a two-year participant observation study of a Norwegian prison (Mathiesen, 1965a; the study is referred to in more detail below pp. 43–4, 130–1).

Reference to instructions, orders, demands from the outside in general, is the first and simplest of the techniques. When ideas and initiatives which are in conflict with system interests are presented, those responsible for maintaining system interests simply refer to the superior authority invested in demands from the outside. The technique implies first that those in responsible positions view the institution as a dependent link in a larger system which has superior authority. Secondly, it implies that they disclaim responsibility for going against new ideas which might bring fresh thinking into the life and system of the prison.

Defining ideas and initiatives which are in conflict with system interests as *irrelevant* is a more complex technique. It is probably especially used when reference to outside demands no longer appears convincing. In the phase of prison history when ideas of community and group therapy were presented (largely in the 1960s), such ideas were frequently dismissed as irrelevant to superordinate principles of rehabilitation in the prison, which at that time, at least in the Scandinavian countries, to a large extent was mechanized industrial work.

Defining ideas and initiatives as *impossible to implement* is a technique which perhaps above all is generated when the irrelevancy argument and technique becomes ineffective. The latter technique may become ineffective or at least difficult to maintain due to solid argumentation, reference to similar ideas and initiatives elsewhere, strong professional pressures, or combinations of these conditions. The user of the 'impossible-to-implement' technique may refer to general conditions in the prison, lack of resources, and a whole series of other factors making the idea or initiative impossible to carry out. This technique was also used, in Scandinavia in the 1960s, in confrontation with community and group therapy ideas. The ideas were defined as interesting, but simply impossible to practise in the prison.

Postponement of ideas and initiatives in conflict with system interests is a technique by which the implementation of the idea or initiative is postponed 'for the time being', on the grounds that it is not (yet) considered 'fully developed'. Regardless of how well prepared a new idea or initiative is, it can never be foolproof, and it is always possible to point to undeveloped aspects. A new idea is 'new' precisely in the sense that it is not yet tried out and tested in all its details. It can therefore almost always be postponed 'for the time being'; it can politely be put on ice, neutralized as a very good and interesting idea which unfortunately cannot yet be introduced in practice because it is not fully developed, fully matured. The initiator may even be encouraged to go on with the development of the idea, for later presentation, because those using the postponement technique can rest assured that as long as careful testing through actual implementation has not taken place, new undeveloped aspects can always be pointed out.

Puncturing of ideas and initiatives is a technique whereby the practical significance of the new idea is diminished, while a front of understanding, interest, and perhaps even enthusiasm for the idea is maintained. The idea is not rejected, not even postponed, just 'given its proper dimensions'. A protest from a member of the treatment staff is 'fully understood', and given its right place in the protocol. By fully accepting the protest through a formal recording of it and nothing more, the protest is effectively punctured. Puncturing of new ideas takes place all the time in total institutions, including prisons.

Absorption is the sixth and final technique to be mentioned here. Absorption implies that an idea or initiative which conflicts with system interests is not even punctured, but in fact picked up. It is, however, picked up and implemented in a way which subtly and imperceptibly changes the new element in it, so that it in practice fits into the prevailing structure without threatening it. But the name is maintained, as well as the impression of having introduced something new which breaks with the previous tradition. This was precisely what happened in the 1960s with the so-called 'group counselling programme' which was introduced in several Scandinavian prisons. The group counselling programme was, after a while, on the face of it, met with considerable openness. With time, however, the programme was imperceptibly and gradually changed to regular study groups in the social sciences, the psychology of everyday life, and so on. The study groups had a clear authority structure, a context of rather bureaucratic rules, etc. They fitted very well into the security system of the prison, without in any way threatening it. But the name, and the impression of something new, breaking with prevailing system interests, was enthusiastically maintained, at least for a while. Group treatment, group counselling, were key words at the time.

In short, through techniques like reference to outside authority, defining ideas as irrelevant, defining them as impossible to implement, postponing ideas, puncturing ideas, and absorbing ideas – techniques of neutralization which come in addition to, or instead of, sheer power and force – system interests produced as demands on the outside, are maintained inside the prison. Through techniques like these, whereby the representatives of the prison subordinate themselves to the prevailing premises of prison management, the prison in a basic sense becomes a conservative institution. Change going against prevailing terms becomes impossible. The conservatism of the prison society is a basic feature of the prison as an institution.

Rehabilitation is Neutralized

The third general point to be stressed here is this: regardless of which of the four rehabilitation components has received primary emphasis, actual rehabilitation has always been neutralized. There is solid reason for saying that throughout its history, the prison has actually never rehabilitated people in practice. It has never led to people's 'return to competence'.

The fact that the prison did not have a rehabilitative function in earlier times, may today be inferred from looking at the concrete methods which were used. The methods used in Amsterdam, which have been described above, as well as the methods in the prisons of the 1800s with their emphasis on disciplined isolation and moral penance, are today entirely abandoned. The fact that today's prison does not rehabilitate, has a very solid social-scientific basis. It comes from three sources.

First, it comes from the studies of treatment results mentioned earlier. A long string of empirical studies has been produced showing that regardless of type of treatment, and even where very intensive treatment programmes are concerned, the results remain pretty much the same, and generally poor. I am thinking primarily of studies measuring 'results' in terms of recidivism. As already mentioned, even treatment experiments with very careful built-in controls show this depressing lack of difference; this type or that type of treatment – the results are to a large extent the same. (Reviews of studies showing this may be found in Christie, 1961; Robison and Smith, 1971; Martinson, 1974; Bondeson, 1975; Greenberg, 1977; see also for example Ward, 1972; Cornish and Clarke, 1975; Trasler, 1976; Brody, 1976). The number of studies reviewed has been very large. More optimistic evaluations have appeared (Kühlhorn, 1986), but the optimism has been effectively countered (Bondeson, 1986). In some cases, those who have studied the programmes may have discarded sensible and well-designed programmes because they have not satisfied every scientific methodological demand (Wright, 1982: 200), and certain variations do exist in the sense that certain types of institutional arrangements seem to suit certain types of offenders better than others (Brody, 1976: 40). But the overall tendency in the reviews of the programmes is entirely clear.

The overall tendency has been summarized in bald terms by Robert Martinson in his now classic 1974 review of the literature. The review covered methodologically acceptable studies in the English language from 1945 through 1967 of attempts at rehabilitation in the USA and other countries. In the report, Martinson dealt with those studies which measured results in terms of recidivism. After having pointed to the methodological complications inherent in the reporting, he concluded:

> With these caveats, it is possible to give a rather bald summary of our findings: *With few and isolated exceptions, the rehabilitative efforts that*

have been reported so far have had no appreciable effect on recidivism.
Studies that have been done since our survey was completed do not
present any major grounds for altering that original conclusion.
(Martinson, 1974: 25)

The critique which had to come after such a statement (Palmer,
1975) has been effectively refuted (Sechrest, 1979). Martinson's
summary still stands as representative.

Secondly, the social-scientific basis comes from our knowledge of
the actual organization of most prisons, nationally as well as
internationally. Above we have taken as our point of departure
actual treatment experiments and attempts. It is these experiments
and attempts which to a large extent do not show the desired effects.
But as a blunt matter of fact, the actual realities in almost all prisons
are extremely far from anything which may be called 'treatment' in
a qualified sense. As mentioned already (Chapter 1), the prisons are
often overcrowded, run-down, and more or less dangerous places to
those who inhabit them. And as a rule they are large, authoritarian
and bureaucratic machines. This is the everyday life of the prison –
very far from any 'treatment situation'.

Thirdly, the basis comes from sociological studies of the prison as
an organization and of the prisoners' community. The very first
large prison study in modern times, carried out in the US before
World War II (Clemmer, 1940), clearly indicated that rehabilitation
is not promoted by imprisonment. The author, Donald Clemmer,
was a sociologist employed in the prison where the study was
undertaken. Through intensive interviews, questionnaires and
observation, he studied the prisoners' attitudes to the law-abiding
society. His data supported the hypothesis that the prisoners were
'prisonized', as he called it, during the prison term. By 'prisonization' he meant the taking on of the folkways, mores, customs and
general culture of the penitentiary. This culture made the prisoner
more or less immune to attempts from the prison in the direction of
readjustment. In more popular terms, according to Clemmer's
study the prison in a cultural sense first of all functioned as a 'crime
school'.

Every prisoner, Clemmer maintained, was subject to certain
universal factors of prisonization. No-one could fully escape it. To
be sure, there were variations. He hypothesized that the shorter the
sentence, the greater the adequacy of positive relationships during
pre-penal life, the greater the number of positive relations on the
outside, the greater the personal independence in relation to
primary groups inside, the greater the personal ability to refuse the
prisoner code, the greater the physical distance inside from inmate
leaders, and the greater the personal tendency to refrain from

certain types of activity which were introductory to the prisoner code, the *smaller* the tendency towards prisonization. The greatest degree of prisonization followed from the opposite ranking on these criteria. Yet not only were many prisoners exposed to a large number of the factors likely to promote a high degree of prisonization: also, the fact that no-one could avoid it entirely, constituted a main point. Clemmer did not conclude that a high degree of correlation necessarily existed between extreme prisonization and later criminal behaviour, but he did suggest the likelihood of a correlation, and he certainly argued that prisonization did not aid rehabilitation.

Clemmer's comprehensive study attracted considerable attention in professional circles, but World War II put a temporary end to research activity. However, after the war the sociological study of the prison gained renewed importance, and around 1960 a series of important studies appeared which in various ways supported Clemmer's initial findings.

The American sociologist Stanton Wheeler carried out a refined questionnaire study in which he tested Clemmer's findings concerning prisonization (Wheeler, 1961). Clemmer was primarily concerned with the early phases of prisonization, that is, with the prisoners' entrance into the inmate culture. His proposition about an association between prisonization and later adjustment was based on the assumption that the processes observed during the early and middle phases of incarceration continue until the inmate is paroled (Wheeler, 1961: 698). Wheeler investigated this assumption by dividing the prisoners in a large American prison into three groups: those who were early, mid-way and late in their prison term. By dividing the prison population in this way, he was able to infer (the study was cross-sectional rather than longitudinal) that prisonization – measured by the prisoners' responses to a series of hypothetical conflict situations in the prison – increased significantly towards the middle phase of their stay, and decreased again when release approached. In other words, prisonization appeared 'U-shaped': the prisoners seemed to 'prepare' for release by to some extent abandoning the inmate norms and values characteristic of the earlier phases. But it is important to note that the 'U-shape' was not perfect: though a reorientation could be inferred towards the final part of the stay, the reorientation was not complete. And since many prisoners are incarcerated several times, it may therefore be inferred that prisonization is a kind of spiral, through which the individual becomes continually more involved in the inmate subculture.

Also around 1960, several studies appeared which not only

suggested a process of prisonization on the part of the prisoners, but which, most importantly, tried to explain why such a prisoner culture appears in the first place (Sykes, 1958; Sykes and Messinger, 1960). The authors discussed the various pains of imprisonment which the incarcerated prisoner experiences. The basic deprivation of liberty itself, the deprivation of goods and services, the deprivation of heterosexual relations, the deprivation of autonomy, and the deprivation of security in relation to other inmates, are so painful that they create a need for a defence. That defensive need is met through the establishment of the prisoners' community with its particular norms and values. Life in the prisoners' community does not remove the pain, but at least it alleviates or moderates it. A common culture protects against the pressures from the environment. This way, the prisoner culture becomes an understandable reaction.

Scandinavian research, from the same period as well as more recent studies, has in part presented findings which rather strongly resemble the American results.

In 1959 the Norwegian sociologist Johan Galtung published a comprehensive study of the Oslo District Prison, Norway's largest prison (450 inmates, quite a bit smaller than any American and British prisons; Galtung, 1959). Galtung served a sentence as a conscientious objector, and based his study on systematic personal observation, but also on systematic interviews with fellow prisoners and staff. Galtung corroborated the finding that the prison term is experienced as extremely painful, in much the same way as in the American studies (despite the fact that Norwegian sentences are on the average much shorter than American ones), and he found tendencies towards prisonization.

In 1965 I published a study of the Norwegian institution for preventive detention, based on two years of participant observation as a sociologist and interviews, as well as questionnaires administered to inmates in the preventive detention institution and a regular prison for long-termers (Mathiesen, 1965a). A main focus of attention in my study were the power relations in the total institution. Because this was a preventive detention institution, the element of psychiatric and psychological expertise was larger than usual. In view of this, one might think that the pains of imprisonment were reduced from the point of view of the inmates. But the facts were opposite: from the prisoners' point of view, their term in the preventive detention institution was experienced as particularly painful. They felt especially stigmatized as a particularly deviant outcast group. As a small indication, they frequently used the term 'the garbage can of society' to describe themselves. And, most importantly, they experienced the psychiatrists and the treatment staff in general as having a particular and dangerous, almost omnipotent, power. In their eyes, the power of the psychiatrists was related to the role of the medical doctors as psychiatric experts in court: most of the prisoners had a so-called security sentence, requiring a psychiatric investigation and conclusion, and those who had been sentenced to a large extent experienced the psychiatrists as the 'real judges'. This particular finding has much more recently also been corroborated by others (Kongshavn, 1987). But the power of the psychiatrists was also related to the importance of their reports and recommendations for or against release on so-called 'free security'. Through these reports and recommendations, the psychiatrists controlled a benefit which was vital to the inmates. The comparative questionnaire data showed that inmates in the treatment-oriented institution experienced the 'total power' of the staff as being much greater than did inmates in the regular prison (Mathiesen, 1965a: 109).

Based on my participant observation data, I did not find the same strong indications of the kind of prisonization or enrolment in a particular prison culture. 'My' prisoners seemed to a greater extent to represent standard, conventional norms and values, like 'most people'. Similar findings have been reported in at least one other Scandinavian (Danish) group of studies (Balvig et al., 1969). But on the other hand, I found other, at least equally problematical reactions to the stay in prison: many prisoners emphasized that the power of the psychiatrists made it quite impossible for them to enter anything resembling a therapeutic relationship with them. And many tried to defend themselves against the particular stigma they experienced, as well as against what they experienced as the omnipotent power of the psychiatrists, by levelling constant and masssive criticism against the institution and the prison system in general. The criticism emphasized that the institution and the system was unjust, ineffective, or both. The inmates emphasized strongly that their rehabilitation, as that term has been defined above, was not promoted, thus criticizing and rejecting the prison on its own terms; that is, for not maintaining or attaining norms and values which in fact are norms and values also of the prison. In other words, there was a deep conflict between staff and prisoners, even though the conflict did not have the character of a cultural cleavage.

Another comprehensive Scandinavian study, from Sweden, has, however, found clear indications of prisonization also under Scandinavian conditions. In her book from 1974, Ulla Bondeson reports (Bondeson, 1974; rev. Eng. ed. 1989) from a questionnaire and interview study performed in thirteen different institutions for women and men (training schools, youth prisons, closed prisons and a preventive detention institution). According to Bondeson, the prisoners were criminalized, narcotized, neuroticized, and generally made to feel powerless during the prison term. And they were to a significant extent prisonized. A comprehensive argot test was developed to study the prisonization process. Bondeson did not find that small treatment-oriented institutions functioned any better than large ordinary prisons. And women were also prisonized during the prison term. Interestingly, she was unable to corroborate Wheeler's 'U-shaped' curve of conformity to conventional norms (see above). She concludes:

> In summary, the prisonization observed during institutional confinement does not regress toward the end of confinement in our material. There is no sign here that the inmates stop identifying with the criminal subculture as the release date approaches. Thus, there are no grounds here for maintaining that an anticipatory socialization to the law-abiding society begins before release. (Bondeson, rev. Eng. ed. 1989: 248)

These are some of the prison studies which have been undertaken. There are also others, and though there are variations, they give the same general dismal picture. (A large study, from the United States, shows a somewhat brighter picture; see Glaser, 1964. The study has been criticized on methodological grounds.) Whether prisonization in Clemmer's classical sense is found or not, is perhaps partly dependent on the method used. Regardless of whether the mechanism is prisonization or not, the studies almost unanimously and clearly suggest or show that the goal of rehabilitation, attached to the prison, is not attained.

This general conclusion was in fact anticipated as early as at the beginning of the 1950s, in an important article by two American sociologists who were also prison administrators: Lloyd W. McCorkle, who was warden of the New Jersey State Prison in Trenton (where Gresham Sykes carried out his above-mentioned study), and Richard R. Korn, who was director of education and counselling in the same prison (McCorkle and Korn, 1954). They created a key concept which summarized the core point in a large bulk of later prison research: police, courts, and especially prisons, argued McCorkle and Korn, imply a *rejection* of the prisoners as members of society. The prisoners' reply to the rejection is to reject those who have rejected them, *reject their rejectors*. McCorkle and Korn put it this way:

> In many ways, the inmate social system may be viewed as providing a way of life which enables the inmate to avoid the devastating psychological effects of internalizing and converting social rejection into self-rejection.

In effect, it permits the inmate to reject his rejectors rather than himself. (McCorkle and Korn, 1954: 88)

Under these conditions, they argued, anything resembling 'treatment' becomes impossible. Even rehabilitation 'based on easing the harshness of prison life' (McCorkle and Korn, 1954: 95) becomes unproductive from a rehabilitative point of view (however important it might be from a humanitarian point of view), because the rejection which the prisoners react to is overarching or immanent in the system, so that new demands and new rounds of hostility are created. A long series of later studies have proved that McCorkle and Korn were right.

One can probably go further, by saying that not only does the goal of rehabilitation remain unrealized in the prison; also, the chances of rehabilitation are in fact reduced, on a long-term basis, among the inmates who enter the 'rejection syndrome' described above. Let me mention here that Ulla Bondeson has studied the long-term effects of prisonization on recidivism (Bondeson, rev. Eng. ed. 1989, Ch. 12; see also Bondeson and Kragh Andersen, 1986; Bondeson, 1986: 422; on the same issue see, in addition, Robison and Smith, 1971: 71-2; Trasler, 1976: 12-13). Recidivism data were collected on the subjects of her prison study after a period of five and ten years respectively. All crimes and all sanctions imposed were registered with exact dates for the whole period. A number of other follow-up data were also registered. The major analysis concentrated on the ten-year follow-up, and recidivism data were related to previous data on prisonization, controlling for some important background variables. The inmates from the training schools were excluded from the study (and a few people from the other institutions had to be eliminated due to incomplete information), leaving two youth prisons, one women's prison, two men's prisons and a preventive detention institution in the study. The time which elapsed from release until a new crime was committed was analysed using techniques for the so-called survival data, noting differences in recidivism periods. In four out of the six institutions, recidivism could be explained by prisonization. Interestingly, the two institutions which deviated were the youth prisons which had many prisoners without prior sentences. Bondeson concludes:

> In conclusion, for the two youth prisons, none of the covariates considered were found to have a significant influence on the recidivism time distributions . . .
> For the other four prisons, a considerable part of the variation among prisons in recidivism time could be explained by the three covariates, argot knowledge, sentences per year, and type of crime . . . Of the three covariates, argot knowledge was the most significant in the final

regression model (p=0.0005), then came sent/y (p=0.001) and finally type of crime (p=0.003). (Bondeson, rev. Eng. ed. 1989: 292–3)

Does Prison Have a Defence in Rehabilitation?

The overall reply to the main question posed in this chapter, 'does prison have a defence in rehabilitation?', may be put very briefly: an overwhelming amount of material, historical as well as sociological, leads to a clear and unequivocal *no* to the question.

The ideology of rehabilitation is as old as the prisons themselves. It has consisted of, and still consists of, four main components – work, school, moral influence and discipline – which at the same time are core elements in a bourgeois, 'Protestant' ethic. The rehabilitative imagination has not reached beyond these four components, and various concrete expressions of the components.

The relative emphasis through time on the four components has been determined by system interests attached to the prisons rather than to any interest in actual rehabilitation of the prisoners. This means that when there has been conflict between the system interests and considerations of rehabilitation, the former interests have systematically won the battle, and received priority.

And just as systematically, the rehabilitation result has failed to appear. This conclusion receives extremely broad support in the extensive treatment research literature, and in a long string of in-depth studies of a sociological kind of the prison as a social system.

Not only can we most certainly say that the prison does not rehabilitate. Most likely we can also say that it in fact *de*habilitates. Actually, today this is often also granted by responsible authorities. I quote an authoritative Swedish source:

> What criminological research nowadays has taught us is, however, that the idea of being able to improve the punished individual through a punishment implying deprivation of liberty, is an illusion. On the contrary, today it is generally acknowledged that these kinds of punishment lead to poor rehabilitation and a high recidivism rate. In addition, they often have a destructive effect on personality. (Regeringens proposition, 1982/83 No. 85: 29, translated from the Swedish by the present author)

It is only reasonable to demand that the authorities now take this correct understanding seriously in practice.

3

General Prevention

General Prevention as a Paradigm

The notion of rehabilitation is one important theory within the main group of penal theories stressing individual prevention as social defence.

As mentioned already, the other main group of theories of social defence takes its point of departure in general prevention, that is, in the notion of preventing not the inmate, but others, from committing criminal acts. As we have also mentioned, general prevention is conceived as processes of deterrence, moral education and habit formation of others.

The general-preventive effect of punishment is to a large extent *taken for granted* in our society. The notion of the general-preventive effect of punishment is so deeply ingrained in the 'common sense thinking' of society, that questions about its actual existence are frequently not raised and remain unasked. In this sense, the notion of the general-preventive effect of punishment constitutes a prevailing *paradigm* in society.

The word 'paradigm' is Greek and means 'pattern'. In the context of the sciences, 'paradigm' stands for a coherent and basic pattern of thinking which influences the research process by emphasizing particular research tasks and particular problems as fruitful and interesting, and by functioning as a scheme of interpretation when empirical data are to be placed in a theoretical context. Marxism may be said to constitute such a 'paradigm' in the social sciences, and structural functionalism another (for more details, see Kuhn, 1962/1970; see also for example Johnsen, 1979). But it is not only in the sciences that we can talk of paradigms. In society in general, and in various societal sub-systems, we may also talk of different paradigms which in varying degrees compete with each other for our attention and loyalty. Far outside the sciences we find coherent and basic patterns of thinking which indicate points of departure for social interpretation, which give direction to thinking, and which function as regulating perspectives for the understanding of the world. The great institutions in society, like the church, the law, the school, and more recently the mass media, are producers as well as transmitters of more or less coherent and basic patterns of thinking of this kind.

To qualify as a paradigm, the pattern of thinking must always to some extent be taken for granted. *Within* the pattern of thinking, questions and issues may certainly be raised – exactly that happens in the scientific context – but the main and basic pattern, the tenets, must be taken for granted. It is not reasonable to say that a pattern of thinking has the status of a paradigm when large and dominant groups in fact cast great doubt on its basic doctrines. Such patterns of thinking are either in the process of losing their status as paradigms, or simply non-paradigms. Conversely, the more a pattern of thinking is taken for granted by those who transmit it, by those who receive it, or by both sides, the more 'paradigmatic' it is.

The question of how paradigms are established in groups or in society, as well as the question of what causes an old paradigm to yield to a new one, constitute complex and interesting issues of sociology of knowledge. We cannot deal in detail with these issues here (some beginning analyses may be found for example in Mathiesen, 1984: 18–122; see also Mathiesen, 1986, Ch. 6). Here we only wish to point out the following.

In Norwegian, British and US society the notion of the general-preventive effect of punishment to a large extent functions as a paradigm. The theory of general prevention constitutes a coherent pattern of thinking. It constitutes a basic system of thinking in the sense that general prevention is viewed as something of a cornerstone in a well-organized society. And the general-preventive effect is to a large extent taken for granted by those who transmit the message as well as by most observers of the communication process.

This is important, for three major reasons. First, because the notion of general prevention is so paradigmatic in society, the most disparate events and actions become meaningful in the light of it. When the crime rate goes down, this presumably shows that punishment has a general-preventive effect. When the crime rate goes up, this presumably also shows that punishment has a general-preventive effect: it shows that the sanctions are not sufficiently severe, and that stiffer sentencing is necessary to reduce crime. When the number of drug offences, registered either by the police or through research, levels off or tapers down, it shows how correct the stiff sentencing practice in this area has been. When the number of drug offences increases, it shows that sentencing should become even stiffer. Numerous other examples may be found of how entirely contradictory events within the field of criminal and penal policy are thus given a unified meaning (for an example from the area of presumed espionage, see Mathiesen and Hjemdal, 1986). Contradictory events and actions *may* have the same motivational basis, but *need* not have it, and the latter possibility is not taken seriously. Rather, new contradictory actions which occur are incorporated and automatically interpreted as supporting the paradigmatic theory in the way indicated.

Secondly, and as an extention of the first point, because the notion of the general-preventive effect of punishment is so paradigmatic, the burden of proof is placed on those (minorities) who question the theory, and not on those who take it as a point of departure and for granted. General prevention is assumed to function; it is the opposite possibility which is in need of proof. Again, we see this in a number of concrete areas. Because the efficacy of harsh punishment is taken for granted in the area of drug offences, the burden of proof is placed on the shoulders of those who have doubts about it. In a sense, a 'reversed burden of proof' constitutes the order of the day. The theory of general prevention thereby becomes a theory which is highly resistant to criticism and objection.

Thirdly, because the notion of general prevention is so paradigmatic, it is possible for the proponents of the theory to take what they consider to be common sense experience of everyday life as their most important point of departure, often with little or no testing of this experience. The grand old man of Norwegian penal law, internationally known for his contributions to the theory of general prevention, has this to say about what he considers to be the main basis for a belief in general prevention:

> The strongest basis for the belief in general prevention is still the well-known experience that fear of unpleasant consequences is a highly motivating factor in most walks of life, and the more highly motivating the more serious the feared consequences are. The notion that this well-known mechanism were to be without importance when the issue at hand is that of whether or not to commit a criminal act, is almost fantastic. (Andenæs, 1977/1982: 229, translated from the Norwegian by the present author)

It should be added that this strong statement comes as a conclusion towards the end of a long article, and after a detailed review of research results which according to the author have not led to any 'breakthrough in knowledge' (Andenæs, 1977/1982: 228).

To this it should in fairness be added that especially during later years, Johs. Andenæs has been among those who have taken the question of the empirical corroboration of the thesis of the general-preventive effect of punishment seriously. We shall return to this below. Despite this, then, the common sense experience of the fear of unpleasant consequences is in fact his 'strongest basis for the belief in general prevention'. He does not stand alone in this emphasis. Others, with a much more unempirical approach, not only have common sense experience as their strongest basis, but as their only basis.

To summarize: the paradigmatic character of the theory of general prevention functions so that even clearly contradictory events and actions are interpreted within the theory, the burden of proof is squarely placed on those who doubt the theory, and pure 'common sense' experiences are accepted as the strongest or even the only basis of the theory. These circumstances do not make it easy to pose the main question of this chapter: 'Does prison have a defence – in general prevention?' You then pose a question which goes straight against the main direction of the paradigm. All the more important is it to ask the question.

Research Results

The first specific question which may be asked, is that of what the research in the area says.

During the last years, research related to general prevention has expanded considerably. Johs. Andenæs is one who has followed research developments closely, and who has summarized its various phases, for instance in an article from 1977/1982 (Andenæs, 1977/1982), as well as in various other works covering special areas. As he says: 'From the middle of the 1960s we have seen a stream of studies, especially from the United States, and nothing suggests that the stream will subside' (Andenæs, 1977/1982: 196). Because Andenæs has also been one of the main proponents of the theory of general prevention, we have reason to look more closely at his contribution.

First of all, Andenæs points to the entry of the economists into the area. Their point of departure, he says, has been different from that of the sociologists: the point of departure has been that the criminal act is the result of a rational choice. In addition, they have been able to employ new statistical methods, developed within economics. Furthermore, he examines studies of the death penalty, studies of differences between geographical regions, studies of the effect of legal change and change in legal practice, interview studies – especially concerning the effect of knowledge of the law and of changes in the law – as well as experimental research. Various areas of social behaviour and a large number of studies are discussed. The question is, then: where do we stand today? Andenæs opens the reply to his own question like this:

In earlier discussions of general prevention we had to rely on unsystema-
tic experience, general psychological reasoning, introspection, and
historical material. Is it possible to say that the last ten years of research
have changed the situation in any basic way? It is not easy to give a clear
answer. (Andenæs, 1977/1982: 227)

The objectivity and the scientific standard of the discussion have
increased, Andenæs says. Furthermore, it has become more
difficult to maintain extreme positions. On the one hand, it is not
easy to deny a general-preventive effect of penal reactions, or to
maintain that their effect is independent of efficient enforcement.
On the other hand, the belief that an increase in penal levels or
police efforts automatically lower the crime rate, appears clearly
unrealistic. But, he concludes:

Unlike research concerning the individual-preventive results of different
reactions, we have not had any breakthrough in knowledge. Research
has given fragments of knowledge which may be used in the control of,
and as supplement to, the common sense like reasoning which we still will
have to rely on. We have a long way to go before research can provide
quantifiable results concerning the effect on crime which is to be
expected from this or that planned change in the system – if, that is, we
ever reach that stage. (Andenæs, 1977/1982: 228)

The conclusion is significant. We have not had 'any breakthrough in
knowledge'. Research has only provided 'fragments of knowledge'.

We shall return later to Andenæs' discussion. First we shall look at
some other reviews of and contributions to the literature.

To Andenæs' examination of research we should add that a
conclusion corresponding very closely to his is reached in a
comprehensive and thorough updated review of the most vigorous
branch of modern research in general prevention: the economic
branch, which we mentioned earlier. The review is provided by the
German researcher Jürgen Frank (Frank, 1986), and takes as its
point of departure the wide range of American studies using
rationalistic economic models and 'cost-benefit' theories. Speaking
generally, the studies show a certain limited deterrent effect of
penal measures, that is, of the chance of being sentenced or
imprisoned and of the punishment level (Frank, 1986: 4–6).
However, and most importantly, the economic models which
constitute the point of departure contain a number of built-in
problematical or doubtful assumptions when it comes to practical
life, which Frank also discusses (Frank, 1986: 15–22). Frank, whose
appraisals are very sober, concludes as follows concerning this
research tradition: the tradition is interesting in so far as it

represents a challenge to other lines of thinking which do not take their point of departure in the idea of the rationalistic, economically inclined cost-benefit orientation; the strictness and formality of its derivations make the tradition clear and concise in terms of central propositions and core statements; and even if it cannot indicate precisely the influence of penal law and legal alternatives, it does provide a framework for analysis of empirical work. 'The question', Frank concludes, 'of whether non-economic approaches are superior in terms of explanatory power and empirical certainty, remains open' (Frank, 1986: 23, translated from the German by the present author).

It may be added that findings in more specialized areas, such as drunken driving, where research has been intensive, are correspondingly uncertain and at best going in different directions (for details concerning drunken driving studies, see Klette's 1982 review). In a comprehensive study, Ross and collaborators surveyed legal developments concerning drunken driving in Finland, Denmark, Sweden and Norway during the 1970s and early 1980s, presenting statistical evidence, where available, on their impact on drinking and driving (Ross et al., 1984). During the period, the first three countries saw important liberalizations of drink/driving laws or legal practice (in Norway, liberalization came after the period), while a rationalization of police controls, in the form of 'random' testing of drivers, was introduced in all four countries. The interventions were analysed by way of interrupted time-series analysis, and the researchers looked for temporary as well as permanent effects, using measures such as crash-related fatalities and injuries, weekend night fatalities, and night-time fatalities. The effects of the legal developments were, on the whole, negligible: the various measures yielded either no changes, changes which were statistically insignificant, or, in the case of Finland, a significant (14 percent) temporary rise in fatalities which virtually disappeared within two months (injuries experienced a significant 2.5 percent temporary decline that lasted nearly a year). The authors concluded:

> From a humanitarian viewpoint, there is much to be commended in the developments of the last decade in the Scandinavian approach to drunk-driving law. The liberalization inherent in this approach has resulted in considerably less misery being foisted on the citizens of these countries, *with no evidence of negative effects on the level of the drunk-driving problem.* (Ross et al., 1984: 480, emphasis added)

However, there is one point which requires a more detailed discussion. In parts of the literature on general prevention a distinction is made between the *level of punishment* on the one hand, and what may be summarized as the *probability of a sanction* on the other. Though the level of punishment seems to show very little or no general-preventive effect, an increase, it is maintained, in the probability of a sanction when a crime has been committed at least has some effect.

In his book *Thinking about Crime*, the American criminologist James Q. Wilson in reality makes this claim (Wilson, 1975/1983). Wilson's point of departure is a defence of the penal system and of prison sanctions. He speaks of the general-preventive effect of punishment/prison in a cost-benefit context and in general terms, and points to various studies showing an effect, though – he seems to admit – a marginal one (Wilson, 1983: 143). If his review of studies is scrutinized, however, it may be seen that what he finds as having a marginal effect, quite systematically is what may be summarized as the probability of a sanction. He speaks of the 'swiftness' and the 'certainty' of punishment, very rarely about the severity of punishment or punishment level.

The distinction between the punishment level or severity of punishment on the one hand and the probability ('swiftness and certainty') of a sanction on the other is made just as clear, or even clearer, in other studies, for example in a large German study of youthful offenders carried out by Schumann and collaborators (Schumann et al., 1987). In a carefully designed empirical project, Schumann and collaborators studied the effect of the expected severity of punishment on criminal behaviour among other aspects. A random sample of 1600 youths aged 15–17 was drawn in the city of Bremen. Sixty-two of these were exposed to a pre-test, leaving a sample of 1538. Two interview schedules were developed, one measuring various possible independent and intervening variables, notably expected punishments and subjective experience of detection risk, and another – administered at least a year later – tapping self-reported criminal behaviour. In addition, information on criminal behaviour on the part of those interviewed was obtained from official records. Altogether 49.3 percent of the sample were reached by two interviews. A detailed analysis is given of those not reached, and of representativeness. The target sample and the group which was reached showed identical proportions of individuals registered for criminal conduct (p. 205). The study showed that the expected severity of punishment had *no* effect on youthful criminal behaviour. Neither, it might be added, had the expectation of youth prison. These negative findings constitute one of the major conclusions of the report, summarized as 'Irrelevance of severity of punishment' and 'Irrelevance of deprivation of liberty' (p. 161). What the researchers did find was that the subjective experience of detection risk had a certain effect, but *not* on the performance of serious crimes, such as robbery, serious physical assault, fraud, and drug crimes, as one might have hoped from a general deterrence point of view. And *not* on the performance of all types of crime which may be classified as trifling crimes, such as various types of theft and temporary illegal use of a car. Effect could only be demonstrated on the performance of *some* types of trifling crimes, such as shop-lifting, trivial physical assault, damage to objects, driving without a licence, and using the subway without paying. And even here, the effect as measured through multivariate analysis is characterized as 'quite modest' (*recht bescheiden*, Schumann et al., 1987: 152). And, let me add, youths who are most likely to be detected, rarely commit such acts. They tend to commit the types of crime which show no general-preventive effect. This is all that can be said in support of general prevention theory in what is probably the most comprehensive empirical study of general prevention in Western Germany, if not in Europe, to date (Schumann et al., 1987; for a summary see Ch. 8).

This German study is particularly important because it focuses on youthful crime, and because it focuses so heavily and sharply on the subjectively experienced detection risk. The detection risk may be said to be the most basic measure of probability of a sanction: without detection or clearance, there will be no sanction, so that the detection risk is a decisive condition for the 'swiftness' and 'certainty' of the sanction. The German study goes further in discussing explicitly the subjective experience of the risk, which is the 'bridge' between the objective risk and behaviour: the objective risk is only likely to have an effect if it is experienced as a risk. With only very partial and quite modest effects of the subjectively experienced detection risk, let alone the level of punishment where no effects could be shown, the theory of general prevention is actually driven into something of a corner.

Yet, by proponents of general prevention, meagre results such as these have been picked up and used as an argument for an expansion of the resources allocated to the police and other segments of the formal control system. Resources, it is maintained, should be allocated in order to increase the actual – and thereby also the subjectively experienced – detection risk, since it has in fact shown some effect, however modest. Today, the clearance rate for crimes reported to the police is generally very low in most industrial countries. For example, the clear-up rate for crimes reported to the police was 23 percent for Norway in 1984. More than three out of four reported crimes, in other words, remained uncleared. There are geographical variations, with the lowest clear-up rate in the large industrialized centres, where the crime rate is highest. The same may be found in other industrialized countries. The argument, then, is that these extremely low clear-up rates must be made to increase. Then the general-preventive effect will also increase and become a reality. This may presumably be attained through increased resources to the police, etc.

Here, however, the proponents of general prevention take a false step. One thing, which the German youth study showed so clearly, is that for the serious crimes, where the detection rate in fact is quite high, the preventive effect of any subjectively experienced risk is non-existent. This strongly suggests that factors other than the criminal justice system determine the existence and development of such crimes.

Furthermore, the extemely low detection rate for the large number of more trivial crimes, which explains the low average detection rate, is a function of social reality itself in industrialized countries rather than of police resources. In our context here, this is the most important point.

In modern, industrialized, urbanized society a series of social factors operate in the direction of making crime *anonymous*. I am thinking of what may be called 'mass crime': theft, car theft, drug use, the less serious crimes of violence, and so on, which are the types of crime where we find a partial and modest detection effect (see above). In industrialized, urbanized society, people are less known to each other and know less about each others' property, offenders more easily find places and areas where they are unknown, areas are without people larger parts of the time, there are more objects, like cars and cottages, the objects are left unguarded more frequently and for longer periods of time, and so on (Høigård and Balvig, 1988: 58–9). The anonymity of these types of crime leads, with a kind of 'sociological necessity', to a low or even extremely low detection risk. The low detection risk follows from the conditions of industrialized and urbanized society, not from a lack of resources to the police. It is probably possible to make the detection risk increase. But there are very powerful societal reasons why the increase in our kind of society will not be significant; possibly, just possibly, unless we develop a pure and complete surveillance and police state, which we would like to avoid for a number of other reasons.

There is an empirical basis for this generalization. By way of summary, Jürgen Frank has this to say about the issue (Frank, 1986: 11): 'Various authors have investigated the influence of police activity on the probability of arrest and sentencing. But no statistically significant evidence could be found for the supposition that an intensification of police activity would increase the arrest and sentencing rate.' This means that *the deterrent, general-preventive effect of an increased detection risk due to increased police resources (and ensuing probability of a sanction, through swiftness and certainty of punishment) would at best be quite modest* – to use the term from Schumann et al. (or marginal, to use the term of the champion of general prevention, Wilson; see above). The Danish criminologist Flemming Balvig has expressed the point in the following way:

> I do not doubt that the clear-up rate could be increased by police activity. I am, however, sceptical to the possibility that it may be increased *significantly* without very great societal costs of an economic kind as well as in other ways. And an increase of a few percentages is probably not of such great interest in view of the fact that the level will be very low in any case. (Balvig, 1980: 63, translated from the Danish by the present author; see also Balvig, 1984b)

Thus, Balvig says, a classical issue of whether or not a high clear-up rate has a general-preventive effect, is solved: 'If it is impossible to attain this high clearance rate, it does not make any difference who is right in this matter' (Balvig, 1980: 66).

With this as a background, we may return to Andenæs' classical review. To repeat, we have not had any 'breakthrough in knowledge', he said. Research has only given 'fragments of knowledge'. The preceding review has provided very considerable support to these conclusions, if by 'knowledge' we mean relationships and significant differences. Largely, we do not find relationships and differences, and if we find them, they are in the main quite modest or even marginal. Which practical conclusion is it, then, that Andenæs draws?

After his discouraging conclusion concerning firm knowledge showing relationships and differences, Andenæs moves on to emphasize the common sense experiences mentioned earlier, in our discussion of general prevention as a paradigm: 'The strongest basis for the belief in general prevention is still the well-known experience that fear of unpleasant consequences is a highly motivating factor in most walks of life . . .'. Despite the total amount of evidence which at best may be characterized as uncertain and unclear, with either lack of relationships or only partial, modest or marginal relationships, 'the belief in general prevention' is maintained in view of 'the well-known experience' of fear of unpleasant consequences. Despite his own careful discussion in the earlier part of his article, showing only 'fragments of knowledge', a discussion which has been clearly corroborated later, Andenæs concludes as if the uncertainty and lack of clarity in the final analysis actually do not count: 'The primary task [of the penal system]', he says, 'must be general prevention, based on a combination of deterrence and moral education – of course within the limits set by the demands of justice and humanity' (Andenæs, 1977/1982: 230).

It would have been much more reasonable to conclude by seeing the uncertain and unclear research results as a significant warning not to take general prevention for granted. Andenæs ends his review by doing precisely that – taking it for granted. Many others do the same.

The serious uncertainty and lack of clarity which at best may be said to exist concerning the effects of general prevention, will be taken as the point of departure below. The discussion will run through the following steps.

First, we shall try to explain why the results show such uncertainty, lack of clarity, and at best such modest or marginal associations. In order to do so, we shall utilize some basic notions from communications sociology.

Next, we shall discuss the moral problems which reasoning in terms of general prevention raise. General prevention does not only raise questions of efficacy, but also questions of morality. In particular, we shall emphasize the moral problem inherent in exposing a few, usually impoverished and stigmatized people, to particular pain in order to prevent others from committing similar acts.

We will then show how the adherents to the belief in general prevention also emphasize the arguments against general prevention mentioned here – when the interests they represent are served by it. In such cases, various types of communication defects, moral dilemmas and so on are emphasized: precisely the kind of factors discussed in this chapter.

We have already discussed the preventive effect of the state's penal policy independently of the prison as a specific type of punishment. We will continue to do so below, because the basic questions are not limited to the use of prison. But in the concluding section of the chapter, the general arguments will be applied specifically to prison as punishment.

General Prevention as Communication

In the context of general prevention, punishment may be viewed as a *message* from the state. First, punishment is a message which intends to say that crime does not pay (deterrence). Secondly, it is a message which intends to say that you should avoid certain acts because they are morally improper or incorrect (moral education). Thirdly, it is a message which intends to say that you should get into the habit of avoiding certain acts (habit formation). The criminal justice system, comprising the prosecuting authorities, the police, the courts and the sanctioning apparatus which includes the prison system, may be seen as a large machine having the purpose of communicating this message to the people. The machinery constitutes one of the state's most important mechanisms for 'talking' to the people about the people's own doings.

The fact that punishment is an attempt to communicate a message, or a set of messages, is acknowledged by the analysts and proponents of general prevention. For example, Andenæs says that 'The communication process from the legislator and the law enforcement agencies to the public is therefore a central link in the operating of general prevention' (Andenæs, 1977/1982: 216–17). Andenæs also states that in 'older penal theory there was not much emphasis on this. It seems as if a correspondence between the objective realities and the comprehension of the individual was tacitly assumed' (Andenæs, 1977/1982: 217).

But even if the communication process today presumably is seen as 'a central link', there is not much emphasis on it. What is emphasized, if anything, is the rather simplistic question of people's knowledge of the law and legal regulations, for example their knowledge of maximum penalties. However, the communication process is a complex process of interaction between sender and receiver, which raises far broader and more complicated questions than just 'knowledge' of the law. Legal and penal theory of general prevention has hardly, if at all, approached these questions.

The questions go to the core of the issue 'does prison have a defence – in general prevention?'

The Politics of Signification

First of all, what do we understand by 'communication'? The concept is complex. In extremely few words, communication stands for *the transfer of meaning* between interacting parties. Transfer of meaning may take place between individuals, groups, classes or whole societies, or between the state and the members of a society. When transfer of meaning takes place between the state and the members of society, which is the assumption of general prevention theory, particular state institutions are responsible for the transmission, and the transmission is usually very predominantly a one-way process – from the state institutions to the people.

But meaning cannot be transferred directly. As the Norwegian sociologists Hjemdal and Risan (1985) have formulated it, we need what may be called 'carriers of meaning' to accomplish the transfer. Carriers of meaning may be words, pictures, bodily postures, facial expressions, etc. Language is of course a crucial carrier of meaning. It is, then, *the carriers of meaning which are transferred*: the receivers must recreate the meaning from the carriers which they receive. This particular point is very significant. The recreation of meaning from the carriers which are received presupposes a common context of symbolic understanding. When such a context is not there, or is insufficient, the recreation of meaning becomes correspondingly broken or deficient. The function of the carriers of meaning in the communication process may be elaborated as follows.

The meaning which people assign to events and objects is not only dependent on how the events and objects 'are'. The meaning which people assign to events, such as new legislation or sentences proclaimed by the courts, or to objects, such as police uniforms or police roadblocks, is not only dependent on how these events and objects 'are' in an external sense. The meaning is also to a great extent dependent on how the events and objects are signified. Without the signs which signify, the events and objects alone would be meaningless. 'Sign' here is used as a synonym for 'carrier of meaning'. The signs 'carry' the meaning. Language is a particularly important set of signs carrying meaning. Other material expressions which may be perceived through our senses may also function as signs carrying meaning.

The signs, whether they are language or other expressions which may be perceived, 'carry' the meaning to the other party, thus creating meaning, only when they function within a context of understanding which is given in advance. The signs, then, become creative of meaning when they function in relation to a background of other signs which provide a pre-understanding; the meaning carried by the signs comes forth and becomes 'understandable' when the sign is seen in relation to the sign system or structure of signs which it enters into. This pre-understanding or structure of signs must be common to sender and receiver if the meaning which is created in the receiver is to be a meaning common to the two parties.

Thus, in a very brief and sketchy way we may say that 'meaning' is produced through the relationship between an external reality (what we here have called events and objects), signs (whether they are language or other expressions which may be perceived), and interpretation (the process by which the sign is seen in relation to the structure of signs which it enters into).

We have here touched on and interpreted some features of the school of thought within linguistics called 'semiology' or 'semiotics'. (Central contributors are Ferdinand de Saussure, C.S. Peirce, Roland Barthes and Umberto Eco; see for example Barthes, 1972; for a general presentation, see Fiske, 1982.) Semiology comes from the Greek *semion* which stands for 'sign', and *logos* which stands for 'teaching' or 'science'. Semiology, then, is 'the general science of signs'.

Thus, it may be said that the state's communication with members of the society, its attempt at communicative transfer of meaning, constitutes a *politics of signification* (to paraphrase Hall et al., 1978). The state's politics of signification are exercised in a long string of institutional contexts, such as the school, church institutions, and in the so-called criminal justice system. And signs which are seemingly small and insignificant may be of crucial importance.

The *school*, in other words, is not just an institution for the inculcation of knowledge, but also an institution which in decisive ways brings signs to bear on reality, or signifies reality, for generation after generation. The designations 'curriculum', 'lesson', 'test' and 'examination' are a few of the very large number of designations of reality, which enter into a structure of signs relevant to the school, and which give definite and general associations in the direction of ascetic duty and discipline.

The *church* is not just an institution which satisfies people's religious beliefs and needs, but also an institution which – historically in at least as decisive a way as the school – has signified reality for generation after generation. The designations 'sin', 'damnation', 'belief' and 'forgiveness' are some of the many designations which comprise a churchly structure of signs, and which give associations in the direction of divine omnipotence and churchly wisdom.

The same applies to the system which – not accidentally – is designated *the criminal justice system*: this system is not just a system which prosecutes and punishes offenders against the law, but is also an institution which, precisely while prosecuting and punishing, very strongly emphasizes a whole series of designations of reality. The designations 'guilt', 'sentence', 'legal procedure' and 'criminal justice system' are some of the many designations used by the 'criminal justice system' which jointly comprise a structure of legal signs giving associations in the direction of thorough, carefully prepared and reasonable treatment of offenders. In the context of this book, the example of the 'criminal justice system' is particularly interesting: it shows how the soothing designations of the system are so ingrained that it is difficult to avoid them even here.

The question of the preventive effect of punishment, and of

prison as punishment, may now be considered within the framework of the politics of signification.

Punishment and Signification

Above we emphasized that meaning is produced through the relationship between an external reality – what we called events and objects; signs – language and other perceivable expressions; and interpretation – the process of placing the sign in relation to a wider structure of signs. Meaning, then, is produced through an interaction between these three aspects or elements.

As a method of implementing general prevention, state-produced punishment is confronted by problems in all three respects. In more detail, state punishment with a view to general prevention fails to the extent that the factual events and objects in question (the legislative measures, the sentencing practice, and so on), the designations used, and the sign structure within which the signification is received and interpreted, deviate from what it takes to make general prevention work.

The general point is that the failure of punishment as the state's communicative practice contributes significantly to explain the unclarity and uncertainty which prevails with respect to the preventive effect of prison.

The Factual: Sentencing Practice, Legislation and Detection Risk

Some star examples exist to which proponents of general prevention frequently refer in support of the theory. The high risk of detection and the severe punishments against breaking the rules (concerning the blackout during World War II, for instance) is one of them. In the Scandinavian context, a particular period without any police in Denmark, also during World War II, is another.

The example of the blackout is referred to by Johs. Andenæs in an article from 1950:

> As an example of rules which are close to 100% effective because the actor must count on every rule violation being detected and consequential, the rules concerning blackout in wartime may be mentioned. Here the purely deterrent effect is sufficient, even without any support from the moral authority which the law normally has. (Andenæs, 1950/1962: 116–17, translated from the Norwegian by the present author)

In the same article he has the following to say about the period without police in Copenhagen:

> In September 1944, the Germans arrested the whole Danish police force. During the rest of the occupation, the police service was performed by an improvised and unarmed team of guards, who were almost completely

unable to do anything unless the perpetrator was caught in the very act . . . Crime immediatedly proved to increase very significantly . . . (Andenæs, 1950/1962: 121)

The high detection risk and the severe punishments in connection with the blackout probably did create conformity. And the sudden and complete dissolution of the whole police force probably did increase the crime rate. (Though it should be mentioned that blackout during wartime is obviously also very much in one's own interest, and that doubts have been raised concerning the effect of the dissolution of the police force in Denmark: it has been argued that the crime figures during this particular period were to be expected simply by extrapolating from the figures prior to the period – see Wolf, 1967; discussed in Balvig, 1984a.) However, as Nils Christie (1971) has pointed out in an important article, such drastic changes in the sanctioning system are certainly not a part of the daily round. On the contrary, they are very unusual, atypical and extreme events within the criminal justice system. Christie formulates it as follows, in connection with court decisions:

> The point here is that almost all of the star examples concerning the effects of general prevention are relevant *to a situation which is completely different from that which confronts the judge* when he is to select the concrete reaction. Normally, the judge must choose between sanctions which are rather close to each other – three or six months imprisonment, or at most between conditional and unconditional sentence – while the examples of general prevention concern dramatic differences between stimuli, such as police control against no police control. (Christie, 1971: 55, translated from the Norwegian by the present author)

The same point is also important in connection with the legislative process. Because the legislative process is complex and slow, the legal rules – for example the punishment limits for given types of offence – are largely changed gradually and/or in terms of details. To be sure, in situations of moral and social panic, change may occur suddenly, and it may be extensive. We shall return later to important examples of this (Chapter 5). But despite the existence of important examples of moral panics, which do say much about instability of the moral standards in society, they (fortunately) do not constitute the everyday life of the legislation process. Furthermore, we have no theoretical or empirical grounds for assuming that legal change based on a panic is particularly effective in terms of general prevention. If anything, the irrationality, frenzy, and brushing aside of elementary principles of due process, which tend to characterize moral panics, probably produce the reverse of the desired effect in the relevant groups where the panic strikes.

From a communicative point of view, what we have pointed to above is of decisive importance. It is unreasonable to expect the choices between sanctions or sanctioning levels which are close to each other, and which constitute the everyday routine of criminal policy, to be picked up and received by the receivers with a meaning corresponding to that of the senders. Disregarding for a minute the mediating links in the communication process, which make communication selective (and which we will return to shortly), *reality* in the message structure is in other words such that the process of picking up the message is difficult: the relatively fine nuances which exist in sentencing practice are based on complex conditions relevant to the particular individuals who are brought to trial. And, in much the same way, complex arguments concerning obedience to the law and the effects of legislation constitute the background for the gradual and/or small changes which occur in criminal law.

The following should be noted clearly. Taken together, and over time, small changes in sentencing practice and legislation may lead to larger-scale changes in criminal policy. Indeed, this is happening today. As mentioned in Chapter 1, the criminal policy of a number of Western countries is currently being tightened up, with an increased punishment level. This is an important part of the background for the congested prisons. The point is that the changes which occur *at a given point in time* are usually relatively small, and based on complex reasoning.

The fact that large-scale changes to a significant extent occur over time through an accrual of small changes, may be generalized to other parts of criminal policy. The development of the Norwegian police constitutes an interesting case in point. In 1970 a general plan advocating major changes in the organization of the police as well as greatly increased resources to the police was presented (Innstilling, The Aulie Report, 1970). Precisely because it was presented as a major plan, it was possible to discuss and criticize it publicly, and the plan was in fact abandoned in the mid-1970s. After the shelving of the plan, however, the police have changed in ways which are very reminiscent of the original proposal. But the changes have occurred gradually, in a cumulative fashion from year to year (Lorentzen, 1977). The gradual changes have not caused any sensation or debate, and today the Norwegian police is completely reorganized and greatly strengthened in terms of power and authority. The significant lesson for us is that a political message structure consisting of small, cumulative steps is more difficult to perceive, pick up, and react to – much like the small steps in a cumulative penal development.

Before concluding this section, let me add that the very low detection risk discussed earlier in this chapter (pp. 55–7), is also an integral part of what we have called the reality of the message structure. In an industrialized, urbanized and anonymized society increased police resources will only change the detection risk in a marginal way. This is a basic feature of modern social reality, which has become a part of the message structure. A detection risk like the one we had during the blackouts of World War II is entirely atypical.

Signification: Filtration and Focusing Above (p. 60) we emphasized that 'reality' – the events and objects which form a part of the message structure – not only constitute actual events and objects, but also simultaneously designations which carry (or fail to carry) meaning. In other words, the actual events or objects cannot be separated from their designations: they simultaneously signify (or fail to signify) a meaning which the senders wish to transmit to the receivers. The signification aspect of events and objects was actually with us in the preceding discussion: the conditions which sentencing practice is based on, and the arguments concerning obedience to the law and the effects of legislation which constitute the basis of new penal legislation, do not find adequate designations through the factual aspects of sentencing practice and legislation.

But the signification process may also be discussed in more direct terms, and with an emphasis on some further aspects. Through which media is information about the law communicated in our society? Primarily through the large mass media, which are complex organizations with internal tensions, conflicts and modes of co-operation, and which, above all, represent interests quite different from that of communicating information about the law. The interests in question may be summarized as a combination of news and sales interests: a combined emphasis on striking news and news that sells. This distorts the information in general which is transmitted, and it certainly distorts the communication of information about crime in the direction of the highly deviant, the violent, and the sexual (Aarsnes et al., 1974; Simonsen, 1976; From, 1976; Hjemdal, 1987; summarized in Mathiesen, 1986; 154–7). And the more or less refined details in legislation and sentencing practice have a very hard time penetrating and becoming recognizable. The process has two related features. First, what may be called *filtration*.

'Filtration' means that the details of legislation and sentencing practice, the choices between sanctions which are close to each other and which constitute the everyday routine of criminal policy, are systematically if not totally left out. Filtration takes place in a number of concrete nodal points in media organizations: in the relationship between the journalist and his or her source, at the internal meetings where long-range priorities concerning news are decided, at the desk where the quick and short-range decisions about priorities are made.

Secondly, what may be called *focusing*. 'Focusing' means that after filtration has taken place, specific attention is paid to what is considered really newsworthy. A magnifying glass, so to speak, is put on the newsworthy. Focusing takes place through decisions about priorities concerning the front page, the selection of pictures, decisions about layout, the use of vignettes calling the reader's or viewer's attention to the story, as well as dramaturgic treatment of the material through the use of serials, the selection of background material, and so on (on the dramaturgy of the media, see Hernes, 1984; Mathiesen and Hjemdal, 1986).

The difference as well as the relationship between filtration and focusing is important. Through filtration, unsensational and un-dramatic material is taken *out*, while through focusing, sensational and dramatic material is moved *forward*. This is the main difference between the two. But as mentioned already, focusing on the sensational and dramatic at the same time takes place *with the background of* filtration; with the background, you might say, of the first preliminary sorting. This is the main relationship between the two. The unsensational and undramatic material which survives filtration remains in the news. But focusing gives it only a relegated position.

There are variations between the media in terms of degree of filtration and focusing. There are, in this respect, differences between the radio, television and newspapers, as well as for example between various newspapers. But the literature on media sociology gives us reason to emphasize that the two processes are accelerating, and that a development is taking place in the direction of uniformity with respect to content. It would lead us too far from our topic to detail the indications and background of this develop-ment (for a discussion of it, see Mathiesen, 1986, Chs IV, VI). Here the point is that the acceleration of the two processes, and the increasing uniformity of media content, provides a background for the generalizations concerning the communication process pre-sented above.

The main point may also be formulated in this way. Due to filtration and focusing, it is primarily the sensational and dramatic 'legal news' which is transmitted through the media, thus reaching the larger population – dramatic changes in legislation, particularly sensational or titillating cases, and so on. The small differences, and the way in which the criminal justice system handles mass crime, which constitute the large bulk of grey, everyday attempts to provide messages with a preventive effect, are only to a very small extent transmitted. Communication of 'legal news' is fundamentally distorted.

The Sign Structure: Context for Interpretation We shall now say something about the third point, the sign structure which the designations enter into and are interpreted through.

By way of introduction: towards the end of his article from 1977/1982, Andenæs makes the following statement: 'I believe very many can testify, on the basis of personal experience, that the risk of detection and negative sanctions play a role in connection with crimes such as tax evasion, smuggling, drunken driving, and traffic violations' (Andenæs, 1977/1982: 229). Andenæs' point of departure, then, is 'personal experience'. It should be emphasized that he clearly restricts the types of crime which his personal experience supposedly throws light on. And he also points out that 'there is of course a danger in generalizing from oneself. Knowledge of other groups and their attitudes is important' (Andenæs, 1977/1982: 229). Nevertheless, personal experience is basic, and equivalent to common-sense reasoning: 'In my opinion, there has been a tendency among criminologists to underestimate the significance of common-sense reasoning about general prevention, based on ordinary psychological facts and the experience of everyday life' (Andenæs, 1977/1982: 229).

The question is, however, whether 'personal experience' is such a fruitful point of departure. What is 'comon-sense reasoning'? Phenomenological sociology gives us a hint. 'Common-sense reasoning' is the world of everyday experiences which are so prevalent, so ingrained in our lives, that they are taken for granted. 'Common-sense reasoning' is built on knowledge which is so much a part of us that we do not question it. What we are particularly prone not to question, is *precisely the generalization of our own experience to others*. We take for granted that others experience the world as we do. We are psychologically unable to pull ourselves out of this pre-understanding and genuinely take a different perspective, seeing the world from the point of view of others.

But if we are to understand the preventive effect, or, rather, the lack of preventive effect, of punishment, this is precisely what we have to do. Lawyers are usually not so skilful at doing it, because their reasoning about facts is so unempirical, and based precisely on 'common sense' (Graver, 1986).

There is a fairly good basis for the following generalization: the higher the crime rate in a given group, the less effective will punishment be as a preventive measure. You could also put it this way: for those who – for other reasons – are safely placed on the 'right' side of the line, the thought of a penal sanction perhaps functions as an added obstacle. For those who – again for other reasons – are squarely placed on the 'wrong' side, the penal sanction is neutralized as such an obstacle.

This generalization has a good deal of empirical support, even if it probably requires further specification. As a point of departure, we know that a large part of an average Norwegian population has committed criminal acts, and not just trifling acts at that (Stange-land and Hauge, 1974). In this sense, crime is an everyday thing. However, we also know that those who *remain* criminally active, and who recidivate frequently and end up with long-term sentences in our prisons, show an accumulation of indices of social and personal problems – alcohol use, poor education, family disruption, etc (Bødal, 1962, 1969; Christie, 1975/1982). And we know that a relatively small group of youths with a wide range of serious problems are responsible for a large part of the more serious juvenile delinquency (Balvig, 1984c). The point here is that when facing people with such a complex and problematic background, a background which, as a life context, increases the probability of criminal behaviour, the preventive effect of punishment is also neutralized. Put briefly and in bold relief: general prevention functions in relation to those who do not 'need' it. In relation to those who do 'need' it, it does not function.

This main point may be placed within our communicative frame of reference. The sign structure which the preventive message lands in and is interpreted within, the context of interpretation within which the signal is picked up and understood, is such that the signal is not effective, and the message not understood as the sender has meant it. With a background in complex problems related to alcohol, family life, work situation and educational situation, which together constitute the relevant sign structure or context of interpreta-tion, the signal is not interpreted as a (threat of a) deterrent sanction or an educational message. Rather, it is for example interpreted as more oppression, more moralizing and more rejection.

Above we have talked about what may broadly be called 'traditional' crime – the usual types of property crime, violent street crime, drug-related crime. A corresponding line of argument may be offered for modern economic crime. That part of the business community which largely keeps away from grey or black economic activity on normative grounds, lives in a normative sign structure or moral context of interpretation which at the same time makes the threat of punishment appear as a deterrent sanction or a sensible educational message. Those who are not kept back on normative grounds, however, live within a normative sign structure which neutralizes the deterrent effect of punishment. Again in bold relief: general prevention functions in relation to those who do not 'need' it. In relation to those who 'need' it, it does not function.

Communication Process and Research Results

In view of what we have said about the factual aspects of messages, the designations that messages are given, and the sign structures within which they are received and interpreted, we may return to the uncertainty and lack of clarity of the research results in the area (pp. 51–8).

The main features of the communication process go a long way towards explaining this uncertainty and lack of clarity. In a communication situation where the factual aspects of the messages are such that the messages are unclear, in a situation where the designations which are provided increase this lack of clarity significantly, and in a situation where the sign structure, the context of interpretation, *among those who are criminally active* is such that the deterrent, educative and habit-forming effect of the messages is neutralized, lack of clarity and uncertainty of research results – and only modest or marginal correlations – is simply to be *expected*.

Lack of clarity and uncertainty as something to be *expected* is overlooked in general prevention research. Rather, these are viewed as regrettable characteristics of the research situation, or characteristics which may be overcome through better research techniques and increased knowledge. In this way, general prevention research adjusts to general prevention as a paradigm, and also to an underlying main view in research in general, which implies that uncertain and unclear results are a function of imperfect research instruments, and that *reality is 'actually' certain and clear*. The expectation of reaching a final result which is certain and clear is deeply rooted in science, and reflected for example in the many statistical tests developed within the social sciences to ascertain certain and clear differences. As far as general prevention goes, the communication process necessarily makes the results uncertain and unclear and the correlations weak at best. This is, you might say, 'preventive reality'.

Thus, the communication process itself becomes a very important background for having far greater doubts about the notion of the preventive effect of punishment than is usually entertained.

General Prevention and Morality

The notion of general prevention does not only raise questions about the effectiveness of punishment. It also raises a basic moral question, and this contains two parts. First, what is the moral basis for punishing someone, perhaps hard, in order to prevent entirely different people from committing equivalent acts?

Here the question is formulated in general terms, and is relevant regardless of who is being punished – whether the person is rich or poor, strong or weak. Quite generally: can we sacrifice one person to make another go free?

The question is raised in penal theory, but its bluntness is frequently softened by an emphasis on various other considerations. Various circumstances, it is claimed, such as the seriousness of the crime we try to prevent in others, the consideration of retribution in relation to the offender we punish, and so on, enter into a kind of aggregated conclusion. At times it seems as if considerations are added to save the final conclusion – the consideration of general prevention. But the moral question nevertheless remains, troublesome and unanswered, however masked.

Secondly, and as a further sharpening of the first problem: what is the moral basis for punishing someone, perhaps hard, in order to prevent entirely different people from committing equivalent acts, when those we punish to a large extent are poor and highly stigmatized people in need of assistance rather than punishment?

There are solid grounds for posing the moral question in the latter, sharper form. Today we know that the penal system strikes at the 'bottom' rather than at the 'top' of society. Largely, the harder the punishment, the poorer and more stigmatized are those exposed to it.

Part of the reason for this lies in a fact we mentioned in the discussion of sign structures. Those who remain criminally active, and wind up with long prison sentences, show an accumulation of social and personal problems (see again for example Balvig, 1984c). Another part of the reason, however, has to do with the functioning of the penal system, notably its systemic tendency to create social inequality.

The prisons are above all filled by people from the lower strata of the working class who have committed theft and other 'traditional' crimes (for the Norwegian situation, see Stortingsmelding Government White Paper No. 104, 1977–78: 188; Christie, rev. ed. 1982: 117; Mathiesen, 1982: 31–2). The class character of the penal system may be explained as the result of a process, through which the formal equality of the law, with systematic exclusion of any reference to class, actually does not function as a brake on inequality.

The first step in the process lies in *the definition of criminal behaviour provided by the law*. The law is equal for everybody, but to 'the extent that our society is a class society, the law will also have this characteristic. The law threatens neither private capital nor international exploitation of weak nations' (Christie, rev. ed. 1982: 118, translated from the Norwegian by the present author). The law threatens, on the other hand, theft and related acts, typically committed by people from the lowest strata of the working class. While the socially damaging transactions and acts of the ship-owner are typically legal or semi-legal, the equivalent acts of the alcoholic vagrant (if they may be viewed as equivalent) are typically illegal.

The second step in the process is *detection risk*. Even if penal law is constructed as suggested above, people from higher strata obviously also commit acts which are punishable. But their illegal acts are usually 'less visible, by taking place within a complex organizational framework and with methods which are extremely difficult to uncover. Breaking-and-entering is so simple in terms of form. The reception of money, or other favours – kept outside the company accounts in return for letting company A rather than company B do a particular job – takes place more quietly and exists in the unclear borderland between gifts and deception' (Christie, rev. ed. 1982: 118–19). The same holds for fraud in connection with grants, companies operating with fictitious accounts, planned bankruptcies, fraudulent investments, manipulation with company capital, environmental crime, etc. These are acts which take place 'within a complex organizational framework and with methods which are extremely difficult to uncover'.

The third step concerns *the unequal ability to settle the matter*, and get it over and done with, if detection and suspicion nevertheless follow. The detected tax evader or VAT embezzler is more easily able to settle the matter than is the burglar or the vargrant. This inequality probably permeates the finest details of the class and stratification system. A Norwegian study of cases of VAT embezzlement reported to the police provides an interesting example. The study showed that the cases of VAT embezzlement reported to the police by the taxation authorities were systematically *small* companies and business people (Hedlund, 1982). There is little reason to believe that large and wealthy companies do not attempt to evade VAT, and never come under suspicion for it by the taxation authorities. The small companies were probably reported because they had a weak economy, thus being unable to come to agreement with the taxation authorities concerning postponement of payment, payment in instalments, and the like.

The fourth step in the process consists of a series of *other selective mechanisms* contained in the operations of the police and the criminal justice system. For example, largely, police activity and resources are geared towards catching the small fry who have committed traditional crimes. Only a minor part of police resources are 'oriented upwards'. And if those who commit 'modern' economic crimes are in fact detected and caught, they are able to pay for a good defence.

This is a summary of some of the most important steps in the process. What, finally, about the courts? Is there also inequality before the courts? Empirically, it is difficult to find out, because we are so rarely presented with similar cases which may be compared. And when we try to 'create' equal cases by traditional sociological methodology, holding various background factors constant, our figures soon become too small for comparisons. A comprehensive study by Vilhelm Aubert (1972, Ch. 8) suggested that low status people were more often given harder sentences when various other factors were controlled. But the numbers soon became small, and one difficulty in the study was that the offences in question were characterized by the legal regulations applying to them, a fact which might hide important differences.

In other words, the answer to the question of whether the courts handle similar cases unequally, does not have an entirely easy answer. But I am not so sure that this question is all that vital. The main point is that the judge *is so rarely confronted by similar cases from different social classes.* Through the process described above, those who are brought before the courts are largely going to be the more or less poverty-stricken performers of traditional crimes. Regardless of whether there is equality before the courts, they are the ones who end up in our prisons.

This brings us back to the question of morality. The systematic process whereby the formal equality of penal law does not function as an effective brake on inequality (but, rather, masks actual inequality), puts the moral question on its sharp edge: if we punish people on the grounds of general prevention, we actually to a very large extent sacrifice poor and stigmatized people in order to keep others on the narrow path.

The point may be elaborated. In part, the legislator's and the judge's use of the argument of general prevention is directed towards other poor and stigmatized people. This is for example the case with respect to drug-related crimes: some poor people are sacrificed in order to keep other poor people on the narrow path. One might have tried to do something fundamental with the general situation of the poor, which might have abolished the criminal offence as such a likely solution. Instead, an attempt is made to discipline the many poor by sanctioning some of them.

In part, however, the argument of general prevention has a rather diffuse direction – in its most general form, the aim is to improve people's general tendency to be law-abiding. This means that quite different categories of people, far outside the range of the poor and stigmatized, are also included as target groups for the message of general prevention, and seen as groups to be kept in line by pain infliction on the poor.

I am not sure which of the two directions of the argument is the more questionable from a moral point of view.

When the Proponents go against General Prevention

We have discussed the uncertain and unclear results of research, various aspects of the communication of the preventive message, as well as general prevention as a moral question. As further elaboration, it is of interest to note that the same arguments against general prevention are emphasized also by the proponents of general prevention – when their interests speak in favour of them.

When those who adhere to general prevention as grounds for punishment, in certain contexts argue against general prevention, the words they use are different from those employed above. But in important respects, the stock of ideas is the same.

In the first place, the uncertainty and unclear nature of the empirical data is suddenly emphasized. Let me illustrate. In a detailed and important article on punishment for drunken driving in Norway a few years back, Johs. Andenæs advocated that prison be used less automatically, with non-prison sanctions in cases of low concentrations of alcohol in the blood. (Andenæs, 1982. At the time the article was written, a minimum of three weeks of imprisonment was automatically given to drivers showing an alcohol concentration of 0.05 percent or more. Legislation has later been changed in the direction advocated by, among others, Andenæs.) What would be the effect, Andenæs asked, of fining rather than imprisoning people showing low concentrations of alcohol in the blood? He opened his own reply to the question with the following statement (Andenæs, 1982: 129, translated from the Norwegian by the present author): 'As *with all questions concerning general prevention*, we also here have to rely on general reasoning, including a good deal of guesswork' (my italics).

Andenæs goes on to present his own views, which we will return to below. Here I only wish to call attention to the *uncertainty* which Andenæs emphasizes as far as knowledge of effects goes. Suddenly, it has become important to emphasize the uncertainty, indeed, to emphasize it in connection 'with all questions concerning general prevention'. These are strong words, used in a context where a major proponent of general prevention finds reason to downgrade the preventive effects of punishment.

Secondly, arguments concerning communication are in reality emphasized (even if they are not used to explain uncertain and unclear empirical results, as we have done). The three main features of the communication process which we discussed earlier – the factual aspects, the importance of the designations, and the context of interpretation – are in fact touched on in the 1982 article by Andenæs, though the concepts used are quite different. For one thing, Andenæs emphasizes how the everyday life of criminal policy in the area of drunken driving in fact consists of small differences which are hardly important in terms of effects. 'One must differentiate', he says, between 'the *total effect* of the penal system for drunken driving and the *marginal effect* following from each component in the system' (Andenæs, 1982: 129). Fines rather than imprisonment for low alcohol concentrations, we are led to understand, would only make a marginal difference. Furthermore, Andenæs emphasizes how a message may not necessarily be received and perceived as it is intended. He refers to a study showing that a majority of a representative sample views the loss of a month's wage as more threatening than three weeks' imprisonment – quite the reverse of the intention of the legislator. The details of the process of signification remain entirely undiscussed. But the basic point that punishment is not necessarily received and experienced as intended, is there. Finally, Andenæs, who in other contexts is quite willing to generalize from 'personal experience', is suddenly wary of such generalizations, referring by clear implication to the context of interpretation. On this issue, he is worth quoting in detail:

> The danger is near at hand that we overestimate the preventive importance of our strict legislation concerning drunken driving, because those who usually participate in public discussions of the issue, generalize from their own experience and from their own acquaintances. Politicians, judges, police officers, professors and traffic experts – these are groups which would feel a sentence for drunken driving as a social catastrophe, and who at the same time are to a considerable extent able to control sudden impulses. We cannot take for granted that what is the case for this circle of people, also holds for other groups, for example juveniles, or people lacking control over their alcohol consumption. (Andenæs, 1982: 133)

There is every reason to doubt that only groups like professors and traffic experts would 'feel a sentence for drunken driving as a catastrophe'. Why juveniles, who have an occupational career ahead of them, and who would lose their driving licence for long periods of time, should not feel the same, remains unexplained. The description is patronizing. But the main point, suggesting the dangers inherent in generalizing from one's 'own experience and from [one's] own acquaintances' is important. As we said earlier: within a sign structure built on alcohol problems, family problems, unemployment problems and educational problems, the signal from the state is not understood as a deterrent sanction or an educational message. Rather, it is understood as more oppression, more moralizing, more rejection. The concepts of sign structure and context of interpretation are not used by Andenæs. Precisely because the basic and general communicative understanding of general prevention is lacking, the contention about dangers inherent in generalizations from 'own experience' may be called upon in a haphazard and facile way – simply when it suits the author's purposes. But the *contention itself* is the same. In connection with drunken driving, Andenæs in fact uses words very close to ours:

> Our strict legislation concerning drunken driving has had a good preventive effect in relation to most drivers. Therefore, the total number of drunken drivers on our roads is small. But these are for the most part people who would have been moderate consumers also without our strict legislation, though they might not have kept under the 0.05 percent limit . . . Alcohol accidents are dominated by people who have used large amounts, and the drivers are to a large extent people with major alcohol problems and serious social maladjustments. The groups in question are poor objects for the deterrent and educative effects of the law . . . In brief: There is reason to believe that the motivating effect of the law is strongest in relation to those who would have represented a modest traffic accident risk even if they had consumed more alcohol than stated by the limit of the law . . . (Andenæs, 1982: 132)

Andenæs here comes very close to our own conclusion, which we put in bold relief once more. General prevention functions in relation to those who do not 'need' it. In relation to those who 'need' it, it does not function.

We have seen that the unclear and uncertain nature of the research evidence, as well as the three main components which comprise the communication process, are actually referred to by a major international proponent of general prevention. Thirdly, it may briefly be added that the same proponent also touches on the moral question. Here he is vaguer, and more consistent with his general view on general prevention, but after having emphasized the preventive effect of punishment as the most important grounds for maintaining a penal system, he goes on to say – in connection with drunken drivers – that 'We do not wish adherence to the law *at any price*. The consideration of general prevention must be balanced in relation to justice and humanitarian considerations' (Andenæs, 1982: 129). In other places, he also touches on the highly unreasonable use of prison grounded in considerations of general prevention for drivers with low alcohol concentrations.

We may well ask: why do not the proponents of general prevention use all of these arguments in connection with other groups – drug offenders, vagrants, criminally active juvenile delinquents in general – where the arguments are just as valid and pertinent? Regarding these groups, it is just as valid to argue that 'we also here have to rely on general reasoning, including a good deal of guesswork' (Andenæs, 1982: 129). It is just as valid to say that we must differentiate between 'the *total effect* of the penal system . . . and the *marginal effect* following from each component in the system' (Andenæs, 1982: 129). It is just as valid to say that punishment may not be received and understood as intended. It is just as valid to say that the 'danger is near at hand that we overestimate the preventive importance . . . because those who usually participate in public discussions of the issue, generalize from their own experience and from their own acquaintances' (Andenæs, 1982: 123), and that we 'do not wish adherence to the law *at any price*' (Andenæs, 1982: 129). But the arguments are left unused and silent in connection with these groups. Taken together, they actually speak very forcefully for a reduction of the punishment level for the groups in question.

So do a number of other arguments in Andenæs' presentation: international comparisons showing that even very significant differences in punishment level for drunken driving do not produce comparable differences in crime level, increased knowledge about the relative effects of various degrees of influence of drink (comparable to increased knowledge of the effects of traditional crimes relative to other social threats like work accidents, traffic accidents and pollution), and so on.

But once more, these arguments are not used. The proponents of general prevention only use the arguments when they want to. It is extremely difficult to understand the principle behind limiting the arguments to drunken drivers with a low concentration of alcohol in their blood.

Does Prison Have a Defence in General Prevention?

We have pursued the question of general prevention through a number of steps. The research results are very uncertain and unclear, showing only partial and modest or marginal effects. The communication process is very defective and abounds with problems, a fact which explains the uncertain and unclear research findings and makes it possible for us to understand that reality in this area – the preventive effect as such – *is* actually uncertain and unclear. The moral question is pressing. And even proponents of general prevention stress these major points when they find reason to argue against general prevention.

Two further points must be emphasized. First, it is the combination of the arguments discussed above which is important. If you only look at the research results, only at the communication process, or only at the moral issue, you might say that the argumentation was weaker. The point is that the three sets of arguments *all point in the same direction*. In social life, there is often conflict between considerations of efficacy and morality: considerations of efficacy pull in one direction, and considerations of morality in another. This is not the case here. On the contrary.

This means that the whole thrust of the argumentation dictates restraint when it comes to the use of punishment as a state method of control and government. The whole thrust of the argumentation strongly suggests an emphasis on alternative methods of government.

Secondly, and in particular, the argumentation dictates restraint with respect to the use of the more painful methods of punishment, in the Western world above all *the prison sanction*, which is the focus of attention in this book.

It is impossible to find solid arguments in terms of general prevention as a base for the international development of the prison sanction which now is taking place (see Chapter 1).

The unclear and highly uncertain research results do not provide a solid argument. What we know theoretically and empirically about the communication process does not provide a solid argument. The consideration of morality does not provide a solid argument.

Rather, if you look at the question from the point of view of general prevention, there is every reason to shrink the prison system, diminishing its use.

The unclear and uncertain research results become all the more important as an argument for this when the issue concerns the use of as harmful and painful a sanction as that of locking people up in prison. What we know theoretically and empirically about the communication process becomes all the more important as an argument for this when the issue concerns the use of as harmful and painful a sanction as that of locking people up in prison. The moral consideration becomes all the more important – in fact, it is placed on its sharpest possible edge – when the issue concerns the use of as harmful and painful a sanction as that of locking people up in prison.

While it *may* be maintained that the combined thrust of the marginal results, the communication deficiencies, and the moral consideration is not all that heavy with regard to less painful and therefore less significant sanctions, at least it becomes very heavy – some would say decisive – when it comes to the harmful and painful prison sanction.

In brief, also in terms of general prevention, prison finds a poor defence. When concluding the chapter on rehabilitation, we quoted an authoritative Swedish source, which very strongly emphasized that the rehabilitative effect of prison is an illusion. The same source continued with an equally strong statement about the effects of the prison sentence as far as general prevention goes. Again, we may conclude by quoting verbatim:

> In line with what we have said above [about the illusion of rehabilitation by means of deprivation of liberty, TM], the point of departure must be that the employment of prison as punishment can only be motivated by what is usually called general prevention, and partly also by views concerning protection of society. However, the effects of the prison sentence in these respects are to a large extent uncertain.

> Thus, all available research results as well as international comparisons show that the development of crime is not related in any definite way to the level maintained in terms of number of incarcerations and their length . . . Actually, it is no exaggeration to say that the significance of criminal policy for the development of crime is in this respect rather subordinate, if you compare it with family and school policy, labour and social policies, the organization of the criminal justice system and its functioning in a broad sense, as well as – naturally – the economic structure and view of man in society. On the whole, it may be said that endeavours to create a solidary society with a better and more just distribution of income, housing, education, work environment, and culture are appropriate for preventing the risks of social maladjustment which often constitute conditions favouring crime. Such endeavours, therefore, are certainly more important than penal sanctions against crimes which have already been committed. (Government Bill 1982/83, No. 85: 30; translated from the Swedish by the present author)

It is only reasonable to demand that the authorities now take their own correct understanding seriously in practice.

4
Other Theories of Social Defence

Other Theories of Individual Prevention

As mentioned several times, the theories of social defence are usually grouped in two: individual and general prevention. Above, we have discussed one important theory of individual prevention – the theory which views prison as rehabilitative (Chapter 2) – and the theories of general prevention (Chapter 3).

As mentioned before (p. 18), this order is not accidental. As the theory of individual prevention in terms of rehabilitation became seriously threatened and put out of ideological action during the 1970s, the theories of general prevention grew in importance, nationally as well as internationally. But the theories of general prevention were also exposed to criticism. Consequently, the 1980s have seen the rediscovery of individual prevention in terms of incapacitation, and to some extent in terms of individual deterrence. The theories are old, but have received new impetus during the 1980s. In short, as prevailing theory has been questioned or put out of action, the criminal justice system and its researchers have produced new varieties of old theories of social defence.

Incapacitation

'Incapacitation' has become an important criminological concept during the 1980s. The concept implies that the offender's 'capacity' to commit new crimes is to be concretely obstructed or reduced through a prison sentence. The basic idea is that the offender is to be incapacitated by being taken out of social circulation. This is precisely why prison, or extended prison, is used in order to incapacitate.

Though we sometimes do find the idea of incapacitation in combination with the notion of rehabilitation, the theory of incapacitation is, in its pure form, stripped of humanitarian ideals emphasizing help to the incarcerated. Because rehabilitation has become so outmoded in the 1980s, we often find the notion of incapacitation in its stripped or pure form.

Below, we shall first in general terms present two basic questions which arise in connection with incapacitation. They may be called *the question of accuracy* and *the question of principles*. Each of the two questions in turn has two aspects which we will be discussing.

Next we shall, more concretely, present two varieties of research and efforts in the area of incapacitation. They may be called *collective* and *selective* incapacitation. We shall look at both varieties in relation to the two basic questions of accuracy and principles.

Finally, we shall draw some conclusions.

Two Basic Questions

The Question of Accuracy In the first place, the theory of incapacitation raises this main question: how accurately is it possible to predict who will commit crimes in the future? The greater the accuracy, the better will incarceration in prison function as a method of incapacitation. The smaller the accuracy, the more poorly it will function.

The question of accuracy contains two subquestions. When accuracy is low, two types of problems may arise.

On the one hand, one may fail to use prison, or extended prison, when facing people with a high recidivism risk. In other words, one may fail to incarcerate – or just incarcerate for a short period of time – people who stand in great danger of committing new crimes. In the international literature, this problem has been called the problem of the 'false negatives': the prediction is negative, in the sense of stating that the offender will *not* recidivate, but the prediction is false because recidivism occurs.

On the other hand, one may in fact use prison, or extended prison, when facing people with a low recidivism risk. In other words, one may in fact incarcerate – or incarcerate for an extended period of time – people who do not stand in great danger of committing new crimes. In the literature, this problem has been called the problem of the 'false positives': the prediction is positive, in the sense of stating that the offender *will* recidivate, but the prediction is false because recidivism in fact does not occur.

In Norway, the criminologist Nils Christie has given the question of accuracy careful attention. In a dissenting statement in a Penal Council Report from 1974 on the treatment of so-called abnormal offenders, he examined the relevant international literature which was available at the time (Straffelovrådet, Penal Council Report NOU 1974, No. 17: 126–46). He distinguished between the standard and less serious offences such as traditional property crimes on the one hand, and the more unusual and serious crimes such as crimes of violence and sexual crimes on the other. It is possible, he argued, to predict with a fairly high degree of accuracy that those who have often committed traditional property crimes will do so again. Prediction is much more difficult for the more unusual and physically speaking more serious offences (Penal Council Report NOU 1974, No. 17: 128, translated from the Norwegian by the present author): 'In view of this, it must be stated clearly that today we do not have any sound basis for predicting later dangerous behaviour at all.'

Christie was especially concerned with the problem of the false positives. As he put it (Penal Council Report NOU 1974, No. 17: 128): 'In particular, we cannot avoid catching a large number who would in practice not have proved dangerous later . . . If we want to catch a few dangerous people, we have to lock up a large group which probably would not have committed anything dangerous at all.'

The Question of Principles To Christie and many others the problem of the false positives – the fact that many who are actually not dangerous will have to be detained if we are to detain a few who are – constitutes a serious question of principle: what is the justification for locking up many who are actually not dangerous in order to secure ourselves from a few who are?

As we shall see later, this question is certainly still with us. But this does not exhaust the question of principles. In addition, and independently of accuracy, the notion of incapacitation raises another fundamental problem of principle.

The problem is this: what is the basis, in terms of principles, for the sentencing to prison for acts which otherwise, without the sentence, may or will occur in the future? The prevention of future acts is here not just a more or less vaguely formulated goal, but the explicit *grounds or reason* for the particular sentence. What is the basis for grounding a sentence in future acts?

The fact that this is a very real question of principle may be seen by the organization of the penal code.

The penal code contains regulations concerning acts which are considered criminal in our society. The regulations have two basic features. In the first place, they provide instructions concerning punishments for acts which the individual has committed *in the past*. The penal code, and the penal system in general, is distinctly past-oriented. It is the acts of the past which are the basis of punishment.

Secondly, the regulations provide instructions concerning punishment for acts *in a narrow sense* which have been committed by the individual. It is the act itself which is the basis of the sentence. So-called irrelevant circumstances, pointing more or less beyond the act, are peeled away. There is an emphasis in sentencing practice on mitigating and aggravating circumstances: age is for example at times viewed as a mitigating circumstance. But the main principle is clear – what you are *sentenced for* is the act in a narrow sense.

The fundamental problem inherent in the theory of incapacitation is that it insists on sentencing to prison for acts which, without the sentence, may or will be committed in *the future*, and that it insists on doing so on the basis of an examination of the individual, and the individual's situation, in more or less a *broad sense*.

When doing so, incapacitation theory breaks fundamentally with the basic principles of penal law. It transforms the consideration of future acts, together with considerations concerning the individual and his or her situation in a broad sense, from being considerations which are accepted as fundamental in a minority of very special cases (as, in Norway, in the use of preventive detention for so-called abnormal offenders, where they are questionable enough: see Aubert, 1958; Christie, 1962; Mathiesen, 1965a; Ellingsen, 1987; Kongshavn, 1987), into being considerations which are to be considered fundamental and normal to the use of prison in general.

The problems implicit in the employment of such a basis for sentencing are understood by many lawyers, who are often less oriented towards efficacy than are politicians and administrators. Lawyers point to the fact that by this emphasis, important principles of 'the rule of law' are broken. Strictly speaking, many of the same basic objections could be entertained against general prevention and the notion of rehabilitation. These theories also contain the built-in presupposition that the offender is partly to be sentenced for future acts – the acts of others or the offender's own acts, which are to be prevented – and that the sentencing takes place on the basis of a set of broad evaluations. I believe the reasons why the basic objections are rarely as explicit in connection with these theories, are, on the one hand, that general prevention has such a strong and widespread ideological foothold and, on the other, that rehabilitation presupposes giving the prison a meaningful content over and above pure and simple incarceration. The ideological foothold of general prevention, and the meaningful content which the prison is supposed to be provided with, make it more difficult to perceive the problems inherent in the orientation towards the future. But actually, they are there.

I have said that the theory of incapacitation breaks with some of the basic principles of the penal code and the penal system. In the penal system, the principles we have mentioned are just as important as, for example, the principle stating that no one is to be viewed as guilty before sentencing is passed. Therefore, it is no exaggeration to say that the notion of incapacitation breaks with the 'ethics' of penal law. The basic principles stating that no one is to be sentenced for an act not yet committed, and that it is the act and not circumstances exterior to the act which the person is to be sentenced for, belong to the basic rules of the penal system.

The notion of incapacitation, then, raises two basic questions, the question of accuracy and the question of principles.

The question of accuracy may largely be said to be a question of *efficacy*, though, as we have seen, it also raises the fundamental question of the 'false positives' – those who are erroneously predicted to new criminality, and who thus are included in the incapacitation programme. The question of principles may be said to be a question of *morality*.

It should be noted clearly that both main questions are questions of degree. Accuracy varies. So do violations of principles: the more one-sided the emphasis on future acts as a basis for sentencing, and the broader the prognostic background, the more the principles in question are violated. The violations would become extreme if the person sentenced had not been found guilty of any past crime, but was only sentenced for future acts, and if no boundaries whatsoever existed concerning relevant background, but a full totality was considered relevant. In the context of the penal system we have not yet come this far in our society – a guilty verdict for a past crime must at least be in the package as partial grounds for a sentence, in order for the process in the penal system to be initiated. But, as we shall see later, there are examples of research which violate the principles seriously enough. Perhaps we are on the road towards the extreme.

We shall now proceed to look at the concrete varieties of research and efforts in the area of incapacitation.

Concrete Varieties
As mentioned above, we may differentiate between two main varieties of research and efforts in incapacitation: 'collective' and 'selective' incapacitation. The distinction, which is a rough division, is used, for instance, in Andrew von Hirsch's recently published work on incapacitation and justice in the penal system (von Hirsch, 1986; see also for example Blumstein et al., 1986).

Collective Incapacitation Collective incapacitation is the simplest of the two. The basic point is that prison sentences, perhaps

extended prison sentences, are given to broad categories of people –
defendants convicted of major felonies, defendants who have
recidivated a given number of times – without any attempt to
predict who are the high risk individuals among them. By removing
everyone in the category from circulation for stated periods of time,
perhaps for particularly long periods of time, an incapacitative
effect will presumably occur.

Internationally, the idea of collective incapacitation was in the
forefront in parts of criminology during the mid-1970s. This variety
of incapacitation theory was therefore partly combined with ideas
about general prevention. The conservative American criminologist
James Q. Wilson was at that time the leading international
exponent of it, in the first edition of his book *Thinking About Crime*
(Wilson, 1975: 173–4, 198–202). Wilson stated that by concentrating
on incapacitating a larger fraction of convicted robbers, especially
the repeaters, at least a 20 percent reduction of serious robbery
would be conceivable (Wilson, 1975: 199).

Wilson, who argued very hypothetically, based his argument
vaguely on a statistical model developed by Reuel and Shlomo
Shinnar (Shinnar and Shinnar, 1975; Wilson, 1975: 200–202; see
also von Hirsch, 1986: 116). Very briefly, the basic point of the
argument seems to be this. A measure was developed representing
the individual offending frequency, i.e. the average annual rate at
which individual offenders commit offences in the community
('lambda'). A high average rate of offending was assumed. Based
on this assumption, sizeable crime reduction effects of across the
board incarceration of given groups of offenders could be predicted.

Actually, however, the rate at which individual offenders commit
offences in the community is *unknown* (though there is a converg-
ence in *estimates* for given offence types, see Blumstein et al., 1986,
Vol. 1: 4). When assuming a lower rate, the calculated effect in
terms of crime reduction decreased dramatically. Evidence concerning a higher or lower rate was not forthcoming. 'As these difficulties
became apparent, enthusiasm for collective incapacitation waned'
(von Hirsch, 1986: 116).

A few years ago, Swedish authorities introduced a reform which
was not meant to throw light on incapacitation, but which in
practice did so. It illustrated well the problems inherent in collective
incapacitation. We shall therefore take a look at it.

On 1 July 1983, Sweden introduced automatic parole on half time
for the large bulk of Swedish prisoners. The main exception from
the new rule concerned offenders convicted to at least two years'
imprisonment for 'particularly serious crimes' directed towards or
bringing about danger to life and health, provided a major risk of

recidivism to the same kind of crime after release could be assumed. In such cases, two-thirds of the sentence had to be served before parole. All other prisoners – the large majority, also many quite serious offenders, since a two-year prison sentence is a long one in Sweden – were to be released on parole on half time. The reform was introduced partly to reduce the pressure on the prisons (see Chapter 1).

The reform had considerable effect on the number of prisoners in Sweden. During the budget period 1982/83, there was an average of 4024 prisoners in Swedish prisons (not including pre-trial detention). For the budget period 1983/84 the corresponding figure was 3505 – a decrease of 519 or 13 percent. If we compare figures on two representative dates, 1 June 1983, one month before the reform was given effect, and 1 June 1984, the decrease was close to 17 percent. The reform constituted an important and interesting attempt to reduce the number of prisoners in the country, and 'shrink' the prisons.

As could be expected, the question was raised of whether the reform had any effect on the Swedish crime rate. The Swedish Council of Crime Prevention did a study to throw light on the question (Ahlberg, 1985).

First, the researchers estimated the number of 'months at liberty' for imprisoned offenders during the second half of 1983, comparing it with what the number would have been if the reform of 1 July 1983 had not taken place. The comparison showed that the country had received an 'addition' of about 3,200 months at liberty.

Next, the researchers estimated the number of reported offences per 'month at liberty' which are normally committed by an imprisoned person during the first year after release. The estimate was based on a study of the documents available for a sample of individuals released during a period prior to the reform. The reason for the choice of the sample was that the individuals who had been released due to the reform had not yet had 'time' to be registered for offences even if they in fact had recidivated.

By relating the 3200 months 'months at liberty' added after the reform, to the average number of reported offences committed per month, the expected number of added crimes during the first half year after the reform was obtained. The total number proved to be a little over 4000 reported crimes.

So-called 'housebreaking' was important in the analysis. During the second part of 1983, an actual increase in the number of housebreakings took place in Sweden. The increase could be calculated to a total of about 2000 offences. There were various reasons for the increase. The contribution of the reform, estimated in the way mentioned above, comprised about 800, or about 40 percent of the total increase, not an insignificant proportion.

What does this tell us about collective incapacitation? Here the duration of imprisonment was *shortened*, while we usually expect it to be increased when incapacitation is the issue. Therefore, the reform says something about incapacitation in a 'negative' sense, that is, something about what Sweden may have *lost* in incapacitative effect.

At first sight, it may seem as if a great deal was lost. About 4000 offences during half a year is no trifle. Neither is a 40 percent contribution to the increase in housebreaking. But first sight is deceptive. The addition of 4,000 offences, and the 40 percent contribution to the increase in housebreaking, followed *after a major collective release of prisoners at exactly the same time*; more precisely, after the collective and immediate release of 13–17 percent of the country's prisoners. Such a discharge is a highly deviant, one-off event; what we must do is to study the incapacitative effect in relation to the normal increase in release, distributed through the year. If we do that, we find that the (lost) incapacitative effect is *minimal*. In line with this, Ahlberg's report concluded that when release was normalized and distributed through the year, the effects would be so small that they would hardly be noticeable in the crime statistics. The future crime level would probably be somewhat higher, but the effect would be marginal. The report formulated this important conclusion in the following words:

> Now, the effects on the number of reported crimes is a phenomenon which will pass rather rapidly. Because so many who had been sentenced to prison were released at the same time, we got an accumulation of crimes of certain kinds for a limited period of time. With time, when release goes back to normal and is distributed evenly through the year, the effects will be of a size which is hardly noticeable in the statistics. Since an incapacitative effect (that effect on crime which follows when people are incarcerated, for example in prison) exists, the future level will, however marginally, be somewhat higher than if prison terms had remained unchanged. (Ahlberg, 1985: 21, translated from the Swedish by the present author)

In short, in connection with the above-mentioned reform, prison sentences became considerably shorter for the large majority of prisoners. Even this sizeable reduction in duration of imprisonment had only marginal incapacitative effects once the transition period was over.

It may be added that material from the United States shows similar results, but from an increase rather than a decrease in prison figures. The Panel on Research on Criminal Careers, chaired by

Alfred Blumstein and sponsored by the National Institute of Justice, published its major two-volume report in 1986 (Blumstein et al., 1986). The panel paid close attention to the issue of incapacitation. Between 1973 and 1982 the number of state and federal prisoners in the United States almost doubled – 'a sort of an experiment in collective incapacitation' (Messinger and Berk, 1987: 774) – yet the crime rate increased by 29 percent. Estimates available to the panel suggested that depending on the assumed individual offending frequency ('lambda'), the rate would have been 10 to 20 percent higher if the almost 100 percent increase in prison figures had not occurred (Blumstein et al., 1986, Vol 1: 124–8; see especially note 8 on p. 125). This may be viewed as a modest gain, but certainly an extremely costly one in view of the dramatic increase in the prison population. Further reductions 'would require at least 10 to 20 percent increases in inmate populations for each 1 percent reduction in crime' (Vol 1: 128). In short, the marginal effect of collective incapacitation is demonstrated anew.

Let me add that a major collective incapacitation study of so-called dangerous offenders in the United States (Columbus), obtained comparable results in terms of estimated effect. Penal policies of varying degrees of severity were compared with respect to likely incapacitative gain. Even the most severe policy, very unlikely in practice due to the costs involved, showed only a marginal incapacitative effect, and would not in any significant way increase the safety of the citizens (Conrad, 1985, Ch. 5).

It should also be added, however, that the Swedish study helped trigger a proposal to go back to normal release on parole on two-thirds time (though with an added proposal to the effect that sentences in part should be shortened instead; Fängelsestraffkommittén, the Swedish White Paper SOU 1986, No. 13–15; see also Chapter 5 below). The half time reform created considerable public debate, and public allegations about an increased crime rate. The allegations were based in part on the effect of the collective release following right after the reform. The conclusions with regard to long-term effect were overlooked. This shows how the public debate through mass media filtration and focusing (see pp. 65–6) may influence criminal policy.

What, then, can be said by way of summary about collective incapacitation as far as accuracy and principles go?

As mentioned earlier, collective incapacitation does not contain any attempts to predict high risk individuals in the given category. Nevertheless, a kind of 'collective' prediction about recidivism is implied. Therefore, the question of accuracy is relevant.

We have already seen that proponents of incapacitation have been unable to demonstrate empirically the individual offending frequency. This fact, which makes effect extremely uncertain, implies also that accuracy is at best just as uncertain, and that there is no guarantee against either many 'false positives' or 'false negatives'. Add to this the major studies in Sweden (Ahlberg, 1985) and the United States (Conrad, 1985), which show that even very sizeable differences in duration of imprisonment suggest only marginal long-term effects on the crime rate and the safety of the citizens, as well as the very modest gains – even when the best of 'lambdas' is assumed – following from the extremely dramatic rise in the prison population in the United States (Blumstein et al., 1986). The Swedish study very directly implies that the contribution to the total crime rate of those imprisoned at any one time is so small that even sizeable differences in duration of sentence show only marginal effect.

But what if we, by some magic, managed to increase 'collective accuracy', for example by finding criteria defining in more precise terms the nature of the particular groups which recidivate? Some Swedish criminologists have recently argued, quite hypothetically, that this might be possible (Persson, 1987). Relying on what they call 'initiated guesses', and on US estimates suggesting that the individual offending frequency is skewed so that a small percentage of offenders commit a large number of crimes (Blumstein et al., 1986: 4), they have claimed that the proportion of the total number of housebreakings, car thefts, and the like, committed by a small group of persistent recidivists, is so large that confinement of this group would in fact reduce the crime rate. What if they are right? The Norwegian police, inspired by recent Swedish thinking, have instituted (in 1988/89) what they call a 'Ten-on-top' policy, using major resources to track down a small but well-defined persistent group of active recidivating criminals. The police argue that the crime rate will taper down by this policy. What if the Norwegian police are right?

The Swedish criminologists, and even more so the Norwegian police, seem to forget that the present generation of offenders is not the last one. New generations of offenders will appear in the streets. This means that a decline in the crime rate, if any, will soon fade. Now, the collective incapacitation experiment could of course be renewed and continued for the next generation, or generations. But since they are persistent, all generations would have to be imprisoned for a long time. This would be the case even though criminal activity tapers off with age. And we would never catch up, because of the ever-present input of new generations. We would, in effect, end up with huge numbers of prisoners in our prisons, whom we would not know exactly when to release, and continued crime in the streets due to the new generations. This is in fact admitted by the Swedish criminologists in question (Persson, 1987: 25), but not taken into consideration when political claims are made.

So much for the questions related to accuracy. The problems of principles are also present. Collective incapacitation implies that whole categories of offenders are sentenced across the board to extended prison sentences in view of an estimate of the probability of preventing future crimes. In other words, the thinking implies a very considerable emphasis, as the very basis of the sentence as such, on acts not yet committed.

In addition, the thinking also implies a certain emphasis on a broad evaluation of the past: even if prognoses are not made for particular high risk individuals, people with many earlier crimes constitute, as we have seen, a particularly important group (Wilson, 1975: 199). Now, emphasizing a prior criminal record is not so uncommon within the Western penal systems, and not such a broad type of evaluation. The issue is put on a much sharper edge when other social factors are taken into account. We shall return to this shortly, in connection with selective incapacitation. But the heavy emphasis on prior criminal record, implied in so much thinking about collective incapacitation, does represent a deviation from the narrow point of departure. The moral issue is clarified by posing the opposite possibility: prior criminal record, and persistent criminal behaviour, could well be viewed as a mitigating rather than an aggravating circumstance. One could argue that since the persistent criminals have suffered so much already, their sentences should be made more lenient (Christie, 1981). This argument, however, is never heard.

And, to repeat, there is very considerable emphasis, as the basis of the very sentence, on acts not yet committed.

Add to this that the individuals thus sentenced to a large extent are poor, socially handicapped, and stigmatized, and the moral issue becomes acute.

Selective Incapacitation   Now to selective incapacitation. The basic point is prediction of high risk individuals within given groups, and the use of imprisonment, or extended imprisonment, selectively for them. The idea is that the high-rate offenders can be identified individually, given sufficient information about past behaviour and other characteristics. It has been maintained that selective incapacitation strategies may lead to significant reductions in crime without increasing the total numbers of offenders incarcerated (Greenwood, 1982: xix).

The notion of selective incapacitation has a long history, back to early attempts to predict crime in the 1920s and 1930s (see e.g. Hart, 1923, in contrast to Warner, 1923; Glueck and Glueck, 1937; for an excellent review which we utilize here, see von Hirsch, 1986: 105–7). The early prediction studies usually took their point of departure in information gathered about samples of offenders. Using statistical techniques, the relationship between various background factors such as criminal background, employment history, and social history on the one hand, and subsequent recidivism on the other, was studied. Usually, recidivism was measured by reconviction or parole revocations (von Hirsch, 1986: 105). On this basis, predictive indices utilizing the factors showing the strongest relationship with recidivism were constructed. The predictive index could then be used for new samples of offenders.

The studies usually showed that a few factors – criminal history, employment history, and the like – could be combined and used as an instrument to predict high risk individuals. At the same time, however, the correlations were weak, with a high percentage of error in the predictions. The proportions of false negatives, those mistakenly predicted not to recidivate, were substantial. So were the proportions of false positives, those mistakenly predicted to recidivate. The rate of false positives was especially high when the forecasts concerned serious criminality (von Hirsch, 1986: 106). A review of five major prediction studies of violence on the part of violent offenders released from institutions, showed that while the proportion of false negatives was relatively low in some studies and high in others (the proportions varied between 8 and 31 percent), the proportions varied from 59 to 86 percent; Monahan, 1981, Ch. 3). The studies in question used clinical forecasts (as opposed to the 'actuarial' or statistical methodology used in many other studies) and long follow-up periods (three to five years). Though the very high proportions of false positives to some degree could be explained as a result of hidden criminality (i.e. the false positives having committed violent crimes which were undetected), the general tendency could hardly be explained in this way (Monahan, 1981: 82–7). The problem stemmed from the fact that violent crimes are rare. The rarer the event, 'the greater will be the tendency to overpredict' (von Hirsch, 1986: 106–7).

In addition, attempts at reducing the problems of the false negatives increased the problem of the false positives, and vice versa (von Hirsch, 1986: 107). The problem of the false negatives could be reduced by making the definition of probable repeaters, the 'bad risks', broader. This way, the certainty of having the actual 'bad risks' included would be higher. But this increased dramatically the already high proportions of false positives. Conversely, the problem of the false positives could be reduced by making the definition of 'bad risks' more restrictive. But this increased the number of false negatives.

In short, the results of the early prediction studies gave little ground for enthusiasm. However, during the early 1980s a new variety of prediction studies was developed – suggesting the possibility of so-called selective incapacitation.

With some exceptions, the old prediction studies had largely tried to predict two categories of behaviour: recidivism as opposed to non-recidivism, regardless of number or type of offence (see, for example, the main conclusion in Glueck and Glueck, 1937, particularly table on p. 141 and text on p. 142, as well as the conclusions drawn on the basis of column 1 as opposed to the other columns in tables on pp. 139–40). Selective incapacitation, however, looks at recidivism to *serious* crime, like robbery and other crimes of violence, and tries to find out who may be expected to commit *many* such crimes in the future. In the literature, they are called the 'high-rate robbers' or the 'violent predators'. These are the offenders to be predicted and incapacitated.

The most important studies of selective incapacitation have been produced at the Rand Corporation in the United States (Greenwood and Abrahamse, 1982; Chaiken and Chaiken, 1982). The Rand studies are based on interviews with a sample of inmates in jails and prisons in California, Michigan and Texas. On the one hand, the inmates were interviewed about their criminal history, employment history, drug use, and so on. On the other, they were asked to report the frequency with which they committed serious crimes such as robberies. A prediction index was constructed on the basis of those background factors which were associated with a high frequency of self-reported serious crimes.

The Rand studies have caused something of a sensation in parts of international criminology. For example, James Q. Wilson, who was a spokesman of collective incapacitation in the first edition of his influential book *Thinking about Crime* (Wilson, 1975; see p. 84 above), switched to selective incapacitation in the second edition (Wilson, 1983, Ch. 8).

However, the problems of accuracy are apparently still very great. As we saw above, the association between the relevant background factors and subsequent criminality was weak in the early prediction studies. The association is apparently not any stronger in the Rand studies. The proportion of false negatives is still substantial. Greenwood reports a very low proportion of false positives. He reports it to be as low as 4 percent (Greenwood and Abrahamse, 1982: 59–60). However, von Hirsch has concretely shown that the result follows from using particular and rather questionable cutting points in the material. It is worth quoting von Hirsch (1986: 110–11):

> Greenwood reports a strikingly low false-positive rate, in the order of only 4 percent. He does this by treating as false positives only those offenders predicted to be high-rate offenders who had, in fact, the lowest reported rates – namely, the most extreme category of false positives. He fails to treat as false positives those predicted to be high-rate offenders who proved to have medium rates, although these also could receive longer incapacitative sentences under his own proposals. When one asks what percentage of supposedly high-rate offenders were thus erroneously classified, the false-positive rate shoots up. Of those offenders in his sample predicted by his index to be high-rate offenders, less than half in fact were so. The remainder showed medium or low rates. The false-positive rate was 56 percent, which shows scant improvement over previous studies. The false-negative rate was also substantial.

Chaiken and Chaiken report similar problems. In particular, they report very openly that the problem of the false positive is very substantial. Thirty percent of those identified as probable high-rate robbers in fact reported no robberies. They conclude that 'this margin of error allows for considerable false identification of some offenders as high-rate robbers – which is more than just a research problem if the criminal justice system acts upon such identifications' (Chaiken and Chaiken, 1982: 23). Though Chaiken and Chaiken are participants in the Rand studies, their conclusion is in reality close to a deadly blow to the accuracy of the predictions. After having pointed out that their findings 'suggest that violent predators are most appropriate candidates for incapacitation strategies' because the 'seriousness of their crimes, the rates at which they commit all crimes, and their violence have an inordinate effect on crime in our society' (Chaiken and Chaiken, 1982: 26), they conclude:

> Nevertheless, we cannot now recommend basing sentencing policy on these conclusions. Giving less serious criminals lighter sentences would probably be cost-effective (on the basis of incarceration cost per crime averted), and any errors in identification result only in unwarranted leniency (which happens also at presentencing stages of the criminal justice system). However, using the models to identify violent predators – even if limited to those convicted of serious crimes – can potentially result in real injustice. In our opinion, the models would make too many false identifications. (Chaiken and Chaiken, 1982: 27)

I insert here that an identical conclusion is drawn in recent Danish studies of juvenile delinquency. In the chapter on general prevention, I referred to a study by Flemming Balvig, which shows that a relatively small group with a wide range of serious social and personal problems are responsible for a large part of the more serious juvenile delinquency (Balvig, 1984c; see p. 68). In another study, Balvig finds a clear association between particular material conditions during adolescence and later criminality (Folmer Andersen and Balvig, 1984). Balvig claims that on the basis of information about material conditions, it is possible to identify categories of juveniles with a high probability of later convictions for criminal offences. But he emphasizes that 'the associations are not strong enough to make even approximate individual prognoses possible' (Folmer Andersen and Balvig, 1984: 12). The associations lead Balvig to a welfare conclusion rather than any conclusion about incapacitation. The importance of changing and abolishing the conditions showing an association with criminal behaviour is emphasized.

Back, now, to the Rand studies. So far we have only reviewed the most important parts of the methodological criticism which have been raised against the Rand studies. They make the accuracy of the predictions highly questionable. In addition, the following well-founded methodological criticism should briefly be mentioned (from von Hirsch, 1986, Chs. 9 and 10):

In the first place, the fact that the Rand studies are based on samples of *inmates*, and that they purport to have found a prediction instrument for the self-reported robberies of *inmates*, constitutes a serious problem.

From a series of studies we know that those who end up in prison are not representative of those committing crime in the community (see pp. 70–2). Those who end up in prison and who report a large number of robberies and other serious crimes – the group for which the Rand studies try to find predictive factors – are therefore not necessarily representative of robbers generally, not even of high-rate robbers. This is supported by the fact that the probability of being detected and imprisoned for robbery is low. Greenwood reports an extremely low probability for the state of California (Greenwood, 1982: xvii), and von Hirsch points out that the probability is small in most American jurisdictions (von Hirsch, 1986: 108; for Norway the probability is higher, but still quite low: in 1984 the clear-up rate was 28 percent for robberies and extortion together). The low probability of detection and imprisonment increases the probability that the robbers who end up in prison are unrepresentative for all robbers. von Hirsch remarks that 'Greenwood's method is thus reminiscent of the researcher who makes "findings" about the drug habits of addicts in a community by studying the drug histories of a limited number of addicts residing in in-patient drug treatment centers. Such findings would likewise be of little or no value, because the addicts in treatment might be wholly unrepresentative of the general population of drug users' (von Hirsch, 1986: 118). It may well be true that high-frequency offenders who are never caught and punished do not exist in large numbers. However, as von Hirsch (1986: 119) points out, this does not exhaust the possibilities of challenging Greenwood's design. For one thing, those who showed an accumulation of predictive factors in Greenwood's sample – unemployment, addiction history, and so on – also showed high average annual robbery rates. But if unincarcerated offenders with the same characteristics had been examined, it might have emerged that 'many such individuals never had high robbery rates or had since lost their criminal initiative' (von Hirsch, 1986: 119). In other words, the high correlation might prove to be an artefact of the sampling procedure. For another: Greenwood assumed a uniform probability of arrest and conviction for given robberies. Actually, however, that probability may vary considerably with background characteristics such as criminal history or drug addiction, and occasional offenders may be responsible for a larger proportion of robberies than recognized. If so, 'the crime-control effect of confining the robbers who do badly on his prediction index would be far more modest than claimed' (von Hirsch, 1986: 120).

Secondly, the Rand studies are strictly speaking 'postdiction' rather than 'prediction' studies, because the criminal behaviour which is to be predicted has already been committed, and is reported in an interview.

One thing is that interviews of this kind may be unreliable. Public records are perhaps even less reliable. Rather, the basic problem with 'postdiction' is this: in the research, information about employment history, drug history, and so on, is obtained through interviews in order to 'postdict' the probability of criminal behaviour. But even if the background factors did show a high ability to 'postdict', it would certainly not necessarily follow that a practicable prediction instrument had been developed. How would we, in actual practice in the sentencing process, go about getting the necessary background information? There would be two possibilities. *Either* we would, like the Rand researchers, have to interview those accused about their employment history, drug use, and so on, and predict and subsequently sentence them on this basis. We can easily imagine how willing the accused would be to give correct information when this use of it become known. Obviously, their willingness would be very low, and the predictive instrument quite worthless. *Or* we would, unlike the Rand studies, have to base ourselves on public records. But we know that public records of employment history, drug use, and the like are very unreliable, and again the prediction instrument would be quite worthless.

Thus, *even* if the accuracy of the prediction instrument had been high, the 'translation' of findings from studies like these to actual practice would be very difficult, if not impossible.

All of the problems mentioned here make the notion of selective incapacitation extremely problematical. The most basic point is that the problems of accuracy are still very large.

The low predictive accuracy is substantiated by several other sources. Christy Visher has undertaken an extensive reanalysis of the Rand inmate survey, concluding that although 'the scale certainly does better than chance in all the jurisdictions examined, one would expect improvement from any scale that invoked the predictors it did and that was fitted to the sample data. There is no indication that Greenwood's scale would perform any better, even in California, than any other scale that has been used operationally' (Visher, 1986: 205). Visher found that using a seven-item scale and a sentence policy that would double sentence lengths for high-rate offenders, the most favourable effect achieved was about 13 percent. This effect was demonstrated for California. In addition, Visher goes on to say:

> the scale used to identify high-rate offenders is more sensitive to the attributes of those offenders in California than to the attributes of high-rate offenders elsewhere. If the same sentencing policy and prediction scale were applied in Michigan and Texas, the crime rate would probably *increase* because of differences in current criminal justice practices and offender populations in the three states. (1986: 205)

And even for California, the reduction in crime would decline for example if the comprehensive self-report data used in the Rand analyses were replaced by less complete official records, or if the model were applied to any new population and especially to a population of all convicted offenders rather than prisoners (Visher, 1986: 205–6).

Visher's reanalysis was performed within the context of the Panel on Research on Criminal Careers. As mentioned earlier (pp. 86–7), the panel paid particular attention to the issue of incapacitation. The panel's conclusions show that selective incapacitation is replete with problems. Though rates of false predictions do vary between various classification scales, the rates are certainly high. And 'with available statistical scales, gains in crime control efficiency through selective incapacitation would be modest at best – a 5–10 percent reduction in robberies by adults, for example, with an increase of 10–20 percent in the number of convicted robbers who are incarcerated' (Blumstein et al., 1986, Vol. I: 195–6). Mention should also be made of other recent reports on the prediction of violence, which clearly indicate that our predictive abilities are very small with regard to juveniles (Hopson, 1987) as well as adults (Steadman, 1987). Peter Greenwood of Rand Corporation still seems to maintain that the available data are sufficient to inform action, though he now appears to advocate early rehabilitation rather than later incapacitation (Greenwood, 1987).

So far, we have only discussed the problems of accuracy, and in general the issues of efficacy, which selective incapacitation raises. We have taken for granted that the notion is morally acceptable. This, however, is certainly debatable.

In the first place, selective incapacitation very clearly emphasizes that sentencing is to be grounded on the probability of preventing future crime. Thus, a future orientation is a major basis of sentencing practice. Secondly, selective incapacitation just as clearly emphasizes a broad evaluation of the past: on the basis of past circumstances, which are far outside the normal realm of a court, prediction of high risk individuals is to be performed. The emphasis on a broad evaluation of the past is much clearer in the selective than in the collective variety of incapacitation. To illustrate the moral problem, we shall take a closer look at the background factors which the Rand studies utilize. Greenwood's prediction instrument contains seven factors (Greenwood, 1982: 50):

1   Prior conviction for the instant offence type.
2   Incarcerated more than 50 percent of the preceding two years.
3   Conviction before age 16.
4   Served time in a state juvenile facility.
5   Drug use in preceding two years.
6   Drug use as a juvenile.
7   Employed less than 50 percent of the preceding two years.

With the above-mentioned factors, Greenwood constructs three categories of predicted offence rates – low, medium and high. The low risk have none or one of the seven factors, the medium risk have two or three, and the high risk have four or more.

What is the moral basis for relying on factors like this to determine a sentence? Prior conviction for the instant offence type is probably not so questionable, being close to the instant offence itself. Prior incarceration, conviction as a juvenile, and time served in a juvenile facility, are farther away, and could just as well serve as mitigating circumstances. Here they only have an aggravating function. Drug history, and especially unemployment, bring us to circumstances which are very far away, and which, if anything, should only serve as extenuating circumstances. Is it reasonable to give a prison sentence on the background, for instance, of unemployment? A practice of this kind would raise a major problem of principles, and be ethically extremely questionable. Unemployment is a structural feature of society, and in addition a feature which in an important way indicates poverty in the individual. If unemployment were to be used as a partial basis for conviction to prison, it would constitute a strong support of the cumulative tendencies in society, for example, the tendencies towards accumulation of new poverty among the already poor.

Even worse – once we embark on this road, the road may be widened. Should race be included among the predictive factors to be used in sentencing practice? Postponements of selective incapacitation deny, apparently on ethical grounds, that it should (Wilson, 1983: 158). But if race turned out to be a predictive factor, what would be the logic of excluding it when unemployment is not excluded? Perhaps the real reason why race so far has been excluded comes out if we separate the question of what proportion of a population commits or participates in crime from the question of how frequently those participating do so. Though race is a demographic factor which differentiates in terms of *participation* in crime, studies so far seem to suggest that it does not differentiate in terms of individual offending *frequency* (Blumstein et al., 1986, Vol. I: 3–5). The implication is that so far race has not been found to be a predictive factor useful for selective incapacitation.

The point may also be formulated in a slightly different way. As practice is today, there is a clear relationship between the use of prison and factors like drug use, unemployment and – in the United States – race among the incarcerated. We place the poorest segment of society behind bars. This relationship in itself constitutes a serious ethical problem as far as the use of prison goes. If this practice were to be amplified by a conscious and planned use of the same factors in sentencing practice, the ethical problem would become acute.

Conclusions about Incapacitation Collective as well as selective incapacitation present major problems in terms of accuracy as well as in terms of principles. Both types of problems of accuracy – the problem of the false negatives and the problem of the false positives

– are present in both varieties of incapacitation.

One of the two major ethical problems – the problem of sentencing on the basis of future acts – is also present in both varieties. The other ethical problem – that of broadening the basis of sentencing to social factors like drug use, unemployment, and perhaps even race – is particularly important in selective incapacitation, where it is acute.

In connection with the problems of accuracy, we may finally ask, why are they so great? In particular, why are we so unable to predict 'dangerousness'? The reason is probably that 'dangerousness' to a significant degree is situational. Individuals, with individual characteristics, commit dangerous acts. But their acts take place, or are released, in a context or situation. If the situation had been different, the act would perhaps, or probably, have remained unperformed, or would have followed a different course. The fact that dangerous acts are a result of a meeting between the individual and the situation, makes it very difficult to predict who will commit dangerous acts and who will not. It also makes it very difficult to predict dangerousness from a sample in one situation (for example in the situation of an institution) to an equivalent sample in another situation (for example after release; see Monahan, 1981: 87). People whom we might think would commit dangerous acts, in fact do not. Others, on the other hand, end up in situations which make them dangerous.

At times, these others may become many. The situation of war is an extreme example: during war, most young men in the younger age groups are dangerous, or potentially dangerous.

Perhaps we should incapacitate our youth, or parts of it? We would hardly, with any accuracy, exterminate the threat of war.

Deterrence

So much about incapacitation. Before concluding the chapter, something should be added about 'deterrence' as individual prevention. The theory of deterrence as individual prevention does not have a position in modern penal theory comparable to that of incapacitation, but a few words are in order.

A couple of the arguments used against prison as a method of general prevention (Chapter 3) may also be used against the notion of prison as a means of deterring the individual offender.

What we said about 'the sign structure' as the individual's context of interpretation of messages (pp. 67–8) is particularly important. We pointed out that the closer we come to the groups which for other reasons are criminally active, the less efficient is punishment as a method of general prevention: the context of interpretation is such that the signal is not efficient, and the message not understood as the sender has meant it. The same may be said about the deterrent effect of prison on the individual offender.

Here, as well, we have a substantial amount of empirical data supporting our generalization. As mentioned in Chapter 2 on rehabilitation (pp. 41–6), a long string of sociological studies of the organization of the prison and of the prisoners' community appeared before and after World War II. The studies of the structure and culture of the prison not only explain why rehabilitation does not take place in prison. They also very clearly suggest that, perhaps barring exceptional individual cases, deterrence does not take place. Whether the studies have uncovered processes of prisonization or other modes of defence against the prison situation and system (see pp. 43–5), they have all along shown that the prison creates deep distrust and marked hostility towards the prison system and its representatives. Culturally defined 'rejection of the rejectors' is hardly a suitable background and context for deterrence. Rather, there are good sociological and psychological reasons for supposing that 'rejection of the rejectors' above all causes frustration and bitterness, which have the opposite effect.

As with general prevention, the defenders of prison argue about individual deterrence on a 'common-sense' basis, implying that they reason on the basis of 'personal experience'. But they have a context of interpretation which is entirely different from that which is produced in the prison setting. To reason on the basis of 'personal experience' is, therefore, also a very poor method in connection with individual deterrence.

To be sure, some studies of recidivism may be cited in support of a certain deterrent effect. I am thinking in particular of Murray and Cox's study of juvenile delinquents in Chicago who were exposed to varying degrees of restrictiveness in treatment (Murray and Cox, 1979; cited in Wilson, 1983: 171–7). What Murray and Cox did is reminiscent of what the students of selective incapacitation did in their context: rather than looking at recidivism as opposed to non-recidivism, they looked at the *frequency* of behaviour per unit of time, and found, to put it briefly, an association between degree of restrictiveness and later frequency of arrest. The more restrictive the treatment, the lower the arrest frequency. The study has, however, been severely criticized methodologically, and even James Wilson, who tries to make the most of it, concludes that 'it cannot be taken as a conclusive study' (Wilson, 1983: 175). 'For one thing', says Wilson, 'we would like to know what happens to these delinquents over a much longer period . . . We would also like to know more about the kinds of offence for which these persons were arrested, before and after court intervention (perhaps they change the form of their criminal behavior in important ways). And above all, we would like to see such a study repeated in other settings by other scholars' (Wilson, 1983: 175). Furthermore, against the Murray and Cox study we have recidivism studies like Ulla Bondeson's (1977) methodologically extremely careful study of crime prevention in the community, where, again to put it briefly, she shows that even with very careful controls of a number of background factors, restrictiveness is inversely related to recidivism: the less restrictive the treatment, the lower the recidivism. In more detail, the study followed 413 sentenced individuals – a random sample of men sentenced to one of three types of sanction during a year in three so-called supervision areas (comprising thirteen different courts) in Sweden – for a two-year period. The three sanctions were supervision combined with institutional treatment, supervision without institutional treatment, and simple conditional sentence. Comprehensive controls were carried out by the aid of a prediction instrument comprising thirty-six variables divided into six sub-indices covering a broad range of individual and social background characteristics. When carefully controlling for risk categories, so that individuals belonging to the same risk categories were compared across the three types of sanction, individuals subjected to supervision with institutional treatment showed the highest recidivism rate, those given supervision without institutional treatment showed a lower rate, and those given conditional sentence showed the lowest rate. A number of possible sources of error were carefully studied without changing the results. The author concludes (p. 335, translated from the Swedish by the present author): 'Thus, we again find that a positive intention in terms of individual prevention seems to lead to *negative* effects in terms of individual prevention . . . The results as far as negative individual prevention goes should, when transformed into practice, lead to a systematic downgrading of the whole penal system, that is, *depenalization*'. (See also Bondeson, 1989, and Bondeson and Kragh Andersen, 1986; Robison and Smith, 1971: 71–2; Trasler, 1976: 12–13.)

From the point of view of individual deterrence, the studies mentioned above at best cancel each other out, so that we can conclude nothing about deterrence. This would mean that we would be unable to use individual deterrence as an argument for prison. Because Bondeson's study is so careful, it seems more reasonable to conclude that from the point of view of individual deterrence, restrictiveness actually defeats its own purpose.

Does Prison Have a Defence in Incapacitation and Individual Deterrence?

The problems of accuracy as well as the ethical problems speak strongly against the argument of incapacitation as an argument for prison. The culturally defined distrust and hostility which is produced in the prison speaks equally strongly against the argument of individual deterrence.

We concluded Chapters 2 and 3, about individual prevention through rehabilitation and general prevention, by quoting a particular Swedish source, Government Bill 1982/83, No. 85 (see pp. 47, 78 above). This chapter may likewise be concluded by comparable quotes concerning incapacitation and deterrence from still another authoritative Swedish source – the White Paper SOU 1986, No. 13–15, which is a major recent report from the Swedish prison committee. The committee summarizes its view on incapacitation with the following words:

> *Incapacitation* as a basis for determining length of sentence has been questioned on the grounds that preventive effects are doubtful, as well as – and perhaps most importantly – from the point of view of justice . . . In our opinion, within the context of usual sentencing practice it is entirely out of the question to open up for the interest in incapacitation of the individual. (Fängelsestraffkommittén, SOU 1986, No. 14: 71–2, translated from the Swedish by the present author)

The committee summarizes its view on deterrence as follows:

> Considerations about which punishment is needed to *deter the convicted individual* from continued crime, should in our opinion not be allowed to influence the fixing of the sentence. The only situation in which this might be defensible, are certain cases of recurrent criminal activity. (Fängelsestraffkommittén, SOU 1986, No. 14: 71)

Thus, the committee gives only very limited support to the deterrence argument, and no support to incapacitation, as far as sentencing goes. The committee summarizes its view on individual prevention in general – rehabilitation, incapacitation and deterrence – with the following words:

> By way of summary, then, we find that neither should individual prevention, i.e., incapacitation, individual deterrence, or the need for care and treatment, be assigned any independent significance when fixing the sentence in the individual case. (Fängelsestraffkommittén, SOU 1986, No. 14: 72)

With this background one may ask: when all of the arguments of individual prevention, and to a considerable extent also the argument of general prevention, are rejected in this way by the most competent authorities of a country, how can this country – in this case Sweden – continue to utilize prison as a core method in criminal policy?

We shall return to this question in the next chapter.

5
Justice

The Circle of Theories

What remains is justice.

Once in a while one may get the feeling that the theories of criminal policy move in a circle. The 'absolute' theories of punishment, where the aim first of all is to fulfil the demands of just retribution, are probably the oldest theories. The law of talion (where the issue is proportionality between harm and punishment, see p. 17), and the principle of culpability (where the issue is proportionality between guilt and punishment, see again p. 17), constitute some of the oldest ideas.

These theories of punishment were replaced by the 'relative' theories, where the aim first of all is to defend society, partly through individual prevention, partly through general prevention.

As the theories of social defence have been put out of action or questioned, the circle back to the theories of just retribution has been closed.

We concluded the preceding chapter by asking, when almost all ideas about social defence have been rejected in a country like Sweden, how can the country continue to utilize prison as a core method in criminal policy? This is the reply: precisely by closing the circle back to the theories of justice. Though, as we shall see, without *fully* managing to leave social defence. A dose of social defence is still in the package, in the form of general prevention. But as I shall try to show, it functions primarily as a dutiful appendage.

The Modern Theory of Justice

Old and New Classicism
The roots of the new theory of justice in penal policy, the theory of the 1980s, goes back to the Age of Enlightenment, to the time of Rousseau and Voltaire. At that time, two demands were emphasized. In the first place, there should be as *little* regulation of human behaviour as possible. Secondly, the regulation which had to be

there should be highly *specified in advance*. The relationship between the offence on the one hand and punishment on the other should be precise, and determined by the seriousness of the offence.

The penal thinking of the Enlightenment has been called 'classicism'. The growth of the bourgeoisie was behind its development. To the growing bourgeoisie, the question of an effective defence against the wide discretionary powers of the feudal lords and the nobility was vital. Classicism became a part of this defence. The basic point was that the citizen and the nobleman were to be given the same sentence when the same offence had been committed. 'To secure this equality, sentencing was given a detailed advance anchoring in the seriousness of the crime, not in the status of the perpetrator or the discretion of the judge' (Christie, 1980: 116).

In more recent history, we find the background of modern theory of justice in the so-called neo-classicism of the 1970s. Neo-classicism was based on the classicism of the Enlightenment.

The American Quakers launched neo-classicism in the early 1970s, in an important committee report (American Friends Service Committee, 1971). In the 1800s, the Quakers had produced much of the ideological support for the Philadelphia prisons, the penitentiaries where the prisoners were to be isolated to do penance. As we have seen, within the parameters of their time, the penitentiaries were oriented towards rehabilitation of the individual. Now the Quakers advocated a view which was almost diametrically opposed to this: determinate sentences fixed on the basis of the seriousness of the crime. During the 1970s, several other major reports were also published which contained the same general emphasis (see for example von Hirsch, 1976).

What about the Nordic countries? Here, neo-classical thinking became important in several state planning institutions. The influence was least noticeable in Denmark and Norway, and very pronounced in Finland and Sweden. In the latter countries, the influence could be seen in two major governmental reports concerning the basic principles and organization of the penal system (Kommittébetänkande, 1976, No, 72 in Finland; in Sweden BRÅ report, 1977, No. 7).

Proportionality beween offence and punishment was an important catch-word in both reports. *Punishment scales* was another, and *the seriousness of the crime* a third. The basic notion in both reports was this: punishment was to be made proportional to the seriousness of the crime. Through proportionality, the offenders were to get the punishment they 'deserved'. This was the core message of just retribution embedded in both reports. On this basis, punishment scales were to be constructed for various offences. Thus, a just and predictable penal system was to be developed.

The Theory of Justice of the 1980s

Modern ideas about justice in penal thinking, in the 1980s, are a further detailing of the neo-classicism of the 1970s. We find the ideas in state policies – for example, in Sweden, in a recent comprehensive set of penal reforms, parts of which are presently in the process of being carried out.

The proposals are contained in the white paper SOU 1986, No. 13–15, 'On Punishment Scales, the Choice of Sanctions, and Release on Parole, etc.' We will have a good deal to say about this white paper, because it is probably the most comprehensive and best developed, state-initiated set of neo-classical proposals to date.

Let us, first of all, try to summarize the argumentation for justice in Fängelsestraffkommittén, SOU 1986, No. 13–15 (from now on, the three volumes are called 1, 2 and 3). The notion of 'punishment as deserved', or 'just deserts', is the very core of the proposals, as formulated, by way of summary, in the first volume:

> We have, then, arrived at the conclusion that neither considerations of general nor individual prevention are to be emphasized when the punishment scales for the various offences are developed. In our opinion, the punishment scales of the offences should instead be based on the gravity or the objectionability of the offences in question. Thus, we view the evaluation of what the offences in general deserve in terms of punishment as a very reasonable point of departure when punishment scales are to be determined. In order to arrive at which punishment scales the various offences should have, one has to rely on some form of reasoning concerning justice. Here proportionality and equivalence become important concepts. By proportionality is meant that the punishment scale should be determined in proportion to the gravity of the offence. Equivalence implies that equally serious punishments are to be used for equivalent types of offences, and may be said to be a consequence of the notion of proportionality. (Vol. 1: 15, translated from the Swedish by the present author)

With this as a general point of departure, the various offences are allotted a 'punishment value', and a distinction is made between abstract and concrete punishment value:

> By the *punishment value* of an offence is meant the gravity of the offence in relation to other offences. Punishment value is, then, a measure of how serious the offence is. The punishment value which is expressed in the punishment scales is the abstract punishment value of the offences in question. The punishment value of a given offence which in fact has been committed, constitutes the concrete punishment value. (Vol. 1: 19)

The punishment values are determined on the basis of the gravity or the objectionability of the offences. Here is what the report says about objectionability as a base:

> As mentioned above, our view is that with respect to developing punishment scales for various acts, we can neither make use of reasoning about general nor about individual prevention. Instead, it is our opinion that the evaluation of punishment values should be based on the objectionability of the various offences. Thus, the point of departure when it comes to deciding the punishment scales for the various offences is to be what the offence generally speaking deserves in terms of punishment. In order to arrive at this, it will be necessary to follow some kind of reasoning about justice, in the sense that we ask what the various offences generally speaking deserve in terms of punishment. (Vol. 1: 19)

The punishment scales are to be developed on this basis:

> Thus, the punishment scale should be determined in proportion to the gravity of the offence, and equally serious punishments should be used for equivalent types of offences. (Vol. 1: 19)

The quotes are complex. The reader is advised to postpone the study of their details: we shall return to them later. Here the main point is that based on a notion of proportionality, a number of punishment values and punishment scales are specified.

The punishment values for ordinary property crimes, says the report, are generally too high and should be placed lower. The punishment value for offences against the person, especially crimes of violence, should on the other hand be placed higher. So should the punishment value for environmental crimes and drug crimes.

Taken together, the proposals imply a certain lowering of the general punishment level. Against this background, the automatic release on parole on half time for a majority of offenders (see pp. 84–6 above) is proposed abolished. A return to two-thirds time is proposed instead. The idea is that the lowering of the punishment level will counterbalance the increase in prison time following from this. Obviously, it is an open question whether such a counter-balancing will take place.

Does Justice Stand Alone?

Before evaluating the reasoning about justice reviewed here, the following question must be raised. Does justice stand completely alone?

The answer is: almost, but not quite. Combined with notions about justice, we also find a certain emphasis on social defence, notably general prevention.

The formulation of general prevention varies somewhat between different documents. Nevertheless, the main features are the same. If we look at the American Friends Service Committee from 1971, the von Hirsch committee from 1976, the BRÅ report 1977, No. 7, and SOU 1986, No. 13–15 – in addition to a recent book, von Hirsch, 1986 (which we also discussed in Chapter 4, because von Hirsch criticizes incapacitation theories) – the common features as well as the variations stand out clearly.

The common features are these. A distinction is drawn between the motivation *for having punishment at all in a society*, that is the motivation for having given acts criminalized, and the motivation for *the concrete organization and use of the penal system*, that is the concrete legislation in terms of punishment scales and stipulation of sanctions through choice of reactions and sentencing.

The motivation for having punishment at all, why given acts are criminalized at all, is to be found in *general prevention*, or at least primarily in general prevention. Arguments about justice probably appear too cold and naked; something socially useful must be added to motivate the infliction of intended pain on people (see American Friends Service Committee, 1971: 61, 66, 149–50; von Hirsch, 1976: 37–44; BRÅ report, 1977, No. 7: 199–200; SOU 1986, No. 13–15 Vol. 1: 14–15, Vol. 2: 67–8; von Hirsch, 1986: 47–60).

The motivation for the concrete organization and use of the penal system, however, is not to be found in general prevention, or, for that matter, in any other socially useful ends. All of the above-mentioned works are very clear on this. The motivation for the organization and use of the penal system, for punishment scales and concrete stipulations of sanctions, is to be found in *the principles of justice* described above. The fact that the motivation is *not* to be found in general prevention, is for example apparent in the following strong statement in SOU 1986, No. 13–15:

> Neither do the results from research on the effects of imprisonment in terms of general prevention inspire any great hopes for the possibility of influencing the volume of crime through adjustments in the use of imprisonment. International comparisons have not shown any tendency indicating that stiffer penalties bring about a lower crime level.
>
> Thus, increased employment of imprisonment is not an effective tool to lower criminality, or even to prevent an increase in crime. To the extent that it is possible to decrease criminality, measures of an entirely different kind are needed. It follows from this that nothing suggests that a reasonable decrease in the use of imprisonment in general is of any importance to the volume of crime. (Vol. 1: 16)

The distinction between the motivation for having a penal system at all, which at least primarily is to be found in general prevention, and the motivation for the concrete organization and use of the penal system, which is to be found in the principles of justice, is fundamental in all of the works referred to here. Within this context of agreement there are also some variations between them. The variations are not so important for our purposes, but we should point out one of them.

In some of the works, particularly the BRÅ report, an attempt is made to create a unity between the prevention motivation for having a penal system at all, and the justice motivation for the organization and use of the penal system. In the BRÅ report, the unity and link is largely established through an emphasis on the educative aspect of general prevention. If the deterrent aspect of general prevention had been stressed, the report says, the concrete sentence would have had to consider the temptation to commit the act. On the other hand, if the educative aspect is stressed, emphasis has to be placed on the punishment value of the offence, and the sanction on the gravity or objectionability of the offence – precisely what punishment scales and concrete sentencing *should* be based on. The implication is that if these principles of justice were to remain unemphasized, the system would not have moral credibility, and would in turn not have an educative function. This way, unity between the two levels is established (BRÅ report 1977, No. 7: 200). Also the follow-up of the BRÅ report, SOU 1986, No. 13–15, emphasized the educative aspect of criminalization, and contains a line of reasoning which resembles that of the BRÅ report (Vol. 2: 64–6).

Other works do not attempt to create this kind of unity between the two levels. The two levels appear as more or less distinct, that of general prevention being a necessary forerunner for the reliance on justice in concrete sentencing: if it were not for the preventive effect of the system as such, we might have abolished all sentencing. Due to the preventive effect, sentencing remains, and is meted out in terms of strict justice. As far as I am able to understand, this is the major line of reasoning for example in von Hirsch's recent work (1986: 47–60).

How should we view the renewed emphasis on general prevention? In the first place, in the literature reviewed here, there is hardly any detailed argumentation for general prevention, with or without an educative emphasis, as a valid motivation for the existence of punishment and criminalization.

The preventive effect as an unmotivated assertion or axiom is even more pronounced here than in the regular literature on general prevention (see Chapter 3 above). Virtually the whole intellectual effort is used in the detailed argumentation for justice as a motivation for the concrete organization and use of the penal system, where the whole emphasis of the various reports and books lies. An example of the axiomatic or taken-for-granted character of general prevention may be found in SOU 1986, No. 13–15, Vol. 1: 14–15: 'We find', the report flatly states, 'that considerations about general prevention obviously are of basic importance for decisions about *criminalization*, i.e. decisions about employing punishment for given acts' (see, likewise, Vol. 2: 67, where 'common sense' is largely referred to as motivation).

Secondly, in several of the works cited, we find a good deal of honest argumentation which actually goes a long way towards saying that the preventive effect of the system as such is in fact limited, or even questionable. Again SOU 1986, No. 13–15, may serve as a (perhaps especially clear) example. The report introduces its general deliberations about punishment as follows:

The main task of criminal policy is . . . to prevent crime. However, in this respect the penal system [*straffsystemet*] is not a particularly effective instrument. Experience in Sweden as well as abroad speaks in favour of this view. There is no relationship between long and severe penal sanctions and the crime level. (Vol. 1: 14)

The first part of this statement speaks rather directly about the very existence of punishment, the penal system – *straffsystemet* – as such. In the last sentence, the statement is moderated, with reference to the punishment level rather than to the existence of punishment. But taken together, a statement like this at least comes close to saying that the effect of the very existence of punishment is questionable.

Thirdly, at least in SOU 1986, No. 13–15, we find examples of imperceptible changes in formulations, from the assertion about the preventive effect of the existence of punishment or criminalization as such, to an assertion that we, in spite of everything, do find a preventive effect of the concrete organization of the penal system.

After having stated that considerations about general prevention are obviously of basic importance for decisions about criminalization (see above quote), SOU 1986, No. 13–15, goes into greater detail about this, among other things by stating that the prevention of crime is 'first of all a responsibility of the legislator, whose task it is to shape [*som har att utforma*] the penal system in such a way that the preventive aspects are given their due credit without injuring the demands of legality and the uniform execution of justice' (Vol. 1: 15). Here the concrete organization of legislation, which was to be motivated solely by arguments about justice, is suddenly, by an imperceptible change, also motivated by general prevention. The question of the preventive effect of the concrete organization and details of legislation is, however, very different from the question of the preventive effect of the very existence of punishment or criminalization. Today, it is much easier to muster support for an affirmative answer to the latter question than to the former. By subtly switching the emphasis from the latter to the former, the idea that even the details of legislation have a preventive effect is, equally subtly, maintained as a part of the argument. In a masked and rather effective way, the idea is kept alive that the concrete organization of legislation is useful also from the point of view or prevention.

In short, the justice orientation in the neo-classical works does not stand entirely alone, but is found in combination with a certain emphasis on social defence, through general prevention. Naked justice cannot stand entirely on its own feet. But the emphasis on general prevention is highly limited, notably to the question of how to motivate the existence of criminalization, the existence of punishment. This is the corner to which the theory of general prevention has been driven, by the pressure of research, by the professional discussion, and by time.

Even in this position, it does not fare well. It stands in the corner, as an axiom without detailed argumentation, in part close to being inconsistent with itself, and with a built-in imperceptible tendency to change level when argumentation does take place.

With this as a background, we may now move on to a more detailed review of the reasoning about justice, the main content of the message, as a basis for using prison. SOU 1986, No. 13–15 is one of the main state-initiated ideological sources, and we shall therefore concentrate on it. But we shall also touch on the most recent international professional contribution – von Hirsch's book, also from 1986.

The Limits of Justice

First, it may be useful to define more closely the *kind* of philosophy of justice which is contained in neo-classical reasoning.

What Kind of Justice?
In his important work on justice, Torstein Eckhoff distinguishes between two basic types of justice (Eckhoff, 1971/1974, Ch. 2). Translating from the Norwegian edition (the terminology in the

English edition is slightly different), one of them may be called 'balancing-of-scales justice'.

In general terms, balancing-of-scales justice concerns the *exchange* of values. The exchange should be in balance, like the scales of the Goddess of Justice. Eckhoff discusses four concrete varieties of such exchange. We need not deal with them in detail; here the main point is that the following two characteristics are common to them all – and, by the same token, to balancing-of-scales justice in general.

First, they imply a right or a duty to some form of retribution (1974: 31): 'By this I mean a right or duty which is conditioned by a transfer and which serves as the basis of a new transfer in the opposite direction or with reversed values.' Secondly, they imply a certain type of equality, that type which emphasizes that the values which are exchanged should have equal weight. Here Eckhoff refers directly to the scales of the Goddess of Justice (1974: 31):

> The principles are also based on ideas of *equality*, demanding that the exchange values shall have equal weight if balance is to be restored. The scales held by the Goddess of Justice symbolize this idea. If the scales do not balance, weight must be laid on the side which has become too light, but not more than is necessary to restore equilibrium.

The other basic type of justice is called 'distributive justice'.

In general terms, and as the name suggests, distributive justice concerns the *distribution* of values. Also distributive justice is based on a notion of equality, but rather than emphasizing equal weight on the part of exchanged values, it emphasizes equal treatment of the recipients of given values. Equal treatment sometimes means absolute equality. It may for example be argued that recipients in a given distribution should have or receive equal-sized pieces of cream-cake, or the same number of months of military service. In other cases relative equality is called for. For example, it may be argued that the relationship between guilt and punishment should be the same for everybody. While balancing-of-scales justice always concerns a relationship between two parties, distributive justice in principle contains no such limit.

It is possible to place the modern justice ideology in penal theory (concretely, the thinking in SOU 1986, No. 13–15) in relation to the main types of justice. In SOU 1986, No. 13–15, a balancing-of-scales justice appears to be basic. The report clearly presupposes an exchange of values with equal weight, a balanced exchange, when it speaks of 'proportionality' between punishment and offence. Distributive justice is something which presumably *follows when a balance-of-scales justice has been instituted*: when balance has been established between punishment and offence, equal treatment will ensue in the sense that the same punishment will be used for equivalent offences. We may quote once more the following except from a quote we have given earlier (Vol. 1: 15; see p. 105 above):

> Here proportionality and equivalence become important concepts. By proportionality is meant that the punishment scale should be determined in proportion to the gravity of the offence. Equivalence implies that equally serious punishments are to be used for equivalent types of offences, and may be said to be a consequence of the notion of proportionality.

The crucial question is, therefore: is the argumentation for a balancing-of-scales justice, the creation of a balance between offence and punishment, tenable?

Through its formulations, the justice defence of prison gives an impression of something highly reliable and precise. Through concepts like 'proportionality', 'punishment value', 'punishment scales', and 'measurement', the justice ideology gives the impression that it is possible to arrive at the length and severity of punishment in a strict, analytical way – in presumed contrast to the vague and imprecise evaluation of individual and general prevention.

In the first place, the presentation gives the general impression that the reasoning is based on stringent scientific logic.

Secondly, the presentation gives the impression that one of the two sides in the calculation of proportionality, the gravity or objectionability of the crime, may be evaluated on the basis of standards which are fixed.

Thirdly, the presentation gives the impression that the other side in the calculation of proportionality, the severity of the punishment which is to balance the crime, may be evaluated on the basis of standards which are absolute.

Fourthly, the presentation gives the impression that the two sides to the balancing operation, the pain infliction of the crime and the pain infliction of the punishment, are comparable entities.

The four impressions are false. Taken one by one, their falsity might perhaps be corrected, or could possibly be disregarded. But we find them together. Taken together and as a sum, they deal a devastating blow to the justice defence of prison.

We shall look more closely at the four points.

Reasoning and Circular Argument
To repeat, the presentation of the justice defence gives the general impression that the reasoning is based on stringent scientific logic.

In sharp contrast to this impression, the reasoning in SOU 1986, No. 13–15, is built on an argument which is fundamentally circular.

Let us use a magnifying glass on some of the quotes given earlier, in our review of the main content of SOU 1986, No. 13–15. The question which is basic to the whole reasoning in the report, is that of how to determine *the punishment value*. As mentioned earlier, the punishment value of an offence is determined on the basis of the objectionability or the gravity of the offence. Objectionability (*förkastlighet*) is primarily related to the offender's culpability, and gravity (*svårhet*) is related to the damage or danger which the act has caused. No precise distinction is drawn between these two aspects, and it is sometimes difficult to recognize the distinction in the text. However, we leave this aside here. The point for us to emphasize is the fact that objectionability/gravity is the basis for the punishment value of the offence. As we quoted on p. 106 (from Vol. 1: 19): 'Instead, it is our opinion that the evaluation of punishment values should be based on the objectionability of the various offences.' This quote is taken from the general discussion of punishment values. The fact that this is how punishment values are to be determined, may also be seen from the discussion of the determination of sanctions:

> The point of departure is the punishment value of the offence which has been committed, which is determined by the gravity of the offence, with special reference to the damage or danger which the act has implied, and the culpability of the offender as it is expressed in the act. (Vol. 1: 22)

There is no doubt, then, that the point of departure for the determination of the punishment value is the gravity or the objectionability of the offence.

Because the determination of the punishment values is the stepping-stone to the determination of the punishment scales, the objectionability or gravity of the offence also becomes the point of departure for the punishment scales. This is also directly stated in the report, as quoted earlier on p. 106 (Vol. 1: 19): 'Thus, the punishment scale should be determined in proportion to the gravity of the offence . . .'. How, then, are we to determine the objectionability or gravity of the offence? In line with what we have said so far, this question is of course decisive.

We learn something about this in Volume 1, in a section which we also quoted on p. 105 (Vol. 1: 19; see also Vol. 2: 131): 'By the *punishment value* of an offence is meant the gravity of the offence in relation to other offences.' This, then, means that the objectionability or gravity (here gravity) of the individual offence is assessed relative to other offences (whereby the punishment value is determined). In other words, the individual offence is viewed within a context of other offences, and the objectionability or gravity of the individual offence is determined through a comparison.

Such comparisons are of course fully in order. The gravity of housebreaking, for example, may well be determined relative to the gravity for example of robbery or rape. But the solution is only provisional: we have still not been told how the objectionability or gravity of these other offences, with which the individual offence in question is compared, is to be determined. We have still not been told what the standard for gravity or objectionability is. So, we must repeat the question: how is objectionability or gravity more precisely to be determined?

The answer is sensational. The gravity or objectionability of the offence, which together provide the basis for determining the punishment value and thereby the punishment scale, are in turn determined by *what the offence deserves in terms of punishment*, that is, the punishment value.

As quoted earlier (p. 106), from Volume 1: 19, directly following the sentence 'Instead, it is our opinion that the evaluation of punishment values should be based on the objectionability of the various offences', we learn that 'Thus, the point of departure when it comes to deciding the punishment scales for the various offences *is to be what the offence generally speaking deserves in terms of punishment*', (emphasis added). The fact that the gravity/reprehensibility of the offence, which provides the basis for the determination of the punishment value and thereby the punishment scale, in turn is determined by the punishment value, is also apparent in several other places in the report. As quoted earlier (p. 105), directly following the sentence 'In our opinion, the punishment scales of the offences should instead be based on the gravity or the objectionability of the offences in question', we learn that (Vol. 1: 15) 'Thus, we view the evaluation of *what the offences in general deserve in terms of punishment* as a very reasonable point of departure when punishment scales are to be determined', (emphasis added).

In both of the quotes the word '*Thus*' (in Swedish two words, *således* and *nemligen*) is decisive. It ties the statements saying that the punishment value/punishment scale should be based on the gravity/objectionability of the offence directly to the statements saying that the punishment scale should be determined by what the offences deserve in terms of punishment, *implying that the latter statements are explanatory or amplifying of the former*.

An interpretation more favourable to the report could be this. 'e report tries to say that the punishment value should be based on the objectionability/gravity of the offence, that the punishment scales in turn should be based on the punishment values, and that 'thus' stands for 'because'. The move from objectionability/gravity to punishment value is important 'because' of the subsequent move from punishment values to punishment scales. But in context it is more complicated. The two quotes, which may be found *in extenso* above (pp. 105, 106) show, I think, that at the very best, the report is extremely unclear on this crucial point, and that the circular interpretation is, to say the least, very near at hand.

In bold relief, a balance is to be established between offence and punishment. The punishment value is determined by the objectionability/gravity of the offence. The objectionability/gravity is determined by what the offence 'deserves in terms of punishment', the punishment value.

When the punishment value is determined by the objectionability/gravity and the objectionability/gravity by the punishment value, it follows that the task of determining what is a 'balance' between punishment and offence is not so arduous.

It may possibly be said that in their more detailed discussion of these issues, in Volume 2 (Chs 11 and 12), the circular argument seems less blatant. But it is certainly there. In the opening of the major chapter on punishment values (Vol. 2, Ch. 11), we learn that the concrete punishment value of a committed offence 'is viewed as a measure of the gravity of a certain committed criminal act' (Vol. 2: 131). In other words, the circular argument is stated very directly. In addition, the principled and basic discussion of independent measures of objectionability/gravity (Vol. 2: 147–9), couched in terms of the interests or values that need protection, is brief and extremely general, a fact which is admitted by the report ('It is hardly possible in a general way to detail more closely how the evaluations of punishment values should occur', Vol. 2: 149).

In fairness it should be added, as an extenuating circumstance for SOU 1986, No. 13–15, that the logic of the circular argument did not begin with this report. The circular argument is, more or less, explicitly, as old as the absolute penal theories themselves, and an important criterion of both old and new classicism. As far as I can see, the neo-classical work which bears least evidence of it is von Hirsch's book (1986). Here, he tries to establish independent criteria of seriousness. The establishment of these criteria contains its own problems which we will return to; here the point is that he apparently tries to limit the circular argument. But even von Hirsch does not avoid it completely. After having discussed on a general level the question of how the seriousness of crime is to be determined, he moves on to give some practical advice to the legislator. And in addition to emphasizing other, more independent criteria, he gives the advice that at 'least as far as typical crimes of theft, force and fraud are concerned, one can develop a rough assessment of their consequences *using the legal definition of the crime* and available common knowledge of its probable effects' (von Hirsch, 1986: 74, emphasis added). It seems just about impossible to evaluate 'the legal definition of the crime' without taking the punishment value into consideration.

In favour of SOU 1986, No. 13–15, it must be said that it advocates a reduction in the use of punishment. So do the other justice-oriented works, from the 1976 Quaker report on. More concretely, SOU 1986, No. 13–15, believes that the new punishment scales which it proposes will imply a reduction comparable to about 300 of Sweden's 4,200 prison places. Such a reduction would not be a bad result, even if we might wish more.

The point, however, is that *exactly the same type of reasoning might have led to a demand for more severe punishments and thereby for an increase in prison numbers*. The circular argument may lead to liberalization in the name of justice, but it may just as well lead to the opposite – in the same name.

This in fact appears to be happening in Sweden. Steps are currently being taken to prolong sentences for recidivists. It is done in the name of neo-classicism and justice. But the actual background is probably the popular demand for collective incapacitation of persistent recidivists, which has developed in Sweden during the last few years (see pp. 88–9). The circularity of neo-classical reasoning makes it possible for such a demand to feed into the planning of the penal system, and influence it – while the name of justice, in the form of adjustments of punishment scales, is maintained.

In this sense, the so-called 'absolute' penal theories are actually perhaps the least 'absolute' of all.

If the idea of balanced justice, proportionality between offence and punishment, is to be meaningful, the gravity/objectionability of the offence and the severity of punishment must at least be defined independently, and not as constituting a circle. If such independence is obtained, however, other problems arise which create great difficulties for proportionate justice.

Gravity, Objectionability and Morality

From SOU 1986, No. 13–15, and other neo-classical documents, it is apparent that crime is also evaluated in *moral terms*. Words like 'gravity' and especially 'objectionability' (used in SOU 1986, No.

13–15) are moral terms, covering damage or harm and culpability or guilt.

Morality as a standard for evaluating crime is, as a point of departure, an independent criterion which breaks the circular conclusion discussed above. However, as a standard it is not fixed, but highly variable, varying with a number of social and social psychological factors and indices (see, for example, Kutchinsky, 1972). It is therefore a very complex basis for establishing proportionality.

This is important because, as mentioned earlier, the second feature of the justice ideology is the general impression of fixed standards which it gives to one of the two sides in the balancing operation – the gravity/objectionability side. Here two main variations will be emphasized. Each of them in turn appears in two varieties.

In the first place, moral evaluation, and with it the perception of the gravity or objectionability of the crime, varies with time.

On the one hand, we find many examples of long-term historical change in moral evaluation and perception of criminal behaviour. The evaluation of blasphemy and homosexuality are cases in point.

On the other hand, we also find examples of short-term and dramatic changes in moral evaluation over short periods of time, so-called moral panics. Moral panics have a complex background. Usually, important interests are first provoked by particular types of behaviour; next, representatives of power and authority structures react to the behaviour; then the mass media (or other prevailing communication systems) find out what is happening, which may make the initial interests still more provoked, which in turn may make the power and authority structures react even more, and so on – in a spiral-like panicky moral reaction. Stanley Cohen (1972) has described the reaction to the so-called 'mods' and 'rockers' in the 1960s in England as a moral panic. The reactions to vagrant alcoholics in the 1970s and to young drug users in the 1980s in Norway, have been described in a similar terminology (Mathiesen, 1975; Christie and Bruun, 1985). All three examples are interesting in that they had legal repercussions. The mods and rockers in the 1960s in England were, after a while, treated by the police in ways which superseded standard rules of law. The Norwegian vagrants in the 1970s, who were no longer incarcerated in forced labour camps after the forced labour system had been abolished in 1970, were met by a panic which almost re-established the forced labour system, and which caused a review of existing regulations concerning 'forced treatment'. And to the drug users the panic in fact became very important in terms of penal level: the maximum penalty for drug offences has, over a period of a few years, increased from 10 through 15 to 21 years in Norway. The maximum penalty is meant for professional drug dealers. Almost always, small users and peddlers are taken – and receive very stiff sentences.

Secondly, moral evaluation, and with it the perception of gravity/objectionability, varies in space.

On the one hand, we find many examples illustrating that moral evaluation and the perception of crime varies between different societies. One example: the view on drunken driving is probably quite different in the United States and Norway. Different cultural contexts produce differences in definition.

On the other hand, we find many examples showing that evaluation and perception varies between groups or subsystems within a society. In a study of parents and sons, the latter aged 15–18, in a typical 'middle-class' and a typical 'working-class' area in Oslo, I found significant differences in evaluation and perception of deviant and criminal behaviour between generations as well as between classes. In the first place, the parents were systematically less accepting and more restrictive to such behaviour than their sons. Secondly, regardless of generation, those with a working-class background were systematically and significantly less accepting and more restrictive than those with a middle-class background. The questions were formulated so as to tap moral evaluation directly – those interviewed were asked whether they personally thought the behaviour in question was 'right' or 'wrong' (Mathiesen, 1966: 23). Studies from other countries, notably the United States and Italy, show similar class differences (Kohn, 1969). In addition to the direct questions about personal opinion, those interviewed were also asked *what they believed would be the opinion of others*. The questions aimed at finding out something about the moral climate in the environment. The parents were asked what they thought boys of their sons' age as well as other parents would think, while the sons were asked what they thought sons of their own age and their parents would think. Among the parents as well as the sons, people from the working class quite systematically experienced the moral climate of the environment as less accepting of and more restrictive towards deviant and criminal behaviour than did respondents from the middle class.

What we have said here about variations over long periods of time, and variations between different societies, is probably less important than are differences over short spans of time and between subgroups and subsystems within a society. It may with some justification be said that the balancing operation of justice must be judged within the context of the concrete historical epoch, and within the context of the concrete society in question. However, it is considerably more difficult to argue that justice may well be allowed to vary over short spans of time, and that rather different views on penal retribution within a society – even between classes – is acceptable.

Let me emphasize: what we have said here does not mean that everything moral varies. To repeat, in the above-mentioned study of parents and sons, I found systematic differences between groups. Nevertheless, a majority among parents as well as sons, and among middle-class as well as working-class respondents, were of the opinion that the most clearly criminal act which they were asked to evaluate was 'totally wrong'. Here the variations between groups, in other words, concerned *differences with respect to the size of the majority*. Similar trends towards consensus have been demonstrated in several American studies, though there is a continuing debate about the extent of the consensus (see von Hirsch, 1986: 65). The degree of consensus probably also varies between societies. In a review of American and Finnish studies, where the latter showed a far higher consensus concerning the relative seriousness of various types of crimes as rated by the law, the courts, the judges and the public, Kutchinsky has suggested that variations between societies may be explained by sociological differences in degree of hetero-geneity, cultural conflict, mobility, and social change (Kutchinsky, 1973). In any case, people's moral evaluation is far from completely fluid.

But neither is it completely fixed. Enough varies, even over short time spans and between groups, to complicate the moral evaluation of gravity and objectionability. If it is true that decreased consensus follows from increased heterogeneity, cultural conflict and social change, many Western countries may even expect an increase in variations during the latter part of the 1900s.

Before moving on, it should be mentioned that in his recent book on 'just deserts' (1986), Andrew von Hirsch has attempted to over-come these difficulties in an analysis of the seriousness of the crime. His point of departure is, as usual in absolute penal theory, partly the harm (the damage or injury done or risked by the criminal act) and partly the culpability (the guilt or intent, motive and circum-stance) that determine how much the offender should be held accountable.

In line with Richard Sparks, von Hirsch first argues that what people *think* about crime should not be the basis of assessing harm, because people may for example *believe* that the harm following from given acts is greater than is actually the case. The proposition is that harm must be assessed on the basis of factual harm, and factual harm may to some extent be studied empirically. However, von Hirsch adds the important qualification that such 'empirical inquiry into criminal harm must be supplemented by value judgments' (von Hirsch, 1986: 66). Partly, different crimes injure different interests which, he clearly implies, must be subject to evaluation. 'There also remains', he goes on to say, 'the other comparably important element in seriousness: the offender's culpability for the acts he commits' (von Hirsch, 1986: 66). The implication is that this element also involves value judgements.

'How then', von Hirsch asks, 'can such value judgments be made?' He goes on to develop a system for gauging seriousness, partly with an emphasis on harm through the ranking of various types of interests, and partly with an emphasis on culpability through the ranking of various degrees of fault (von Hirsch, 1986: 63–76). In this way von Hirsch attempts to give the determination of the seriousness of crime a factual character. And on the positive side it must be said that he does gain something in clarity. But it should also be stressed very clearly that he places great emphasis on 'value judgements', with respect to harm as well as culpability. When doing so, *he is necessarily into the question of moral evaluation of crime*. It is very difficult to understand how he, or the hypothetical legislator, avoids moral evaluation with all of its problems – other than by masking: by giving it the appearance of something non-evaluational. We have quoted a little of the following before, but may now quote it in context:

> I think a rulemaking body can take a number of practical steps that will enable it to formulate a workable, if not perfect, seriousness scale for use in its guidelines. At least so far as typical crimes of theft, force, and fraud are concerned, one can develop a rough assessment of their consequences using the legal definition of the crime and available common knowledge of its probable effects. One can also make commonsense moral judgments [sic!] about the relative importance of the rights and interests that different crimes invade. One can grade culpability at least according to whether intentional, reckless, or negligent conduct is involved . . . (von Hirsch, 1986: 74)

Moral evaluation is clearly in the package.

Add now, to the above mentioned variations over time and between groups, the large number of dramatic differences in resources and life chances which exist between individuals and groups in society.

As mentioned in another context (p. 93), those who remain in a criminal career and who end up with long-term sentences in our prisons, present an accumulation of problems – alcohol problems, drug problems, lack of education, unemployment, and so on. And to a large extent they come from the lower strata of the working class. The acts which are evaluated as particularly grave and objectionable, and which on that basis result in long prison sentences, are thus committed by people who are extremely poor in a wide sense of the word. The more we get to know their poverty, the more difficult it is to maintain the evaluation of their acts as being so reprehensible. Is an act committed in material distress so blameworthy? Is an act committed in social or psychological distress so blameworthy? The assessment of gravity and objectionability, which is complicated by the fact that moral evaluations vary in time and space, *becomes extremely difficult when vital conditions like these are taken into account.*

The classical approach, for example in SOU 1986, No. 13–15, to a large extent peels away such considerations, bringing them in only as mitigating circumstances or so-called 'reasons of equity' (Vol. 1: 22). If we let them 'sink in', however, moral evaluation as such becomes very difficult.

We know that the closer we come to the life of those who are filling our prisons, the more clearly we see their poverty in terms of resources and life chances. The implication is that the vantage-point, more precisely the proximity to he or she who has committed the act, is an important dimension. The significance of the vantage-point becomes decisive when we move on to discuss the severity of punishment.

Severity and Vantage-point
To repeat, the justice ideology in the third place gives the general impression that the other side in the balancing operation of proportionate justice, the severity of punishment, may be evaluated on the basis of standards which are absolute. However, what constitutes a severe punishment, and what is more or less severe, is bound up with, dependent on, and therefore relative to one's vantage-point – more precisely, to one's distance from the situation and the individual concerned.

Through the years, a large number of studies have appeared gauging people's views on the severity of punishment. The results from a Norwegian study are interesting from our point of view. In a nation-wide public opinion survey on criminal policy towards juveniles (Mathiesen, 1965b), the following general question was asked: 'Do you think juvenile delinquents nowadays are largely treated too severely, not severely enough, or about right?' The distribution of replies showed a highly punitive attitude: only 2 percent thought the treatment was too severe, a large majority of 67 percent thought it was not severe enough, 21 percent thought it was about right, and 10 percent did not reply.

If the matter is pursued in somewhat greater detail, however, the replies change. The following somewhat more detailed question was asked: 'For each of the measures on this card, I would like to know whether you think it is used too often, about right, or too rarely towards juvenile delinquents'. On the card were listed 'withdrawal of charges, no trial', 'borstal, juvenile institution', 'treatment by doctor, psychologist, and the like', and 'punishment by prison'. In other words, the question was detailed concerning measures, but the issue was still 'juvenile delinquents' in general. The replies contained more nuances than did the replies to the first, completely general question – 49 percent thought punishment by prison was used too rarely. But slightly more, 51 percent, thought treatment by doctor, psychologist and the like was used too rarely, and a rather large proportion, 31 percent, thought that borstal and institutions for juveniles were used too rarely. Even withdrawal of charges or no trial received a substantial proportion when compared with the replies to the first, completely general question: 20 percent thought that withdrawal of charges, etc, was used too rarely.

If the matter is pursued in still greater detail, the replies contain still more nuances. In a third question, we asked not only for details concerning measures, but also for an evaluation of various types of 'juvenile delinquents'. The question and the results are given in Table 5.1.

Among the delinquency types mentioned in the table, property crimes/car thefts are more frequent among young people, robberies are clearly less frequent, and rape, at least as a reported crime, is rare. Concerning the most frequent delinquency types, we find that measures other than punishment by prison/unspecified punishment have a very prominent position, and that people have rather liberal views. For 'housebreaking' as well as 'car theft' with a value of 2000 Norwegian crowns (£180; note that it concerns 1962 crowns/ pounds), compensation is mentioned more often than punishment by prison/unspecified punishment. For 'housebreaking', warning, withdrawal of charges, reprimand, and conditional sentence are also mentioned more often than punishment by prison/unspecified punishment, and for 'car theft' such reactions – which must be considered quite liberal – are at least mentioned by a sizeable proportion. It is worth noting that even among those who gave the 'not severe enough' reply to the most general question about reactions (67 percent, see above), punishment by prison/unspecified punishment is not mentioned more frequently than other measures, but has to share the first place with others.

Table 5.1 *'A person of 20 has committed a first offence. What do you think should be done with him if it concerns –?' (%)*

	Housebreaking (value ca. 2000 kr)		Auto theft (value ca. 2000 kr)		Robbery (value ca. 2000 kr)		Rape	
Punishment by prison	15		20		37		51	
Unspecified punishment	13	28	14	34	19	56	22	73
Compensation	32		43		20		–	
Warning, withdrawal of charges, reprimand, conditional sentence	17		9		6		1	
	18	35	11	20	7	13	2	3
Borstal, juvenile institution	4		5		7		3	
Treatment, observation	2		1		2		10	
No reply	11		11		12		12	
Unclassifiable	9		9		8		7	
N	(2101)		(2101)		(2101)		(2101)	

The percentages do not add up to 100, because respondents may have mentioned more than one reaction.

There are many problems attached to the interpretation of answers like these. But the results at least suggest quite clearly that the closer the respondents come to the situation and the individual in it, the greater the number of nuances and the more liberal the view of punishment.

It may be added that if we change vantage-point even more, and move from a representative sample of the population making statements about the treatment of others, to a sample of prisoners in Norwegian prisons making statements about their own treatment, the tendency noted above becomes even clearer. In an interview/ questionnaire study one of the questions the inmates of two Norwegian long-term prisons were asked was: 'Do you think the sentence you got was just compared to what you had done?' As many as 75 and 65 percent in the two prisons said 'no' (Mathiesen, 1965a: 160). Though some of these respondents may possibly have implied that the sentence was too light, most of them probably implied that it was too severe. The percentages may be compared with the other extreme, the proportion of the general population saying that the treatment of young offenders was too severe. We recall that the latter percentage was 2.

International studies suggest the same tendency as far as vantage-point is concerned. In a study of a random sample aged between 18 and 75 in the Swedish city of Malmö in 1975, Ulla Bondeson asked a general question about the respondents' views on punishment in the country. Eight percent replied that punishments were too severe, 55 percent that they were too light, and 22 percent that they were about right, while 18 percent gave other answers or did not reply (Bondeson, 1979: 135). Next, the respondents were asked a series of concrete questions about various types of behaviour which were either criminalized or which might be considered morally objectionable. Among other things, the respondents were asked what they personally thought the sanctions for these types of behaviour should be. On this level, the responses were more nuanced. Bearing in mind Kutchinsky's point that there may be national differences in the degree of consensus between the law, the courts, judges and the public (Kutchinsky, 1973; see p. 119), Bondeson's own summary of her findings may well be quoted:

> Space prevents a review of the various questions, but certain tendencies may be pointed out. Generally speaking, it may be said that the public has a rather nuanced legal view; they consider certain types of behaviour as more serious than does legislation and court practice, while they view others as less serious. Thus, the answers give no general support to Illum's contention that legal consciousness is unstructured and lacking content. But neither can we say that they support the contention that the public generally speaking demands 'stiffer measures against the criminals'. (Bondeson, 1979, translated from the Swedish by the present author)

Again it is instructive to add a comparison with inmates. In Ulla Bondeson's study of inmates in a number of Swedish institutions, 51 percent responded that punishments in general were too severe, while 6 percent responded that they were too light (Bondeson, 1974: 438, see also Bondeson, 1975: 135). The percentages may be compared with the proportions of the general population of Malmö responding that punishments were too severe (8 percent) and too light (55 percent). The findings are diametrically opposed. Mention should also be made of Bondeson's systematic comparison, as far as views on punishment go, between Scandinavian studies of prisoners and of general populations (Bondeson, 1974: 439–41). Though variations do exist between studies and between subgroups within the general population samples, these variations are clearly smaller then the difference between inmate samples on the one hand and the general population samples on the other. She concludes that there are 'striking contrasts' (Bondeson, 1974: 440), in the direction discussed here, between prisoners and general population samples.

In short, though there are tendencies towards consensus concerning the severity of punishment, there are also important and very significant variations. In particular, views vary with the vantage-point, that is, with the nearness to/distance from the situation and the individual in the situation. My interpretation of these differences is: the greater the distance, the more superficial we become, and the less we understand of the pain of punishment. Conversely, the smaller the distance, the more we understand. This interpretation is supported by other research findings from other contexts. Stanley Milgram (1965) observed, in an experimental situation, that the greater the distance created between a person ordered to inflict a certain kind of pain and the victim, the more willing the person is to follow orders about inflicting the pain. Nils Christie showed that the greater the distance which Norwegian guards in Norwegian World War II concentration camps managed to construct between themselves and their prisoners, the more willing they were to use heavy power, and even torture (Christie, 1972). This does not mean that close relations may not contain repression and violence. This we know from the private sphere, especially the family. Whether nearness leads to understanding, or not, probably depends on the context. In the public – often state – sphere, where the point of departure is bureaucratized impersonal relations, greater proximity to the victim will make it easier to understand.

In the area of criminal policy, a political conclusion would be that of reducing the distance, so that people might *see* the situation at close quarters and be able to empathize: a conclusion which is easy to make in principle, and more difficult, in our society, to carry out in practice.

To summarize, it is complicated to evaluate, in moral terms, the gravity and objectionability of the crime (see the preceding section). Taken alone, this would probably be a complication one could live with, also because there is, after all, a considerable degree of consensus concerning the moral evaluation of different crimes. Added to this, however, comes the relative character of the severity of punishment, especially its dependence on the vantage-point. This means that it is also, and even more, difficult to evaluate what is a 'correct' punishment value as far as severity goes. Together, the two 'sides' in 'punishment as deserved', thus contain major built-in problems.

Before moving on, it should be mentioned that von Hirsch (1986) has tried to argue in a way which, as I understand it, is supposed to neutralize the importance of the vantage-point, and with it the importance of the relative, for the severity of punishment. Earlier (pp. 119–20), we saw how he has also attempted to neutralize the problems of morals and values involved in evaluating the gravity/objectionability of the crime. Thus, he apparently seeks to neutralize the problems existing on both 'sides' in the balancing equation between gravity/objectionability and severity.

Concerning the severity of punishment, von Hirsch relies on a distinction between what is called 'cardinal' – or basic – and 'ordinal' – or rank-ordering – magnitudes of punishment. The issue of the cardinal magnitudes of punishment is the question of what absolute levels of severity should be chosen to anchor the penalty scale. The issue of the ordinal magnitudes is the question of how crimes should be punished relative to each other.

According to von Hirsch, the task of finding the cardinal magnitudes, the anchoring points of the punishment scale, is the first thing which must be performed. Then, when this is done, the ordinal magnitudes, the steps of the scale, may be determined within the limits of the cardinal anchoring points.

The presentation gives the impression that the cardinal magnitudes are objective or absolute. The word 'anchoring' gives the clear connotation that the points of departure of the punishment scale may be anchored like a boat in harbour. How, then, are we to find the anchoring cardinal magnitudes? To this question von Hirsch gives no satisfactory answer.

To begin with, von Hirsch says that justice, or 'just desert', is only a limiting principle for decisions concerning the cardinal magnitudes, whereas it is a determining principle for decisions concerning the ordinal magnitudes within the limits of the scale. The idea that 'just desert' is a limiting principle for the cardinal values, means that the cardinal points may not be determined in a precise way on the basis of justice. The points are only limited by, and cannot transcend, what is reasonable in terms of proportionality.

But how are these limits to what is reasonable in terms of proportionality to be fixed? About this von Hirsch gives nothing but vague hints; in fact, it may be said that the question is quite open (von Hirsch, 1986: 43–4). Though he does try to find his way with some examples, we find no real method which the legislator can use in practice.

Furthermore, the fact that justice only is to be a limiting, and not a determining, principle for the fixing of the cardinal magnitudes, implies, as von Hirsch openly admits, that other considersations also affect the choice of magnitudes. Which considerations? Mainly one: prison resources, availability of prison space, which, according to von Hirsch, one should be able to consider in combination with 'normative judgments about cardinal proportionality' (von Hirsch, 1986: 96; see also 100–101). The point is that the cardinal magnitudes should first be tentatively fixed on the basis of availability of prison space. Then one should examine whether this 'line, thus tentatively located, is consistent with cardinal proportionality constraints' (von Hirsch, 1986: 96). In some cases, with little prison space meeting acceptable standards, so that even serious crimes remain unpenalized by imprisonment, the latter considerations would imply that prison space should be increased. In other cases, where extensive prison facilities exist so that even lesser offences are punished by imprisonment, prison space should be decreased by the same token.

However, such a reliance on prison space as an additional criterion is tantamount to introducing a criterion – prison space – which is historically determined through the economic and political history of a country or a state (von Hirsch speaks of states in the US). As a point of departure for fixing the basic – the absolute, the cardinal – anchoring points for a punishment scale, this is in itself very unsatisfactory. Certainly, if Italian, German, or Norwegian prison space were taken as a point of departure, one would arrive at so-called absolute, cardinal anchoring points very different from the American, so that there would actually be little absolute, cardinal, or anchoring about them. Furthermore, and most importantly, by adding 'normative judgments about cardinal constraints', or further location of the cardinal magnitudes 'consistent with cardinal proportionality constraints', von Hirsch is simply begging the question: these proportionality constraints are the very constraints to be determined, they are the cardinal magnitudes which we are searching. Thus, we are in fact left empty-handed.

von Hirsch must be aware of these problems. In fact, he makes the following forceful reservation in connection with the question of the cardinal magnitudes: 'True, there is no uniquely correct solution to anchoring the penalty scale' (von Hirsch, 1986: 100). But, von Hirsch thinks, considerations like these make the procedure 'rational in the sense of being coherent and backed by reasons based on a general conception of deserved punishment' (von Hirsch, 1986: 101).

However, because the assessment of the limits to what is

proportionately reasonable, which the cardinal magnitudes cannot transgress, remains so problematical and unanswered, and because the above-mentioned supplementary criteria are so problematical[1], the considerations rather make the procedure *appear* rational. The suggested procedure masks reality. Actually, the problems of the vantage-point and relativity are just as much there.

The Content of Imprisonment

As mentioned earlier, the justice ideology in the fourth place gives the general impression that the two sides in the balancing operation between crime and punishment, the pain of crime and the pain of punishment, are comparable entities.

The difficulties associated with this presupposition, and with the construction of the proportionate justice in general, are brought out in extreme form when the actual content of imprisonment is reviewed more closely.

The Pains of Imprisonment   Among criminologists today, the pains of imprisonment are strangely forgotten in the great output of works on incapacitation, harm and culpability, cardinal and ordinal magnitudes, and so on.

Yet the description and analysis of the pains of imprisonment has a tradition in criminology and sociology. One of the early, and still one of the finest, descriptions was given over thirty years ago, by Gresham Sykes in his *The Society of Captives* (1958). There is reason to go back to this early work, and remind ourselves of it (see also Christie, 1981; Foucault 1977).

Sykes uses the word 'pain' to avoid the tendency to regard pain as something belonging to the past and as something belonging only to the body. The first pain which Sykes discusses is the pain involved in the very deprivation of liberty. 'Of all the painful conditions imposed on the inmates of the New Jersey State Prison, none is more immediately obvious than the loss of liberty' (Sykes, 1958: 65). One thing is the fact that the individual's movements are restricted. Much more serious is the fact that the inmate is cut off from family, relatives and friends. The freedom to enter and maintain such relationships is not always utilized when the inmate is on the outside. But that the freedom to do so *is* there, is the main point, and its absence 'is painfully depriving or frustrating in terms of lost emotional relationships, of loneliness and boredom' (1958: 65). Much more than this, confinement represents a 'deliberate, moral rejection of the criminal by the free community' (1958: 65), which is a constant threat to the inmate's self-conception. We might add here that the deprivation of liberty is an 'onion-shaped' system, with mechanisms of isolation inside the prison, and isolation within the isolation inside the prison.

The second pain discussed by Sykes is the deprivation of goods and services. Minimum material needs are usually satisfied in the prison. 'But a standard of living constructed in terms of so many calories per day, so many hours of recreation, so many cubic yards of space per individual, and so on, misses the central point' (1958: 68). In modern Western culture, material possessions are so large a part of the individual's conception of himself or herself 'that to be stripped of them is to be attacked at the deepest layers of personality' (1958: 69). It is true that the material poverty experienced on the inside is not always greater than the poverty which the inmate experiences when in the outside community. But the systematic *deprivation* of goods and services on the inside constitutes a systematic and highly threatening attack on the individual's self-conception.

The third pain is the deprivation of heterosexual relationships. This is obviously much more than a physiological problem: 'the psychological problems created by the lack of heterosexual relationships can be even more serious' (1958: 71). The status of male – or female – is called into question. Basically, one is shut off from the other sex which by its very polarity gives the world of one's own sex much of its meaning. Since we seek our identity partly in the picture of ourselves which we find reflected in the eyes of others – Cooley's 'looking-glass shelf' – a diffuse but serious threat is brought to bear on the prisoner's self-image (1958: 72).

Fourthly, there is the deprivation of autonomy. The prisoner is deprived of autonomy by being 'subjected to a vast body of rules and commands which are designed to control his behavior in minute detail' (1958: 73). It is true that self-determination is withheld in many areas of life. But regulation by a bureaucratic staff is felt far differently than regulation by custom. The loss of autonomy is total and imposed, and for these reasons less endurable. The question of self-conception again becomes central: the detailed and often inexplicable regulations 'descending from the bureaucratic staff involve a profound threat to the prisoner's self-image because they reduce the prisoner to the weak, helpless, dependent status of childhood' (1958: 75).

Fifthly, there is the deprivation of security. The 'individual prisoner is thrown into prolonged intimacy with other men who in many cases have a long history of violent, aggressive behaviour' (1958: 77). It is an anxiety-provoking situation even for the hardened recidivist. At least in Norway, the anxiety is reflected in the fact that a number of prisoners explicitly wish to live in isolation cells. Isolation, then, appears as the lesser evil. In addition, there is the anxiety provoked by living with the staff – living with search squads, sudden searches, sudden interrogations by the narcotics police, and so on.

'Imprisonment, then, is painful', Sykes concludes (1958: 78). In criminological texts today, these pains of imprisonment are often – at best – just listed, as common knowledge to be taken for granted. By being taken for granted, they are often left out of criminological concern and consideration. This is why we have brought them out again in some detail here. Though there are certainly variations between the prisons of different countries, and between different prisons, these basic and general deprivations are there to a greater or lesser extent.

To the list of pains comes the *power* which the prison wields in and over the lives of prisoners. The prison controls a wide spectrum of formal as well as informal benefits and burdens which are important (strangely disregarded as unimportant, incidentally, by Gresham Sykes), at times even vital, in the lives of the incarcerated.

From the outside one might think that the benefits and burdens controlled by the prison are not so important. From the outside, the difference between an isolation cell and a regular cell may appear small. So may the difference between six and eight crowns per day as allowance. In any case, the cell is cramped and the allowance small. Seen from within, however, much of this appears differently. Seen from the inside, differences which appear small from the outside are often magnified or enlarged and in part receive vital significance. The enlargement from within of differences which appear insignificant from the outside has been emphasized in several prison studies, partly from small and relatively open prisons (Mathiesen, 1965a), and partly from larger, closed prisons (Kristof-fersen, 1986). Kristoffersen, a Norwegian social anthropologist who worked as a guard in the Oslo District Prison, has significantly given his dissertation the suggestive title *The Tyranny of Trifles*. The enlargement from within follows as the prison context becomes the prisoners' comparative frame of reference. In so far as prisoners manage to maintain the outside community as frame of reference, they may also maintain the outside view of inside differences. In so far as they do not manage this, but take on the prison frame of reference, they also take on the inside view. This is the normal course, at least in long-term prisons (Mathiesen, 1965a: 76–80). Then the difference between six and eight crowns *does* become important.

Added to this is the fact that the prison controls benefits and burdens which outside observers should also be able to grasp as significant. Correspondence with or without censorship, leaves granted or not granted, release on parole or continued imprisonment, and so on, are all vital benefits and burdens controlled by the prison or by superior authorities. This does not mean that they function as effective rewards and punishments from the point of view of the staff, who aim at getting the prisoners 'in line' (which is the reason why Sykes disregards them as unimportant from the point of view of power). But through the eyes of the prisoner, whose aims are different, staff control over them indeed implies power (Mathiesen, 1965a; see also Goffman, 1961).

It is important to realize that the decision-making system of the prison is to a large extent discretionary. The rules which the prison has to abide by are to a significant degree elastic – in informal Norwegian terminology called 'rubber band rules'. Partly for this reason, prisoners lack effective legal methods with which to control and limit the decision making of the prison. Elsewhere I have characterized the power of the prison as *patriarchal*: in the context of the discretionary possibilities, it is of the same basic kind as power in a feudal structure, and the power of the feudal lords. Within the structure of the legally based modern bureaucracy, crucial legacies of the past are in other words alive and thriving (Mathiesen, 1965a, Ch. 6).

In view of the important, often vital benefits and burdens controlled by the prison, the discretionary, patriarchal decision-making structure of the prison implies an enormous power potential in the eyes of inmates.

Justice and the Content of Imprisonment   In this section we have discussed some of the pains of imprisonment, and, as an extension of this, power and the execution of power. Together, the prison becomes painfulness reduced to a system. Our question is this: how is such painfulness to be 'weighed' in the balancing operation of proportionate justice?

The point is that a 'weighing' of one set of pains by means of another can hardly be done. It may certainly be said that crime exposes others to pain. At least, this may be said when the victims are individuals, and it may especially be said for the minority of individuals who are the victims of violent crimes. As we have now seen, those who end up in prison for such acts are also exposed to pain. The two 'versions' of pain are, however, *not commensurable entities. Therefore, it is not possible to 'weigh' one by the other, as if we were operating with a pair of scales, in a construction of punishment values, punishment scales, and final proportionality or balance.*

On the one hand, a car is stolen, a house is broken into, a robbery has perhaps taken place. People have been deprived of goods, in some cases integrity and health. On the other hand, if placed in prison, the person who has committed the act is systematically deprived of liberty, goods and services, heterosexuality, autonomy and security, as well as being exposed to a formidable execution of power in every detail of life. I am not saying that the pain which the victim of crime is exposed to is insignificant – though I must confess I do think this is so in a fair number of cases. Neither am I saying that the pain which the prisoner is exposed to appears greater than that which the victim receives – though again I must confess I do also think this is so in a fair number of cases. All I am saying is that the pains are so *different* that they cannot be compared, at least not in so precise a way as to provide a basis for punishment values, punishment scales, and proportionality or balance of punishment.

How much deprivation of liberty, medical services, self-esteem and personal autonomy is necessary to balance the breaking and entering of a home or the vandalism of a summer house? The two 'versions' of pain, in this hypothetical example, contain so many complex factors, and such a strong element of subjective experience, that proportionate justice, the balancing-of-scales justice, breaks down.

Does Prison Have a Defence in Justice?

We have moved through a series of issues. Let us try to tie them together.

At the time when physical punishments were replaced by imprisonment, a transformation of punishment took place – punishment became a question of *time taken from the individual*. The basic premise for the idea of meting out proportionate justice through prison is the notion that the punishment value attached to criminal acts may be measured in terms of *time taken from the individual*. The further notion is that the time taken from the prisoner has two characteristics.

First, time is seen as an objective entity, in the sense that it is intersubjective – that is, it counts in the same way for all of us. In our society, we have agreed on a common measurement of time – in seconds, minutes, days, months and years.

Secondly, time is seen as a ratio scale. Courses in methodology generally operate with four scaling levels. In the first place, they operate with the nominal level, where the measurement only implies that the units are classified as mutually exclusive categories – for example gender. Secondly, they operate with the ordinal level, where the units also are rank-ordered – for example social status. Thirdly, they operate on the interval level, where the unit of measurement also makes it possible to measure the distance between the categories – for example temperature as measured according to the Centigrade scale. And fourthly, they operate with ratio scales, which also have an absolute zero point so that the ratio between different units may be compared – for example weight, where you can say that ten pounds is double five pounds (Hellevik, 1977). Prison time is assumed to have an absolute zero point, as weight. Thereby, it is supposedly meaningful to say, for example, that a ten-year sentence is double a five-year sentence.

When the time which is taken from the prisoner thus is viewed as objective and as measurable on the ratio level, it is possible to develop a system of proportionality, a balancing-of-scales justice. A particular act is to receive three years' imprisonment as retribution, another six years. By the same token you have said that the latter act doubles the former in terms of gravity or objectionability, and that a balance has been established between misdeed and punishment.

However, both of the basic premises for prison time break down.

In the first place, prison time is not objective or intersubjective: there is no agreement on what prison time means. Crime is bound up and varies with moral convictions. The severity of punishment is bound up with and relative to the vantage-point, especially proximity. The meaning of prison time, the meaning of two months, two years, twenty years of imprisonment, is therefore morally relative and relative in terms of perspective. This fact is reflected in the great international differences which exist concerning the evaluation of the importance of prison time. If prison time were objective, various nations should converge towards the same punishment times. We know that they certainly do not converge, but show dramatic differences.

Secondly, prison time actually does not constitute a ratio scale: the content of imprisonment is characterized by pain and application of power. Pain and power do not have an absolute zero point. Therefore, it is not meaningful to compare and say that this pain is twice as painful as that pain, and this application of power is twice as great as that application. If the content of imprisonment is taken seriously, as it should be, imprisonment slides down the series of scaling levels. We are not even faced with an interval scale; at best, the pain and the application of power are rank-ordered in 'more' or 'less'. This is also where cautious generals, like Andrew von Hirsch, in theory want to place the justice of punishment (see p. 126, about ordinal magnitudes). But in actual legislation and sentencing practice an untenable ratio scale is clearly presupposed, and it is impossible to see how discussions like that of von Hirsch are to prevent legislators and judges from continuing to presuppose it. In fact, if anything the pseudo-scientific character of the discussion is likely to stimulate it. Furthermore, we are often not even faced with an ordinal scale, but with a pure nominal scale: fourteen days in an isolation cell is different from a refused leave or the censorship of letters, but not necessarily any 'better' or 'worse' than a refused leave or censorship. This becomes manifest when we move from evaluating punishments like this in round and general terms, to evaluating them on the background of concrete information about the situation of the inmates. That situation varies, which implies that isolation may be terrible in one situation, whereas refusal of leaves and censorship may be terrible in another. In other words, differences in context often make the nominal scale the only correct scale.

In order to use time as punishment, legislators and judges take away all such issues, abstracting time from them. You could put it this way: time is treated as a category lacking content.

Mathematicians may treat time this way. To mathematicians, time *is* abstract. When legislators and judges do the same, they abstract time from the realities involved – the variations in the moral evaluation of the misdeed, the importance of the vantage-point for evaluating the severity of punishment, the pain, the application of power, and thereby the incommensurability of misdeed and punishment.

When legislators and judges do this, they mask reality, and give the impression that prison has a defence in a balancing-of-scales justice.

All of the factors we have mentioned pull in the same direction, showing that prison in fact does not find a defence in justice.

Note

1. In addition to prison space analysed as indicated above, von Hirsch also mentions a variety of incapacitation which he thinks should be emphasized.

   As pointed out in Chapter 4 above, von Hirsch argues very forcefully and convincingly against incapacitation, in its collective as well as its selective form, as a motivation for prison as punishment. But towards the end of his own book (from Ch. 13 on), in the final discussion of 'just deserts', he surprisingly introduces a third variety of incapacitation, called 'categorical incapacitation', which in a way is supposed to lie 'between' collective and selective incapacitation. He wishes to combine this variety of incapacitation in a synthesis with 'just deserts'. In contrast to collective incapacitation, which, he says, aims at felonies or major felonies in general in an attempt to obtain an across-the-board incapacitative impact, categorical incapacitation is targeted at particular categories of crime. And in contrast to selective incapacitation, which aims at individual offender characteristics associated with recidivism, categorical incapacitation aims at finding which crime categories are linked with higher recidivism rates. In addition, gravity is considered: the question is which crime categories are associated with high rates of *serious* recidivism. An attempt is made to combine the emphasis on the recidivism of the given category with the emphasis and due regard for justice. The point is to develop aggregate sentencing policies that achieve differential reductions in crime while being consistent with concerns for equity and justice in sentencing. More precisely, tentative guidelines with 'desert' principles exclusively in mind should first be developed. The anchoring points on the penalty scale should subsequently be reset so as to reflect non-selective crime control aims, notably categorical incapacitation (1986: 161). But the adjustment should not be so large as to infringe on limits established by cardinal proportionality, and any change should not disturb the comparative ordering of punishments within these limits (von Hirsch, 1986: 161–2). The idea is based on the work of Jacqueline Cohen (1983).

Two objections seem pertinent. First, categorical incapacitation seems to be a subtype of collective incapacitation. At least, it is extremely difficult to understand how categorical incapacitation differs in principle from collective incapacitation, with the same hazards – as von Hirsch, as far as I can understand, partly seems to admit (von Hirsch, 1986: 165–6), especially when saying flatly that until 'more is known about categorical incapacitation effects, for example, I would think it would be premature to attempt the inclusion strategy of which I have spoken' (1986: 166).

Secondly, the attempt to combine categorical incapacitation with considerations of justice seems extremely artificial from a practical, legislative and sentencing, point of view. Legislators live and work in live and turbulent political contexts, making the kinds of abstract mental operations or exercises suggested here extremely remote. This von Hirsch in fact admits when saying that the inclusion of preventive concerns 'should depend on the commission's capacities and the atmosphere in which it operates' (1986: 166).

Another attempt to combine just deserts with incapacitation should also be mentioned. Norval Morris and Marc Miller have suggested that prediction of dangerousness – in effect of assaultive criminality – is permissible within stated and broad desert limits (Morris and Miller, 1983). 'We argue', Morris and Miller say, 'that punishment should not be extended or imposed on the basis of predictions of dangerousness beyond what would be justified independent of that prediction. Thus, concepts of "desert" define the upper limits of allowable punishment' (Morris and Miller, 1983: 6). They grant that predictive accuracy is low – with the best possible predictions they expect to make one true positive prediction of violence to the person for every two false positive predictions. But, they argue, this does not mean that the two false positives are 'innocent': 'In sum, that the person predicted as dangerous does no future injury does not mean that the classification was erroneous even though the prediction itself was wrong' (1983: 20–21). They analogize to dangerous objects – unexploded bombs during postwar days in London: most bombs did not go off and were thus 'false positives', yet they had a high *potential* to detonate and were certainly dangerous (1983: 18–19).

The argumentation contains several flaws. First, the basis for accepting low predictive accuracy is untenable. A vast body of theory and knowledge, from phenomenology to Weberian sociology, warns against analogies between the actions of human beings, with intentions and consciousness, and the movements of physical objects. Furthermore, and partly because of this difference, we know vastly more about the actual dangerous potential of physical objects like bombs than we do about such a potential on the part of human beings. Morris and Miller in effect do not take the inaccuracy of predictions seriously, but overlook it and treat it as if accuracy and knowledge reigned despite the prediction results.

Secondly, and most importantly in our present context, Morris and Miller do not give any indications as to how and where the desert limits, beyond which prediction presumably should not bring us, are to be determined. They argue that there is a range of just punishments for a given offence, that the concept of *not undeserved* punishments should properly limit the range of utilitarian considerations, and that 'within a range of not unjust punishments' different levels of dangerousness may be taken into account in sentencing (Morris and Miller, 1983: 37). But this does not solve the problem of the anchoring points, which is left just as unanswered. By arguing for incapacitation within broad and actually unstated desert limits, Morris and Miller in fact stand in danger of promoting increased punishment levels in the rhetorical name of justice – exactly what is happening in Sweden (see pp. 88–9, 116).

6

The Future of Imprisonment

The theories of individual prevention – rehabilitation, incapacitation, individual deterrence – are unable to defend the prison. Neither is the other major theory of social defence – the theory of general prevention. And neither is, finally, the theory of justice. The prison does not have a defence, the prison is a fiasco in terms of its own purposes.

This is what we find when we carefully and in detail *take stock* of the prison. It forcefully raises the question of what is to be done with the prison. Before trying to answer that question, it is necessary to look at another: since the prison is a fiasco in terms of its own purposes, why do we have prisons at all?

The Ideology of Prison

In a very general sense, it may be said that we have prisons despite the fiasco because there exists a pervasive and persistent *ideology of prison* in our society.

Ideologies are belief systems which render social life meaningful and legitimate. An ideology of prison exists which renders the prison as an institution and a sanction meaningful and legitimate. The ideology of prison contains two major components – a supportive and a negating component.

The Supportive Component

Some fifteen years ago, I argued that the prison serves four important ideological functions in advanced welfare state capitalist societies (Mathiesen, 1974: 76–8).

I called the first of them the *expurgatory function*. I saw the prison as an institution within which a proportion of the unproductive population of late capitalist societies could be housed, controlled and conveniently forgotten. I saw the prison, in this perspective, as part of a much larger expurgatory system – comprising a wide range of institutions and institutional arrangements.

The second function was the *power-draining function*. Those who are purged away, I argued, are placed in a structural situation where they remain unproductive non-contributors to the system containing them. Unlike the factory's dependence on the workers' contribution, which gives the workers power because they can withdraw the contribution, the prison is not dependent on the prisoners' contribution.

The third function was the *diverting function*. Socially dangerous acts are increasingly being committed by individuals and classes with power in society. Those caught by the punishment machine, and especially those placed behind bars, are, on the other hand, very largely traditional criminals from the lower working class. The heavy-handed use of prison against them, I argued, diverts our attention from the dangers flowing from those in power.

The fourth and final function was the *symbolic function*. I saw the symbolic function as closely related to the diverting function, but with a difference: when those caught by the punishment machine are imprisoned, they are stigmatized as black. Against this background the rest of us, on the outside, may define ourselves as all the whiter, though also we are certainly grey or black.

A basic underlying notion in the analysis was that though other types of institutions and institutional arrangements have these functions too, the prison in a unique way combines all of them. Therefore the prison survives, even in situations where other institutional types are dismantled.

I viewed these functions as ideological in the sense mentioned above. Nowhere do we see more clearly that ideological functions have material underpinnings (Mathiesen, 1980). In terms of observable consequences, the prison physically helps to bifurcate society between the 'productive' and the 'unproductive'; it sets up a structure which, quite observably, places the prisoners in a powerless situation; it also sets up a structure which places members of one class in such a situation that the attention we might pay to the members of another is diverted; and it uses a variety of physical – but not only physical – methods to stigmatize the members of the former class. But the functions as such are ideological: they make prisons appear meaningful and legitimate.

Through the fifteen years which have passed since the above analysis was presented, I have not seen analyses or data fundamentally contradicting the significance of the functions summarized here. I would today add a fifth function, perhaps equally important, which I would call the *action function*: the prison, and imprisonment, is the most observable type of sanction in our society. In earlier times, bodily harm was the most observable type. Our society has passed beyond that sanction. The prison, however, is equally observable, not on the individual level, but as an institutional entity. In this sense there is continuity and change between the two types of sanction. They are similar in the sense that they both 'stand out', as positive, observable signs that something is done. They are dissimilar in the sense that the former sanction is observable in individuals, and the latter in establishing a physical arrangement covering large numbers of people. The change is in turn continuous with a changed society: modern society, with its size and complexity, in this context requires collective solutions. By relying on the prison, by building prisons, by building more prisons, by passing legislation containing longer prison sentences, the actors on the political level of our own times thus obtain a method of showing that they act on crime as a category of behaviour, that they do something about it, that something is presumably being done about law and order – to quote the title of a recent book. No other sanction fulfils this function as well.

The analysis may be tied to the introductory discussion in Chapter 1. There we emphasized that the three major stages in the development of prisons may be viewed as institutional attempts to discipline disturbing or threatening population categories, brought forth by basic upheavals in society, in our own time by an important legitimacy crisis on the part of the state (see pp. 11–14). The various theories of punishment and prison which we have reviewed in the preceding chapters are ideologically acceptable and rationalized formulations of such a perceived need for discipline. The functions introduced here explain why the prison continues to exist and thrive despite the fact that the need, formulated so acceptably and rationally, is not met.

The Negating Component
The ideological functions discussed above constitute a 'supportive' ideological component in the sense that they imbue the prison with something positive. The prison performs something. The ideology of prison also contains what we may call a negating component, that is, a component through which the fiasco of the prison in negated.

Negation of the prison's fiasco takes place in three important public spheres in society – in the widest public sphere, consisting above all of the whole range of modern mass media; in a narrower public sphere, consisting of institutions directly engaged in crime prevention such as the police, the courts, the prosecuting authorities and the prisons themselves; and in an even narrower sphere consisting of particular professional groups, for example in research.

The three public spheres are, simultaneously, systems which supposedly perform the task of continually keeping institutions such as the prison under review and control. The first sphere may be called the 'outer' feedback circle of control, the second may be called the 'inner' feedback circle, and the third may be viewed as a kind of 'kernel' circle. Therefore, the negation which takes place of the prison's fiasco is particularly serious.

In the first public sphere or feedback circle, negation takes place through what I will call non-recognition, in the second through what may be called pretence, and in the third through disregard.

In the widest public sphere or 'outer' feedback circle, *non-recognition* of the prison's fiasco takes place all the time. In the newspapers, on television, in the whole range of media, the prison is simply not recognized as a fiasco, but as a necessary if not always fully successful method of reaching its purported goals. The prison solution is taken as paradigmatic (see pp. 48–51), so that a rising crime rate is viewed as still another sign showing that more prison is needed.

In the narrower public sphere or 'inner' circle – in the police, the courts, and so on – there is also a good deal of non-recognition of the fiasco. But the fiasco is also partly recognized as such. The various earlier quotes from authoritative Swedish sources are indications of this. Many in the police, in the courts, in the prosecuting authorities, know. But *pretence* takes over: the participants pretend that the prison is a success, though in fact it is not and they more or less know it. Pretence in this sense may be found throughout the police, the courts, and so on. Why? Because without it, much of the work done by people and institutions within this sphere would appear meaningless and counterproductive.

It is important to realize that the boundaries between the wider and the narrower public spheres are perforated, so that the pretence in the 'inner' circle feeds into the non-recognition pattern in the 'outer' circle, perhaps in many ways creating it, or at least supporting it. There is, in other words, an important interaction between the two spheres.

In the narrowest public sphere, or 'kernel' feedback circle consisting of professional groups such as researchers and others, there is probably non-recognition as well as pretence. But for professionals, and indeed for researchers, it is more difficult not to recognize the fiasco, and it is – in view of very traditional professional and research ethics – more difficult to pretend or lie that success reigns when in fact a fiasco is recognized. But here *disregard* partly takes over: the ineffectiveness of prison, and the deep troubles involved in establishing proportionate justice, which are well known, are overlooked: simply not discussed or treated in the context of the functioning of the penal system as a whole. The prison as such is conveniently forgotten in some of the discussions.

Again, there is interaction between the various spheres: the boundary between the narrowest sphere and the two other spheres is perforated, so that the disregard in the narrowest sphere spills over into the other two, strongly supporting pretence as well as non-recognition there. The disregard of the facts of the fiasco supports, if not creates (that would imbue researchers with too much influence), the development of mythology in the other spheres.

Let it be emphatically stated that not all research has the quality of disregard. There is, certainly, a large body of research of a fact-finding, critical kind; if there was not, this book could not have been written. But it should be recognized that the information reception centres in the other spheres – journalists in newspapers, etc, as well as police chiefs, judges and so on – actually seek confirmation rather than information, so that the message of disregard is quite *selectively* transposed in the other spheres, in line with the convictions and needs in those spheres. This makes the responsibility of those disregarding the facts of the fiasco all the greater.

While non-recognition in the widest and pretence in the narrower sphere are probably reasonably acceptable notions to many readers of a book like this, the process of disregard in the narrowest sphere, especially in the research branch of it, requires some further detailing. We shall return to this detailing shortly.

What is to Be Done?

In one sense, what is to be done is a simple question. The fiasco of the prison rationally requires a contraction of the prison, and an eventual abolition of it. From a practical point of view, however, the question is obviously not so simple. The strategic problem is acute.

When approaching the question, it is essential to keep the *ideological* character of the functions and defences of the prison in mind. The purging, power-draining, diverting, symbolizing, and action-signifying functions of the prison make it appear meaningful and legitimate, and throughout the spectrum of public spheres or feedback circles, a pervasive ideological mystification packages this legitimacy further.

With this as our point of departure, we shall proceed by sketching some possible steps, keeping in mind that this is the beginning of an analysis rather than a final one.

From Where?

First, from where can an attack on the ideological defence of the prison be expected? I am thinking of countries like Norway, Sweden and Britain. In a wide sense of the word: from the left, from social democracy and leftwards. Why? Because the left, in this wide sense, fosters an ideology which directly counters the prison solution, and which would, if taken seriously, basically challenge the presumed meaningfulness and legitimacy of prison.

I am thinking of the ideological components, common to socialists in a wide sense and social democrats, consisting of *solidarity* and *compensation*.

Solidarity refers to instrumental – task-oriented – and expressive – empathic emotional – relationships between two or more actors, whether in a group, a social rank, or a social class. Solidarity also implies that politically or socially weak members of the group, the rank, or the class are included in the sense that tasks are to be performed for them and emotional support is to be given to them.

Compensation refers to mechanisms which in a concrete way carry solidarity into practice. The process of 'cumulation' – the 'Matthew principle' (Matthew 13.12), whereby the rich are getting richer and the poor poorer – is basic to late capitalist social structure. Cumulation in this sense is seen in a number of dimensions in society. Compensation is the opposite process, whereby weakness is compensated so that the process of cumulation is subdued or reversed (Aubert, 1976).

It would be a left socialist position that social democracy in societies like the Norwegian, the Swedish or the British, is failing in solidarity, and failing in effective methods of compensation. It would be a left socialist position that effective solidarity and compensation requires fundamental changes in the capitalist market production system and economy, since it is a system and an economy which so forcefully maintains the unsolidary and unrelenting tendency towards cumulation. But social democracy at least caters to *the ideology* of solidarity and compensation, which is important for our purposes here. As pointed out, the ideology runs directly counter to the prison solution, challenging its legitimacy.

Let us for the moment simplify matters, leave the issues of victimless crime, etc, untouched, and concentrate on so-called 'traditional' crime – a vague category, to be sure, but a category which is meaningful because it refers to the kinds of acts committed by those who fill our prisons. Occurrences defined as traditional crime regularly involve two parties – the victim and the perpetrator. A wide range of research results suggest that though there certainly are variations, both of these parties may to a considerable extent be characterized as *politically and socially weak*. This is the case whether the occurrences take place in inner-city areas in Britain, in particular sections of Stockholm, or among drug users along the Aker river is Oslo. To a large extent, traditional crime is a confrontation between the weak.

The prison solution is, first of all, solidary *neither with the victim nor with the perpetrator*. It is, secondly, compensatory *neither with the victim nor with the perpetrator*.

Its lack of solidarity and compensatory relations with the perpetrator is not suprising: the perpetrator is considered the guilty party, and subjected to intended pain. More surprising, or at least more contrary to theory, is its lack of solidarity and compensatory will towards the victim. There is much talk about the victim, but little action, and the prison as such gives the victim nothing. This is the case as far as current victims go. But it is also the case with potential victims, precisely because the prison does not rehabilitate, deter, or incapacitate.

In both directions, then, the prison is a fundamentally unsolidary and uncompensatory arrangement, on full collision course with basic socialist and social democratic tenets. Conservative political ideology, on the other hand, with a fundamental emphasis on individual initiative (rather than solidarity) and regulation through market forces (rather than through compensation), is not at odds with the prison solution. Rather, it is in line with the prison.

Thus, only the left fosters an ideology which runs counter to the prison, and the struggle against the prison ideology can only be started from the left.

From What Sources of Knowledge?
Secondly, from what sources of knowledge can the left draw inspiration for the attack on the ideology of prison? As I see it, there are two major possible sources. The first of them has, in the British context, called itself 'left realism'. Let us take a look at it.

Left Realism? Left realism may be viewed as a school of criminology and thinking about crime and crime control which has developed through the 1980s. Historically, it started off as a reaction to tendencies within radical, critical and left criminology. It viewed, and still views, good parts of such criminology as 'left idealism', and has advocated a realist – albeit still a left – orientation as an alternative. Though the term left realism is British, it has parallels in other European countries. Yet it seems to be more of an integrated school in Britain than elsewhere.

In terms of stated purpose, left realism is dedicated to the cause of socialism, and therefore near at hand as a possible source of knowledge for socialists and social democrats in an attack on the prison solution. In the British context, one of the first major publications advancing the views of left realism was Ian Taylor's *Law and Order, Arguments for Socialism* (Taylor, 1981). This book has been followed up by a number of publications through the 1980s, among them John Lea and Jock Young's *What is to be Done about Law and Order?* (Lea and Young, 1984), Richard Kinsey, John Lea and Jock Young's *Losing the Fight against Crime* (Kinsey et al., 1986), Roger Matthews and Jock Young's *Confronting Crime* (Matthews and Young, 1986), as well as numerous other works (see for example Taylor, 1982; Lea, 1987; Matthews, 1987; Young, 1987; Young, 1988).

The major arguments of the new realists are frequently repeated through the major publications, and may, without too much simplification, be summarized in a few basic tenets.

First, it is forcefully maintained that the left, including good parts of what has become known as critical criminology, minimizes the problem of conventional working-class crime (see, for example, Lea and Young, 1984: 11, 102–3; Kinsey et al., 1986: 59–60). A contrary, right-wing opinion, uncritically dramatizing the crime rate, also exists, and the left realists insist that a realistic criminology must navigate between these currents. But particular attention is paid to what is considered the idealistic minimization on the left of the significance of crime. It is maintained that a so-called 'left idealist position' on crime sees working-class crime as more or less an illusion, 'orchestrated by the ruling class in order to engender moral panic which distracts the population from the real problems which assail them' (Lea and Young, 1984: 102–3), and as 'media-instigated events without any rational basis' (Young, 1987: 338). Within this context, much attention is paid to the question of the causes of traditional crime, with reliance among other things on subcultural theory and theories of relative (rather than absolute) deprivation (Lea and Young, 1984), and on 'deconstruction' of crime into various aspects of the criminal process (Young, 1987). It is maintained that the most fundamental tenet of so-called realist criminology is to be 'faithful to the phenomenon which it is studying' (Young, 1987: 338), that is, crime; yet it is emphasized that the trouble with criminology is that it cannot explain crime (Young, 1987: 338).

In the context of the issue of the aetiology of crime, it is also maintained that the left mistakenly views traditional crime, for example among black youth, as a part of a political – colonial – struggle. This is also an idealization of crime. 'Those', it is said, 'who refer to the 'social and political nature' of the criminality of a minority of black youth have yet to demonstrate its contribution to the struggle for social justice as opposed to the demoralization and weakening of the struggle' (Lea and Young, 1984: 134).

Secondly, it is forcefully maintained or implied, in major publications, that the police force has to be the core institution in a socialist criminal policy. But, the authors insist, it should be a reorganized police, channelled away from the path of military-style policing, with an emphasis on minimal policing and on local democratic control – which will also make the public actively interested in providing the police with the information they need in the fight against crime. It is maintained that 'only an informed socialist policy, involving the restructuring of the relations between police, local community and local government, is likely ever to make our cities tolerable places for working-class people to live in' (Kinsey et al., 1986: 36), and that 'only a reorganization of policing and its aims and methods, coupled with the democratic control of police forces by local government, will offer a way forward in the fight against crime' (Kinsey et al., 1986: 56). The emphasis on the police, and the insistence that the police may be changed in the way suggested, goes back to a view of the state. 'For the left idealists', it is claimed, 'the state is the direct instrument of the ruling class' (Lea and Young, 1984: 101). The state, it is maintained, comprises much more of a constructive role.

Thirdly, and finally in this enumeration of salient points, there is an insistence on 'a continuity in radical criminology from its early days through left idealism into realism' (Young, 1988: 175). This continuity exists despite the basic flaws listed above in what is purportedly left idealism, and also despite other flaws in such idealism – idealization of oppressed groups, an unwillingness to come to terms with sociological positivism, a tendency to see crime as a mere epiphenomenon of social control mechanisms, and an unwillingness to deal with reform (Young, 1988: 174–5). The point of the continuity seems to be that the idealist tendencies, though they have not disappeared, have over time been overruled and set aside by so-called left realism, which incorporates important elements of the past without entering its purportedly oversimplified notions. Left realism, it is maintained, is not politically constrained, which makes it possible to trace crime to features of social structure and to enter, if necessary, a full-blown critique of policing and other aspects of the administration of justice. It is sensitized to the fact that crime statistics are partly products of behaviour and evaluation on the part of control agencies. It is committed to the view that the aetiology of crime also has a subjective component, especially the experience of justice and injustice. And it is committed to warning that the causes of crime, the construction of criminal statistics and successful intervention cannot take place without consideration of politics and morality (Young, 1988: 175–6).

In short, left realism seems to take on itself the task of developing a realist *paradigm*, combining an emphasis on a realistic appraisal of crime as a problem and police control against it with an emphasis on historical notions from critical criminology purged of what is considered their unrealistic excesses and exaggerations (interpretation of Young, 1988). The new paradigm is meant as an attempt to compete with administrative criminology (of the Home Office branch in Britain) as well as with conservative right realist criminology (of the James Q. Wilson branch, see pp. 84, 91, 99–100), both of which presumably converge with so-called left idealism in concentrating on social control rather than the aetiology of crime.

How shall we appraise the attempt of the so-called left realists? Three major objections, or clusters of objections, may be raised.

First, much of what is said about so-called left idealism is *either untrue or grossly exaggerated*.

It may have been true, at one time during the emergence of international critical criminology, that the impact of behaviour defined as traditional crime was underestimated, that traditional crime was viewed merely as part of a political struggle, and that the state – including the police – was conceptualized as a direct instrument of the ruling class.

But, for one thing, these underestimations, views and conceptualizations were, in so far as they could be found, fruitful ways of turning traditional views and conventional wisdom about crime and the police upside down. In their critique, the so-called left realists overlook the historical significance of sharp paradigmatic breaks. Indeed, and rather strangely, some of them overlook their own historical role in such prior breaks.

For another, if the exaggerations did exist at one time, they are certainly toned down now, while the so-called left realists in an undocumented way continue to write as if the status quo was 1968 and not the late 1980s (see, again, Young, 1988). As Maeve McMahon has pointed out (as far as the purported underestimation of crime goes), 'Young's portrait is more a caricature', which 'glosses over the complexity, diversity and insights of the critical criminologies' (McMahon, 1988a: 113).

Particular reference should be made to the purported conspiratorial nature of left analyses. To repeat, crime is presumably seen as a total illusion 'orchestrated by the ruling class in order to engender moral panic' (Lea and Young, 1984: 102; see above). The concept of 'moral panic' (Cohen, 1972) has proved very useful in analyses of waves of opinion about crime and deviancy. It has been used to pinpoint the process whereby even widely divergent interests, for example in a community, under certain conditions come to interact in a fashion which stimulates each of them to develop in a particular direction, so that a total opinion movement results. I have yet to see an analysis utilizing the concept of moral panic in which crime is simply conceptualized as an illusion purposely set in motion by a ruling group with the explicit aim of creating a panic. Along the same line, allegations about views to the effect that 'the state is the direct instrument of the ruling class' (Lea and Young, 1984: 101; see above), run directly counter to the existence of major and serious attempts to analyse, for instance, the complexities and divisions within the state as a system of control (see, for example, Scraton, 1987).

Secondly, while the misrepresentation of critical criminology runs across the board of the left realist tenents outlined, *specific substantive problems are also contained in the various tenets, and in the relationship between them*. These problems are more important than any misrepresentation of adversaries. Briefly, the so-called left realists maintain that inner-city crime can only be explained by a reliance on a theory of relative deprivation combined with subcultural theory. Relative deprivation refers to the excess of expectations over opportunities. Subcultural solutions are seen as products of relative deprivation under conditions of marginalization.

Indeed, it is true that these concepts, and the theoretical perspectives emanating from them, have proved useful as partial explanations of deviance, especially in American sociology. And Young and collaborators emphasize an important point when arguing that the frustration stemming from relative deprivation may help explain for example the difference between the 1930s, with their relative absence of riots (but with a high degree of politicization) despite high levels of unemployment, and the present period (Lea and Young, 1984: 218–19). The team is able to substantiate that crime is endemic to late capitalism. Yet the strong insistence that absolute deprivation is of no importance for an understanding of crime does become a problem. For one thing, there is an element of arrogance in it: as long as the poor do not know any better, and have nothing to compare with, problems presumably do not arise. This is not stated by the so-called new realists. But it may be inferred. More importantly, the insistence on the unimportance of absolute deprivation seems to underestimate the sociological significance of such deprivation – for example the role of absolute poverty and want in structuring concretely aspects of city life so that it is conducive to, for instance, criminal behaviour. Finally, the insistence makes for easy disregard of the possibility that differential interaction between absolute and relative deprivation may produce differential results. Relative deprivation under conditions of extreme want may create one type of behaviour pattern, relative deprivation in a situation of abundance another. In short, the so-called left realists criticize other parts of the left for a simplistic reliance on absolute deprivation and poverty as an explanatory factor, but seem to be trapped by a similar simplification in their own one-sided insistence on relative deprivation.

The so-called left realists maintain that the rise in crime rates following from economic marginality and relative deprivation has become bound up in a vicious circle with a drift to military policing. This is why they call for minimal policing and police accountability through community control. A major volume is dedicated to the detailing of how this goal is to be reached (Kinsey et al., 1986).

Nowhere does the term idealism seem more appropriate. The authors call for a radical reorganization of the police and a limitation of their powers, coupled with a policing system in line with public needs. But rather than outlining a strategy for this, we largely find an outline of the ideal of it.

Maximum public initiation of police action and maximum access to the police, minimal police-initiated action, and minimum use of coercion are, we learn, to be obtained through a combination of legal, political and organizational changes (Kinsey et al., 1986: 189). But the legal, political and organizational changes suggested remain on the level of stated ideals. The legislative framework of minimal policing 'would seek', we learn, 'to define the limits of minimum necessary coercion', 'to define the precise extent of police powers', and 'to minimize the role of police-initiated activity while maximizing that of the public' (Kinsey et al., 1986: 193). The minimization of police intervention in public life, we learn, 'can only be achieved by a fundamental restructuring of the working conditions of the uniformed patrol officer' (Kinsey et al., 1986: 199). It is 'essential', we learn, for the success of minimal policing to establish within the police forces a practice of what might be termed 'generic policing' (Kinsey et al., 1986: 201). And so on.

Statements of ideals may be very important at specific junctures. We shall have occasion to call on ideals later in this chapter, arguing that a restoration of ideals in the area of criminal policy and crime control is now of the utmost importance. But reference to ideals becomes deeply disturbing in an analysis which explicitly purports to eschew (and which indeed also ridicules) ideals, and which claims to replace them with something purporting to be merely and entirely operational steps to obtain organizational change.

There is, furthermore, a highly problematic relationship between the 'crime' part of the so-called left realist argument and the 'police' part of it. As far as I can see, this problematic relationship goes to the core. The crime part of the argument provides an analysis of the social aetiology of crime. We have looked briefly at some difficulties inherent in the analysis, but leave those aside now. Here the main point is that the analysis of the aetiology, and the constant insistence on such an analysis as well as the critique of others for not being sufficiently insistent in this respect, is simply forgotten when it comes to remedies: the remedies are contained in crime control through policing, and almost only in crime control through policing. To repeat, 'only a reorganization of policing and its aims and methods . . . will offer a way forward in the fight against crime' (Kinsey et al., 1986: 56; see above). There are references to the aetiology of crime, such as the absence of an alternative politics for marginalized youth (Lea and Young, 1984: 270–73), but the references are not central. Central is the police – *despite the whole analysis of social causation.*

Thus, the analysis breaks in two – where the analysis of social aetiology should lead to social remedies, it rather leads to more policing, more formal social control. As formulated by Maeve McMahon, 'the revelation of the working class as victimized gives rise to calls for more intensified policing of them' (McMahon, 1988a: 119).

Thirdly, there is, throughout so-called left realism, *hardly any discussion of the sanctioning system, and little or no discussion of the prison.* This is a decisive omission: it implies that we are not told how those brought into the criminal justice system through intensified policing are to be dealt with. And it brings us to the critical concern of this book.

The concern with the prison has been an ingrained feature of critical criminology. In so-called left realism, the interest in it seems to have diminished over time.

In his opening 1981 volume on law, order and arguments for socialism, Ian Taylor was still preoccupied with it. In a major part of a chapter entitled 'Reconstructing socialist criminology', he discussed the prison movement in Britain and Scandinavia, focusing on issues of rehabilitation, justice and abolition (Taylor, 1981: 125–46). Later volumes have contained less.

In the central 1984 volume on what is to be done about law and order (Lea and Young, 1984), there is precious little about it – except a few brief pages towards the end (Lea and Young, 1984: 266–7), under the title 'We must take crime control seriously', in which it is stated that left realism is in fundamental disagreement with conventional as well as left idealist approaches to crime control. The draconian penalties of the law-and-order lobby only make matters worse, and the idealists, we learn, presumably turn their back on the problem. A left realist crime control programme, we are told, must comprise alternatives to prison which help integrate the offender, pre-emptive deterrence rather than intervention by punishment after the event, and minimal use of prison: prison should only be employed 'in those circumstances where there is extreme danger to the community' (Lea and Young, 1984: 267). The volume contains no discussion of the difficulties inherent in introducing effective alternatives to prison, or, for that matter, what 'alternatives' might mean, no strategy towards the proposed minimization of prison, and no guidelines for the 'circumstances' where prison should be used (especially nothing about the wide range of work on the difficulties of predicting danger, see pp. 89–96 above).

Further volumes contain even less. In the 1986 volume on losing the fight against crime (Kinsey et al., 1986) there are a few scattered references to the prison: an introductory lament to the effect that the ineffective prison service now has the highest prison population in British history (Kinsey et al., 1986: 2), a statement to the effect that 'tougher sentencing is largely ineffective as a deterrent' (Kinsey et al., 1986: 57), and statements to the effect that the state should be 'rolled back' in areas where its effect is detrimental, such as in the detention centres and the long-term prisons (Kinsey et al., 1986: 205). The scattered references suggest a dislike of prisons, hardly more. In the volume on confronting crime, also from 1986 (Matthews and Young, 1986), there is indeed a discussion – of unemployment, crime, imprisonment and prison overcrowding (Matthews and Young, 1986: 72–96). But the authors are Steven Box and Chris Hale – hardly identifiable with the school. And in contrast to the left realists, who assert that blacks are in fact increasingly involved in street crime, they suggest that the sentencing of young black unemployed males has become increasingly severe.

Other than this, in the major volumes there are brief references, little more. This is a good example of the 'disregard' of the fiasco of the prison, mentioned earlier, which may be found in the narrowest public sphere of research and science (see pp. 140–1).

The contribution which comes closest to more than disregard, seems to be a recent small piece by Roger Matthews (Matthews, 1987), where it is stated that 'among the issues which radical realism has raised but not yet adequately addressed' is, among other things, 'the question of punishment' (Matthews, 1987: 379). It is pointed out that radical realism is under pressure to provide a viable alternative. But, it is also stated 'imprisonment in one form or other will remain for the forseeable future' (Matthews, 1987: 393). The listing of the limits of incarceration alone, it is claimed, can lead to complacency. Two points are made in this connection.

First, we learn that 'what is conspicuously absent in the endless critiques of the prison is a set of rational principles for the organization of punishment and a systematic analysis of how such principles might determine who goes to prison, for what purpose and for how long' (Matthews, 1987: 393). The author, in other words, asks for justifications and conditions for imprisonment. But he asks without even referring to the host of difficulties involved for example in the neo-classical and the incapacitation-oriented approaches to punishment, which try to elaborate precisely such justifications and conditions (see Chapters 4 and 5 above), and he asks while in fact stating, on the next page, that the 'justice model' has introduced an increasingly unjust system of punishment (Matthews, 1987: 394). His demand for principles determining who is to go for what and for how long, thus becomes extremely confusing.

Secondly, because prison invariably has a negative effect on those currently incarcerated, serving in fact to maintain a high level of crime (Matthews, 1987: 393–4), we learn that it is 'necessary to put rehabilitation back on the agenda' (Matthews, 1987: 394). 'There is thus an urgent need', we learn, 'to reaffirm rehabilitation and to investigate forms of incarceration which . . . might provide constructive modes of punishment which could ultimately help to re-integrate offenders into social life. . . . Such an emphasis upon rehabilitation involves not only devising forms [of] incarceration which are more constructive and reformative but also ensuring that incarceration is only used when no worthwhile alternative is available' (Matthews, 1987: 394).

This vaguely formulated reversion to the rehabilitation ideology is provided in bland contradiction to the whole range of hard evidence concerning rehabilitation in prison (see Chapter 2 above), without so much as touching on the problems inherent in combining rehabilitation and intended pain delivery, and without even suggesting the principles for establishing the rehabilitation programmes in question.

This is Roger Matthews' struggle against the 'impossibilism' of the so-called left idealists.

To summarize and conclude: so-called new realism in several ways seriously misrepresents critical criminology. Its attempt to explain crime and its attempt to provide a model for minimal and accountable policing each contains serious problems. There is a problematic relationship, and a hiatus, between the emphasis on the social aetiology of crime and on policing as *the* solution to the crime problem. And as far as the prison solution goes, there is either more or less complete disregard of the issue, or a vaguely formulated emphasis on notions – long since seriously questioned in prison research – which supposedly might vindicate the prison solution.

The latter two points are the most serious. The strong emphasis on policing, albeit in a new form, gives the whole argument a thrust towards renewed formal control. This thrust is given additional and full impetus by the fact that the prison, as a pivotal and consequential part of the criminal justice system, remains untouched and/or presumably rejuvenated. It is hard not to agree with Stanley Cohen, who has said that the school has regressed 'into the assumptions of the standard criminal law mode of social control' (Cohen, 1986: 131). With a view towards doing something to crime, which is the school's major focus of attention, the thrust points to a bleak and unpromising future, along a very traditional road. So, more specifically, does the thrust with a view towards doing something about the fiasco prison.

Are there other sources of knowledge from which the left can draw inspiration for the attack on the ideology of prison? There is one source. History.

History   When we are situated in the context of the present, that present easily appears unchangeable and permanent.

Yet, when situating ourselves outside the context of the present, we know that the present becomes past, and that present and prior present, past, may differ. In fact, we know that with time, the prior present, or past, may and frequently does differ drastically from the present present. There is continuity in history. But there is also change.

There is abundant evidence of this in the area of penal policy, over shorter as well as longer periods of time. Concretely, there is empirical evidence from history showing that major penal systems have been *frozen* in size, *reduced* in size, *partially abolished*, and *fully abolished*.

All four possibilities exist because the development of penal systems, and the size of the populations in them, is not an automatic reflection of external changes such as simple alterations in the crime rate (see pp. 8–9 above), but determined by political choices – however conditioned these choices may be by structures and processes in the environment.

Let us look briefly at material showing the viability of the four possibilities.

In 1985, the notion of a *freeze* on prison construction was introduced in a plenary sub-session of the VIIIth United Nations' Congress on the Prevention of Crime and the Treatment of Offenders (Mathiesen, 1985). The background was the mounting prison figures, and huge construction projects, in many countries. The need for a halt and a rethink was emphasized. The reaction among the delegates was telling. No proposals or recommendations came out of the initiative, but there was widespread interest and, unusual in the UN context, applause. Perhaps the applause came from the younger parts of the delegations. In any case, a straightforward proposal for a freeze on construction appeared to be received as something of a relief in the bureaucratic context of the United Nations. A number of delegates asked for more information. And information could be given.

In Chapter 1 we saw that prison figures are on the rise also in the smaller European countries like Sweden, Denmark and Norway, and that the rise is taking place despite efforts to the contrary. But for the purposes of this chapter, the finer details of the efforts to the contrary are of some interest. To repeat (pp. 84–6), Sweden in practice froze its prison population in 1983 by introducing half time parole for the large bulk of the country's prisoners. And this happened, as we have seen (pp. 86), without any serious detriment to the population. It implied that through several years in the 1980s, the Swedish prison population remained below its size in 1982. We have seen that the reform created a debate and may, on rather invalid grounds, be reversed (p. 87). And it should be emphasized that in early 1989, prison figures are again exceeding figures from 1982. This, however, does not detract from the fact that in practice, it was possible to institute something like a freeze for some years.

Denmark has a similar experience, using different methods. In 1982, Denmark introduced maximum punishments for a number of property crimes in addition to reducing the minimum time for release on parole and liberalizing the rules concerning drunken driving. The reduced maximum sentences for property crimes were intended to reduce the general sentencing level by one-third. The total daily average number of prisoners, which had been increasing since 1977, fell in 1982 and stabilized at the new level during the following year. It did not last – the new rules concerning sentencing levels still left much discretion to decision-making bodies, and figures are again rising. But the fact that a stabilization could occur is suggestive, showing concretely that relatively undramatic measures may make a difference to the prison population.

The details of the Swedish and Danish experiences mentioned here suggest that with a little more stamina in given proposals, and with a somewhat greater emphasis on mandatory rather than discretionary rules, it might have been possible to stabilize given prison populations for a longer period, or at least stabilize or control their increase.

Notable examples suggest that major *reductions* of prison populations, over long periods of time, are possible.

In an important contribution entitled *Prisons and the Process of Justice*, Andrew Rutherford has examined three historical instances of major reductions (Rutherford, 1986) – England 1908–1938, Japan 1950–1975 and the Netherlands 1950–1975.

In all three countries during the relevant periods, prison populations were significantly reduced and sustained at a new low level. In Rutherford's analysis, two general explanatory conditions emerge. First, in all three countries, 'key decision-makers shared a profound scepticism as to what benefits, if any, derive from imprisonment' (Rutherford, 1986: 145). A detailed review of this scepticism and questioning is provided for all three countries. For England, an intriguing account of Winston Churchill's particular role is given. Secondly, 'the responses to crime by officials engaged throughout the criminal justice process' (Rutherford, 1986: 146) were important. In the Netherlands and Japan, the courts were insulated from the impact of increasing numbers of offenders due to actions taken by the public prosecutors, notably their tendency to dismiss charges. In addition came a widespread intolerance of overcrowding. In England, on the other hand, the critical intervening tactic was the movement away from custody in sentencing practice by the courts. Thus, different personnel sectors were involved. But the role of personnel engaged in practice throughout the system was a common denominator.

We may speculate whether the *combination* of scepticism on the part of top level decision-makers and activities at the grass roots of the system was important. Sustained reduction was perhaps made possible by the fact that the two levels functioned in the same direction. Perhaps top level scepticism alone is rather easily followed by reductions or standstills which are temporary, while sustained reduction requires that the two levels function in an integrated fashion.

Notable historical examples also exist of *partial abolitions* of penal systems. Two such examples may be mentioned briefly.

The first is the abolition of forced labour in Norway (for details, see Mathiesen, 1974: 90–97). As mentioned in Chapter 1, a Norwegian reform in 1970 decriminalizing public drunkenness only had a temporary effect on prison figures. But for the purposes of this chapter, the finer details of the events are again of some interest. Forced labour, introduced by the so-called vagrancy act of 1900 which criminalized public drunkenness, was primarily used against vagrant alcoholics, and implied that alcoholics could spend years in institutions within the prison system. Though the latter part of the 1960s was generally characterized by rather conservative trends in criminal policy, the period saw a mounting criticism, from a spectrum of professional quarters such as medicine, law and criminology, of the forced labour system. It was characterized as unjust as well as ineffective. The Norwegian prisoners' organization was rather efficient in collecting and channelling this criticism, which penetrated into political decision-making bodies as well as the practising grass roots of the criminal justice system. In 1970, a unanimous *Storting* (Parliament) decided to abolish the system, a decision which at the time implied a major reduction of the prison population (250 out of the country's 2000 prisoners). And though the abolition was neutralized later in terms of total prison figures, this particular category of people – particularly impoverished, destitute, homeless alcoholics – *never came back to the system*. In the present context, this is a significant conclusion.

An important feature emerges from the relative success of the Norwegian vagrancy act example. An abolition of this part of the system required not only scepticism towards the system at the top level, and not only agreement at the grass roots within the system, but, additionally, widespread support of and strong pressure for change from professional groups outside the system. In the climate created through the interaction between those three corners, abolition succeeded. But it should also be noted that the pressure for change came primarily from the professions. The wider lay community was not as intensely involved. We shall return to this point later.

Norway is a small country, with a small-scale system. The second example refers to a large country with a large system – the dissolution of the training schools for youthful offenders in Massachusetts. The story has been told before, and is well known

(Rutherford, 1974; see also Rutherford, 1986: 121). Building on a prior period of strong criticism of the training schools or youth prisons, a particular commissioner of the Department of Youth Services – Jerome Miller – closed the schools of the state in the course of 1972, and was able to show an important and sustained reduction in institutional populations. From the example some patterns emerge which resemble those characterizing the abolition of the Norwegian vagrancy statutes. The strong prior criticism in the environment is one of them. Furthermore, somewhat like the vagrancy example, Jerome Miller apparently had political backing from above, and was able to communicate and channel his message through important mass media. Contextual aspects of the situation as well as political relationships favoured the commissioner's abrupt abolition.

We have referred to freeze or standstill, reduction, and partial abolitions. Are there, finally, examples of full abolition, in which total penal or sanctioning systems have been abolished? There are, and we see them if we distance ourselves a little more from our own present.

In an intriguing piece on the memories of abolitionist victories of the past, the German criminologist Sebastian Scheerer reminds us that 'there has never been a major social transformation in the history of mankind that had not been looked upon as unrealistic, idiotic, or utopian by the large majority of experts even a few years before the unthinkable became reality' (Scheerer, 1986: 7). He points to how magnificent the extension of the Roman empire was, and how victoriously its armed forces fought the Huns, twenty-five years before its fall. 'And when', Scheerer writes, 'in August 476, the last of the West Roman emperors was quietly ordered to retire, there were no dramatic changes in everyday life, even though this was the end of an empire that had lasted for more than a millennium, and that had been believed to be invincible' (Scheerer, 1986: 7). Who, in their own present, could see that this was happening?

Scheerer goes on with another example, closer to our issue: the same holds true, he argues, for modern slavery. An estimated 15 million Africans were brought to the New World between the fifteenth and the nineteenth centuries. Slavery became an indispensable feature of world trade. In the early 1800s, only a few decades before the formal abolition of slavery (in the US in 1865), 'abolitionists were still few in number and widely regarded as awkward customers' (Scheerer, 1986: 7). Slavery had succeeded in looking extremely stable almost until the day it collapsed. Who would have thought, at the time, that it was going to fall completely? The conditions which advanced the abolition of slavery are complex and probably not fully unravelled, but we certainly know that political choice and decisions were deeply involved.

A third example to be added here is that of the European witch hunts. Who would have believed, in 1487, when Heinrich Institor Krämer and Jakob Spränger published their major theological and legal dogmatic work on witches, *Malleus Maleficarum* (or *The Witch Hammer*), that the institution of witch hunts would some day disappear, as in fact would the Inquisition itself?

In contrast to the examples of the Roman empire and slavery we are, with Krämer and Spränger, in the early phase of the period in question. Before writing their important work, they had used all their enthusiasm and energy to have as many witches as possible taken to the stake, but had met much resistance, partly to the claim that it was necessary to liquidate so many witches, and partly against their own competence as judges. The two inquisitors even had to swallow that secular authorities sometimes protected witches (Alver, 1971: 25). And to cut a long story short, in their embarrassment they turned to Rome, where Pope Innocent VIII resided, to complain, and on 5 December 1484 Innocent issued his papal bull on witches, *Summis Desiderantes Affectibus*, which provided the decisive churchly sanction to the witch hunts. With the bull as basic authority, the two inquisitors wrote *The Witch Hammer*, which essentially was a handbook on witch hunting. The work contained a dogmatic argument for and proof of the existence of witches (including a counter-proof of the popely *Canon Episcopi* from the 1100s, which had expressed the view that a belief in nightly travel with and to demons was imagination), a detailed treatment of the desecrating acts committed by witches, and, thirdly, a legal manual on witch hunting. Within a period of thirty years the work was printed in fourteen editions (the second edition including a reprint of Pope Innocent's bull), and it became profoundly important as a theological–legal basis for the subsequent witch hunts in Europe. Who would have thought, at the time, that all of this would one day wither and be gone?

And even towards the end of the witch hunts, the institution's demise must have been difficult or impossible to imagine by many, partly because the popular belief in witches remained strong. In a major work the Danish historian Gustav Henningsen has described and analysed the beginning of the end of the witch hunts in the region of Northern Spain in the early 1600s (Henningsen, 1981; see also Henningsen, 1984; Lea, 1906/1966, Vol. IV, Ch. IX).

The beginning of the end came 100 years earlier in this region than in the rest of Europe. The Inquisition, first established in the 1200s as a special force to combat heresy, and organized in Spain during the late 1400s, was at the height of its power. With a point of departure in Navarra in Northern Spain, Henningsen describes the Spanish branch of the special force as a huge spider with a wide net of intelligence services, secret police forces, sentencing authorities and arrests, organized in nineteen (later twenty-one) tribunals throughout the enormous Spanish empire. The tribunals entered a network of definite and bureaucratic communication lines to the super spider in Madrid, *la Suprema*, the Inquisition Council. The beginning of the end came, in fact, among the bureaucrats within this enormous organization.

When the members of the local tribunal agreed, *la Suprema* rarely intervened. But when there was disagreement, extensive communication with the central authority would ensue. Henningsen describes in detail how liberal inquisitors in Northern Spain in the early 1600s, notably a certain inquisitor Alonso de Salazar Frías, began to doubt certain aspects of the witch crazes, the frenzied waves of persecution of witches. The background was an auto-da-fé in Logrono in 1610, which also Salazar had set his name to, where eleven witches had been burnt during the presence of 30,000 spectators. Following the auto-da-fé, and at the initiative of *la Suprema*, Salazar and his aides undertook a major empirical investigation of Basque witches, interviewing over 1800 individuals. To Salazar the question of proof was central, and he found no proof whatsoever of witchcraft. Rather, he found that the best weapon against the appearance of large numbers of witches in fact was *silence* ('I deduce the importance of silence and reserve from the experience that there were neither witches nor bewitched until they were talked and written about'; Salazar as quoted in Lea, 1906/1966, Vol IV: 234). But the other members of the local tribunal did not agree, and the dissensus necessitated communication with *la Suprema*. *La Suprema* had a long tradition in restraint in terms of sentencing witches (as did, in fact, the Italian Inquisition – the major European persecutions predominantly came in areas outside the jurisdiction of the Inquisition), with a practice of pardoning those sentenced to the stake by the local tribunals. Liberal views thus had a sounding board in *La Suprema*, and generalized doubt was beginning to be cast over the issue. In the end, *la Suprema* decided to follow Salazar's recommendation to suspend the witch cases, asking him to prepare a new set of instructions for the handling of witches. The instructions were adopted, with almost no changes, by *la Suprema* in 1614. A liberal inquisitor with support from above thus became instrumental in the subsequent abolition of witch burning and, indeed, hunts, in a way interestingly reminiscent of the professionals involved in the prison reductions and abolitions of more modern times mentioned earlier in this chapter.

Obviously, major social forces outside individual liberal inquisitors were essential in preparing for abolition. We do not know enough about these forces (Henningsen, 1984: 37), which worked differently from parallel forces in the late 1400s. Much greater research effort should be placed on scrutinizing the social conditions fostering such abolitions. It would add importantly to our stock of knowledge about how to achieve results today. The important point here, however, is that political choice and action again was part of the process, and that the vanishing of the witch hunts (and, as I have said, of the Inquisition itself, finally abolished in Spain in 1820), indicates the *realism* contained even in the total abolition of major and whole penal and sanctioning systems.

But, before closing this section: though the Roman empire has disappeared, is it not true that new empires have emerged? Though slavery has vanished, does not discrimination and repression exist? And though the old witch hunts are gone, have not new ones developed?

Undeniably so. Functional equivalents to patterns which are gone have come about. Though on a much larger scale, this is a bit like the return to new trends of imprisonment, perhaps of other groups, in the more limited examples of freeze, reduction and partial abolition of prisons referred to above. Three points, however, should be made.

First, there are degrees of difference between the old and the new witch hunts. There is a degree of difference between being burnt at the stake in the Europe of the 1500s and being politically persecuted for leftist sympathies in the Europe of the 1980s. In our own present, such degrees may not constitute an important part of our phenomenology, but if we place ourselves a little outside, we see them. This is not meant to be taken as a unilinear improvement theory. The Europe of the mid-1900s suggests how problematic such a theory would be. But it is meant to propose the taking of degrees of difference as something important.

Secondly, in so far as equivalents to patterns abolished develop, I would suggest that this is part of the historical process and thereby of the political struggle as an unending activity. Political struggle consists of hard work oriented towards victory and change, but not towards finality. Victory and change later abated or for that matter neutralized do not invite despair but new political struggles on a new level.

Thirdly, perhaps more may be done to prevent return to prior conditions. Perhaps, in fact, this is also one of the lessons of history. We shall return to this possibility shortly.

Through What Steps?
Backed by history as a major source of knowledge and inspiration about the viability of another course, we may finally ask: what concrete steps should be taken to attain a different course?

It probably depends somewhat on the particular course. Andrew Rutherford is probably right in saying that a freeze or standstill policy is not in the long term a viable alternative in expanding prison systems, but more of a short-term relief from population pressures (Rutherford, 1986: 172). Also, this is in line with the evidence on prison expansion presented in Chapter 1. Partly for this reason, the course should be more radical. In 1986 Rutherford proposed a 50 percent reduction as the target for the English prison population by 1990. The three examples of successful prison shrinkage which Rutherford analysed (see above), accomplished such a reduction. It would have brought the number of English prisoners per 100,000 inhabitants down to the range of 35 (Rutherford, 1986: 174). The wide variations which exist between different European countries in terms of numbers of prisoners per capita, with several countries certainly having under 50 prisoners per 100,000 population, make such a goal entirely practical. I have recently targeted a close to full abolition of the Norwegian prison system by 2010, the year when our neighbouring Swedes have decided to close down their last nuclear power plants (Mathiesen, 1987). This target is less practical, in view of the counterforces, but in principle it is attainable. In any case, the goal for socialists and social democrats in countries like Britain, Norway and Sweden could well be set to *a contraction of two-thirds of the prison population* within our century.

The steps with which to reach such a goal may be discussed on two levels, the level of legislation and the level of what may be called policy preparation. Policy preparation presents the most complex issues, and will demand most of our attention.

Legislation   Concrete legislation would have to depend on the country concerned, and its legal and penal context. But a *widening of the range of non-imprisonable offences* on the one hand, and a *narrowing of the scope of the criminal law*, providing for a civil rather than a criminal solution and redress, on the other, are two essential and supplementary legislative roads. The former is frequently referred to as 'depenalization', the latter as 'decriminalization'. Rutherford has called attention to the former (Rutherford, 1986: 182–3), the Dutch criminologist Louk Hulsman very forcefully to the latter (Hulsman, 1986; see also Rutherford, 1986: 183–4).

In addition to these major legislative ways, legal measures such as a lowering of maximum sentences, an increase of early release measures, and a strict programme of prison closure, would be important supplementary methods. Prison closure would be vitally important in order to prevent returns to prior prison policies. One particularly important danger should be kept in mind – the tendency for legislation to have unintended consequences. In particular, there is considerable evidence suggesting that the introduction of so-called 'alternatives to prison' may actually have a 'net-widening' effect: rather than bringing very many people out of the prisons, they may actually bring new people into a wider control system (Pease et al., 1977; Blomberg, 1977, 1978, 1980; Klein, 1979; Chan and Ericson, 1981; Dittenhoffer and Ericson, 1983; Chan and Zdenkowski, 1985; for theoretical discussions, see Cohen, 1979, 1985). The process is hardly inevitable, and recent reassessments of, among others, Canadian data suggest moderations of the general conclusion (McMahon, 1988b). But the danger should be kept clearly in mind. It suggests that the attack on the prisons should come *before* rather than after the alternatives, alternatives to prison should be *preceded* by depenalization and/or decriminalization. As Rutherford has pointed out, this reverses conventional wisdom regarding alternative sanctions 'which is that when these are made available, less use will be made of custody' (Rutherford, 1986: 168). It may be noted that in both of the major partial abolitions referred to earlier in this book, the abolition of the Norwegian forced labour system and of the Massachusetts training schools, this 'deep-end strategy', attacking the prison solution first, was explicitly followed. Indirect evidence suggests that other major abolitions in history have followed a similar course (Henningsen, 1981).

Policy Preparation   Policy preparation comprises the social and political preparation of the wider community or society for the change in question. The more radical the target change is, the more vital is policy preparation. Without it, the necessary legislation will remain wishful thinking, only follow haphazardly, or follow but create a change which will not last.

The lack of long-term permanence in major reductions or abolitions of earlier times is partly explainable in terms of lack of policy preparation of the wider societal context. As we have seen, several of them (apparently even the abolition of the Spanish witch hunts), were initiated 'from above' by key professionals and professional levels, without major and systematic attempts to prepare the community. The implication of policy preparation is to move the issue, in a preparatory way, beyond the initiated professional circles into the community. This may partially be done by attitude preparation, but, most significantly, also by introducing measures which in a better way satisfy relevant needs in the community.

When discussing policy preparation, I envisage a socialist/social democratic government in power, in charge of the considerable resources necessary for preparatory work. This is not the situation in Britain today, but it is the situation in Sweden and has recently been so in Norway, and it is obviously a possible option in the British future. The reader may feel that in the light of today's political situation, and of how social democracy is developing at least in Sweden and Norway, I am demanding quite a bit of such a government. But we should demand quite a bit, and are entitled to do so.

Policy preparation has to go back to *the ideology of prison* and to *the socialist ideology*, discussed as basic and conflicting ideological frameworks in the opening part of this chapter, and take cognizance of their full significance. Briefly put, the ideology of prison has to be *countered*, while the socialist ideology has to be *built*.

The ideology of prison contains, as we have said, a supportive component in the form of a series of ideological functions which the prison fills, and a negating component in the form of a series of denials in various public spheres of the fiasco of prison.

The two major components of the ideology point to the necessity of two types of work to counter the ideology – 'counter-functional work' and 'counter-denial work'.

First a few words about *counter-functional work*. The expurgatory, power-draining, diverting, symbolic and action-signifying functions of prison are functions in the public sphere. This is the implication of their being ideological. They are, in a sense, a series of impression managements: without them, those we wish to be purged of would be visible to us, they would be more vocal, we would not be as easily diverted from the real dangers in society, we would not be as able to see ourselves as white, and we would not be as falsely relieved that something is being done about crime. Counter-functional work would imply massive allocation of resources to information and attitude campaigns concerning the existence and dubiousness of these unauthorized functions: the dubiousness of segregating people under conditions which only increase their propensity to crime, the dubiousness of not giving them a voice, of seeing them as the major danger, of seeing ourselves as falsely white, and of being falsely relieved that something is done.

Easy to communicate? Obviously not. From communication research we know that mass media communication – which would have to be extensively used – is more efficient in confirming than in changing existing attitudes (Klapper, 1960; Mathiesen, 1986). But we also know that attitudes *may* be changed. This is a viable possibility if mass media communication is intensely supplemented by interpersonal communications – at the workplace, in the neighbourhood, in the schools. The labour unions, as part of the socialist and social democratic cause and as builders of the ideology, would have to be called upon. Extensive resources would have to be spent on communication at this level.

Essential in the communication effort would be the task of *making the prisoners visible to us*. As mentioned earlier in this book (pp. 121–5), nearness creates nuances, nearness makes for understanding. It is the invisibility of the prisoner which makes it possible to maintain the ideological functions of the prison. Visibility is the Achilles' heel of the functions.

Counter-denial work is also work in the public sphere. It would imply that the range of denial mechanisms – non-recognition, pretence and disregard concerning the fiasco of the prison – would have to be effectively countered. The information and attitude campaigns suggested above would also have to include this task. Counter-denial work would have to contain two major components.

First, exposure of *the denial*, whereby the mechanisms of denial would have to be made known, would be necessary. Such exposure might be painful to those actively participating in non-recognition, pretence and (perhaps especially) disregard of the fiasco of prison. One would have to be prepared for political conflict.

Secondly, and as a parallel, exposure of *the actual fiasco* of prison would be essential. Something has already been done in this respect. The rehabilitative fiasco of prison has probably already been effectively exposed, at least in the Scandinavian countries. The deep problems and fiascos contained in general prevention, incapacitation and justice are certainly less widely known. It is in these respects that denial in its various forms is particularly forceful. Exposure would have to take place in the wide variety of communication contexts mentioned earlier. Again, major resources would have to be allotted to the task.

Not only would counter-functional work and counter-denial work have to be integrated. Both would in turn have to merge with the second major feature of policy preparation – that of building the socialist ideology in this area.

As we have said, the socialist ideology, broadly speaking, also comprises two major components, those of solidarity and compensation. Compensation refers to methods of practising solidarity.

The building of solidarity through compensation is vitally important. The countering of the prison ideology through counter-functional work and counter-denial work negates the prison, says 'no' to it. Standing alone, the negation is unlikely to succeed. Supplemented by the construction of solidarity and compensation, the negation has a chance to succeed, because in sharp contrast to the prison solution, it will give something important to both of the major parties – victim and perpetrator – in the conflict. Both parties are vitally in need of solidarity and compensation, because both are, as we have seen, politically and socially weak. Two generalized types of work emanate from this – 'victim' work and 'offender' work.

Victim work may be oriented to 'current' and 'potential' victims, as current victim work and potential victim work.

In the Scandinavian countries, there has been some movement in the direction of added resources for individual victims, especially in the form of economic compensation for certain types of crime. But the movement has been very slow and small-scale. Three major kinds of solidary compensation to current victims may be envisaged.

For one thing, automatic and full material compensation – automatic in the sense that it should be released immediately, and full in the sense that it should be used to the fullest extent across the spectrum of offences. In view of the poverty of the offenders, such compensation would have to be the duty of the state. It is actually fantastic that advanced social-democratic states like Norway and Sweden have not long ago introduced automatic insurance, from birth, against crime, but has left the question of insurance to the individual's private initiative. Very modest fees, as part of a taxation package, would be enough to cover the costs.

Furthermore, symbolic compensation is needed – new rituals of sorrow and grief, resources for processing or going over what has happened, new ways of conferring what may be called status compensation, that is to say compensation for lost dignity.

Finally, social support-network establishments around victims, sometimes physical shelters, the latter perhaps modelled on women's crisis centres in the Scandinavian countries, are required.

A number of victims will want little more than economic compensation. Some will want a great deal of symbolic compensation and social support, for example in the forms suggested here. Socialists and social democrats have so far used far too little of their imagination on developing compensatory solidarity in these respects.

Two major kinds of solidarity with potential victims may be envisaged, the first in a broad sense paralleling material compensation to current victims, the second paralleling symbolic compensation and social support.

For one thing, what may be called 'vulnerability relief' should be emphasized. Though the average statistical chance of becoming a victim is very small for street crime in general, some population groups are more vulnerable than others. Vulnerability may be relieved thrtugh a series of material arrangements, community organisation measures and similar street level innovations. This would be tantamount to work oriented towards crime prevention at the street level. It would take the place of ineffective general prevention and incapacitation on the part of prisons. But in line with socialist ideology, the work would have to have a structural sociological rather than a policing profile.

Furthermore, what may be called 'anxiety relief' would be of the utmost importance. Anxiety over crime has become a major welfare problem, perhaps especially in some groups which are not highly vulnerable. At the back of it lies selective dependence on current mass media images, lack of alternative channels of communication, and flare-ups of moral panics around concrete events, revolving around kernels of truth. The kernels of truth are meant to be met by the vulnerability relief suggested above. Socialists and social democrats have done almost nothing with the irrationalities – the task of anxiety relief. It may be provided through some of the same comunication mechanisms and types of measures as may current victim work and vulnerability relief for potential victims.

So much, here, about victim work. Like victim work, *offender work* may also be oriented to 'current' and 'potential' offenders; current offender work and potential offender work.

Current offenders ending up in prisons, which are our focus of attention here, tend to show signs of extreme poverty in three generalized respects, parallel to the dimensions of poverty among victims.

Their material situation is regularly acute, and coupled with illness, drug addiction and distress. Their symbolic standing, in their own eyes and in the eyes of others, is the lowest possible. And their social situation is characterized by isolation and cultural poverty.

It is especially with a background in the extreme and general poverty among a large majority of those caught and imprisoned that the so-called new realists' call for intensified policing as the only or main method of combating crime becomes cool and empty of compassion.

The material standing of these people may be fundamentally changed through relatively simple and fairly modest material inputs. Their symbolic standing and social situation requires more imagination. But rituals may be envisaged which confer new standing and status in early and middle, as well as late phases of the individual's development. One small example: the Norwegian chaplain Leer-Salvesen suggests, in a study of Norwegian murderers (Leer-Salvesen, 1988), that the usual radical isolation of murderers during the protracted remand phase is probably the most detrimental thing which can be done to an individual in acute need of working through sorrow and refinding status. This is an example from within the prison. Outside the prison, which is our focus of attention, rituals conferring standing and status may range from reorganized and non-bureaucratic interaction patterns with state and municipal agencies to the establishment of networks conferring new status to specific individuals in need of it.

What would potential offender work consist of? A great deal of stored knowledge exists concerning the sociological correlates to intensive criminal behaviour. As mentioned earlier, there is research evidence strongly suggesting that a relatively small group of juveniles with a wide range of serious social and socio-personal problems are responsible for a sizeable proportion of the more serious juvenile delinquency (Balvig, 1984c; p. 93 above). This evidence would constitute an important point of departure. The task of introducing compensatory mechanisms with a view towards cancelling out the correlates on the community level would be near at hand for socialists and social democrats. This would involve a new housing policy, a new educational policy, a new youth policy, to mention a few examples.

Another approach would be intensified policing. This would imply intensified proactive police control: control before crime occurs. While few people would object to having police officers in an ordinary way patrolling the streets, a policy of intensified proactive police control as a major strategy would run counter to basic principles of legal security also cherished in modern socialist thinking, and counter to – and creating conflict with – important parts of the community. It is the structure of the community, and its material and social foundations, which are in need of change.

Correlates are not necessarily causes. It should openly be admitted that we do not know enough about the effects of the sociological correlates on behaviour defined as crime, and about the effects of altering the correlates. But altering them contains a welfare value of its own – in itself important to socialists and social democrats. And the whole weight of the evidence (pp. 55–7) suggests that intensified police control solves little. The sensible policy is therefore to begin with the alternative.

This is, to use a favourite phrase of the so-called left realists, to take crime seriously.

The kinds of policy preparation suggested above, meant to prepare a major contraction of the prison system within a few years, would have to *move alongside and contextualize* the contraction, and be stepped up as the contraction gained momentum through concrete legislation.

It would cost money. But there would also be savings ahead. The prison business is extremely costly. In the financial year 1985/86, the budget for the Norwegian penal system was 498 million Norwegian crowns. The parallel budget for the British penal system was £822 million (Sim, 1986: 41). Cut by two-thirds during the 1990s, roughly 330 million 1986 crowns, or £540 million 1986, would be saved *per year*, and could be spent on countering the ideology of prison and on building the ideology of socialism – on counter-functional work, counter-denial work, victim work and offender work.

In the beginning of the period, more money would have to be spent than saved, because prisons would not yet be closed down (and also to allow a period for pensioning of staff). Towards the end of the period the budget might – with one important exception – well balance. The exception would be potential offender work. This work, which would involve whole new policies in housing, education, and so on, would be costly. But it would be a part of a generalized socialist policy, and as I have said have a value of its own, over and above crime prevention.

Closing: The Near and the Distant Future

Above we have been discussing the near future – the rest of our century.

Let us for the last time draw on history, and recall once more that major repressive systems have succeeded in looking extremely stable almost until the day they have collapsed. With this in mind, the thought that policy preparation in the near future may trigger further effect in a future more distant, may be more than wishful thinking. Victim work and offender work will certainly prove far more satisfactory than prison, and we may envisage further contraction, possibly abolition.

This would be congruent with the whole weight of the evidence on prisons. In actual fact, anything else is tantamount to acceding to irrationality. But full abolition would perhaps require that we stretch even further, towards an even fuller restructuring of our thinking about crime.

In this book and this chapter, I have used the concept of crime, and I have assumed the continued existence of criminalization, although much more narrowly drawn. But it may be argued that for prison fully to lose its irrational grip, the very concept of 'crime' has to be abandoned as a tool.

There are, as Louk Hulsman says, problematic situations, which today are criminalized. These problematic situations have an aetiology and a course of development. And they may be handled in a wide variety of much more civilized ways than today.

This, obviously, is still only on the drawing board. But the exercise of thinking away crime as a conceptual tool, and of opening up for imaginative rethinking of the whole handling of problematic situations, should be intriguing to social scientists.

And challenging to politicians.

References

Aarsnes, S.G., Fuglevik, Tor, Hesstvedt, Ola, Johansen, Viggo and Myklebust, Gunnar (1974) *Kriminalitet til salgs. En rapport om presse og kriminalitet* (Crime for Sale. A Report on the Press and Crime). Oslo: Institutt for kriminologi og strafferett, Universitetet i Oslo, Institute Series No. 28.

Ahlberg, Jan (1985) *Effekter av halvtidsfrigivningen: vad hände med brottsligheten under hösten 1983* (Effects of the Half Time Release: What Happened to Crime During the Fall of 1983). Stockholm: BRÅ Forskning.

Alver, Bente Gullvåg (1971) *Heksetro og trolldom* (Witch Faith and Witch Craft). Oslo: Universitetsforlaget.

American Friends Service Committee (1971) *Struggle for Justice: A Report on Crime and Punishment in America*. Prepared for the American Friends Service Committee. New York: Hill & Wang.

Andenæs, Johs. (1950) 'Almenprevensjon – illusjon eller realitet?' (General prevention – illusion or reality?), *Nordisk Tidsskrift for Kriminalvidenskab*, 38: 103–33; also published in Andenæs, Johs. (1962) *Avhandlinger og foredrag*. Oslo: Universitetsforlaget, pp. 109–32.

Andenæs, Johs. (1974) *Alminnelig strafferett* (General Penal Law). 2nd rev. ed. Oslo: Universitetsforlaget.

Andenæs, Johs. (1977) 'Nyere forskning om almenprevensjonen – status og kommentar' (Recent research on general prevention – status and comments). *Nordisk Tidsskrift for Kriminalvidenskab*, 65: 61–101; also published in Andenæs, Johs. (1982) *Fra spredte felter*. Oslo: Tanum-Norli, pp. 196–239.

Andenæs, Johs. (1982) 'Straffeutmåling i promillesaker' (Sentencing in drunk-driving cases). *Lov og Rett*: 115–37.

Aubert, Vilhelm (1958) 'Legal justice and mental health', *Psychiatry*, 21: 101–13.

Aubert, Vilhelm (1972) *Likhet og rett* (Equality and Law). Oslo: Pax.

Aubert, Vilhelm (1976) *Rettens sosiale funksjon* (The Social Function of the Law). Oslo: Universitetsforlaget.

Austin, James and Krisberg, Barry (1985) 'Incarceration in the United States: the extent and the future of the problem', *Annals of American Political and Social Science*, 478: 15–30.

Balvig, Flemming (1980) *Tyveriernes mørketall. Studier over tyvsforbrydelsen III*. (The Dark Figures of Theft. Studies of Theft III). Copenhagen: Kriminalpolitisk forskningsgruppe, Justitsministeriet.

Balvig, Flemming (1984a) *Kriminalitetens udvikling i Danmark før 1950* (The Development of Crime in Denmark before 1950). Copenhagen: Kriminalistisk Institut, Københavns Universitet.

Balvig, Flemming (1984b) 'Opklaringsprocenten – et mål for retssystemets effektivitet?' (The clear-up rate – a measure of the efficiency of the criminal justice system?). Report at Nordisk seminar i rettsstatistikk, Leangkollen. Copenhagen: Nordisk statistisk sekretariat.

Balvig, Flemming (1984c) *Ungdomskriminalitet i en forstadskommune* (Juvenile Delinquency in a Surburban Community). Copenhagen: Det kriminalpræventive råd.

Balvig, Flemming, Dalå, Ole, Poulsen-Hansen, Svend, Rømer, Harald and Wolf, Preben, (1969) *Fængsler og fanger* (Prisons and Prisoners). Copenhagen: Paludan.

Barthes, Roland (1972) *Mythologies*. New York: Hill & Wang.

Blomberg, Thomas (1977) 'Diversion and accelerated social control', *Journal of Criminal Law and Criminology*, 68: 274–82.

Blomberg, Thomas (1978) 'Diversion from juvenile court: a review of the evidence', paper presented at the 1978 Annual Meeting of the Society for the Study of Social Problems, San Francisco. Manuscript.

Blomberg, Thomas (1980) 'Widening the net: an anomaly in the evaluation of diversion programs', in M. W. Klein and K. S. Teilman (eds), *Handbook of Criminal Justice Evaluation*. London: Sage, pp. 527–92.

Blumstein, Alfred, Cohen, Jacqueline, Roth, Jeffrey A. and Visher, Christy A. (eds) (1986) *Criminal Careers and 'Career Criminals'*. Washington, DC: National Academy Press.

Bondeson, Ulla (1974) *Fången i fångsamhället. Socialisationsprocesser vid ungdoms-vårdsskola, ungdomsfängelse, fängelse och internering*. Stockholm: Norstedts. (Rev. Eng. ed., *Prisoners in Prison Societies*. Oxford: Transaction Publishers 1989.)

Bondeson, Ulla (1975) 'Evaluation of correctional treatment: a survey and critical interpretation of correctional treatment studies in Scandinavia, 1945–74'. Lund: Lunds Universitet.

Bondeson, Ulla (1977) *Kriminalvård i frihet. Intention och verklighet* (Offender Care in the Community. Intentions and Reality). Stockholm: Liber.

Bondeson, Ulla (1979) 'Det allmänna rättsmedvetandet – en legal fiktion' (The general sense of justice – a legal fiction), in U. Bondeson (ed.), *Rationalitet i rättssystemet*. Stockholm: Liber, pp. 123–43.

Bondeson, Ulla (1986) 'Frihetsberövandets verkningar – sakkunniga och experter' (The effects of the deprivation of liberty – consultants and experts), *Nordisk Tidsskrift for Kriminalvidenskab*, 73: 415–25.

Bondeson, Ulla and Kragh Andersen, Per (1986) 'Application of a survival model to recidivism data', paper presented at the XIth World Congress of Sociology, New Delhi.

Box, Steven and Hale, Chris (1982) 'Economic crisis and the rising prisoner population in England and Wales', *Crime and Social Justice*, No. 17: 20–35.

Box, Steven and Hale, Chris (1985) 'Unemployment, imprisonment and prison overcrowding', *Contemporary Crises*, 9: 209–28.

Brody, S. (1976) *The Effectiveness of Sentencing: A Review of the Literature*. London: HMSO. (Home Office Research Study, No. 35.)

BRÅ's kriminalpolitiska arbetsgrupp (1977) *Nytt straffsystem* (A New Penal System). Stockholm: Brottsförebyggande Rådet, No. 7 (BRÅ report 1977, No. 7.)

Bugge, Kjeld (1969) *Fullbyrdelsen av frihetsstraff i det 18. århundre. Fengselsvesenets historie nordenfjells i det 18. århundre* (The Execution of the Deprivation of Liberty in the 1700s. The History of the Prison System in the Northern Regions in the 1700s). Oslo: Universitetsforlaget.

Bødal, Kåre (1962) *Arbeidsskolen og dens behandlingsresultater* (The Borstal and its Treatment Results). Oslo: Universitetsforlaget.

Bødal, Kåre (1969) *Fra arbeidsskole til ungdomsfengsel – klientel og resultater* (From Borstal to Youth Prison – Clientele and Results). Oslo: Universitetsforlaget.

Bødal, Kåre (1971) 'Farlig ungdomsfengsel?' (Dangerous youth prison?). Oslo:

Feature article, *Dagbladet*, 8 July 1971.

Bødal, Kåre (1984) 'Kriminalitetsøkning, straffeutmålinger og fengselskøer' (Increase in crime, sentencing practice and prison waiting lists). Manuscript. Oslo: Justisdepartementet.

Chaiken, Jan M. and Chaiken, Marcia R. (1982) *Varieties of Criminal Behavior – Summary and Policy Implications*. Santa Monica: Rand Corporation.

Chan, Janet B.L. and Ericson, Richard V. (1981) *Decarceration and the Economy of Penal Reform*. Toronto: Centre of Criminology, University of Toronto.

Chan, Janet and Zdenkowski, George (1985) *Just Alternatives. Trends and Issues in the Deinstitutionalization of Punishment*. Sydney: Australian Law Reform Commission, Reference on Sentencing. Working Paper.

Christie, Nils (1961) 'Reaksjonenes virkninger' (The effects of sanctions), *Nordisk Tidsskrift for Kriminalvidenskab*, 49: 129–44.

Christie, Nils (1962) 'Noen kriminalpolitiske særforholdsreglers sosiologi' (The sociology of special measures in criminal policy), *Tidsskrift for samfunnsforskning*, 3: 28–48.

Christie, Nils (1971) 'Forskning om individualprevensjon kontra almenprevensjon' (Research on individual prevention as opposed to general prevention), *Lov og Rett*: 49–60.

Christie, Nils (1972) Fangevoktere i konsentrasjonsleire. En sosiologisk undersøkelse av norske fangevoktere i 'serberleirene' i Nord-Norge i 1942–43 (Prison guards in concentration camps. A sociological study of Norwegian prison guards in 'the Serbian camps' in Northern Norway 1942–43). Oslo: Pax. (MA dissertation 1952.)

Christie, Nils (1975) *Hvor tett et samfunn?* (How Dense a Society?). Oslo: Universitetsforlaget. 2nd rev.ed., 1982.

Christie, Nils (1980) 'Nyklassismens skjulte budskap' (The hidden message of neo-classicism), in S. Heckscher, A. Snare, H. Takala and J. Vestergaard (eds), *Straff och rättfärdighet. Ny nordisk debatt*. Stockholm: Norstedts, pp. 116–34.

Christie, Nils (1981) *Limits to Pain*. Oslo: Universitetsforlaget.

Christie, Nils and Bruun, Kettil (1985) *Den gode fiende. Narkotikapolitik i Norden* (The Suitable Enemy. Drug Policy in the Nordic Countries). Oslo: Universitetsforlaget.

Clemmer, Donald (1940) *The Prison Community*. New York: Holt, Rinehart and Winston.

Cohen, Jacqueline (1983) 'Incapacitation as a strategy for crime control: possibilities and pitfalls', in M. H. Tonry and N. Morris (eds), *Crime and Justice: An Annual Review of Research*, Vol. 5. Chicago: University of Chicago Press, pp. 1–84.

Cohen, Stanley (1972) *Folk Devils and Moral Panics. The Creation of the Mods and Rockers*. London: MacGibbon & Kee.

Cohen, Stanley (1979) 'The punitive city: notes on the dispersal of social control', *Contemporary Crises*, 3: 339–64.

Cohen, Stanley (1985) *Visions of Social Control. Crime, Punishment and Classifications*. Cambridge: Polity Press.

Cohen, Stanley (1986) 'Community control: to demystify or to reaffirm?' in H. Bianchi and R. van Swaaningen (eds), *Abolitionism: Towards a Non Repressive Approach to Crime*. Amsterdam: Free University Press, pp. 127–32.

Cole, Charles Woolsey (1939) *Colbert and a Century of French Mercantilism*. New York: Columbia University Press.

Conrad, John P. (1985) *The Dangerous and the Endangered*. Lexington: Lexington Books.

Cornish, D.R. and Clarke, R.V.G. (1975) *Residential Treatment and its Effects on Delinquency*. London: HMSO. (Home Office Research Study, No. 32.)

Council of Europe (1986, 1987, 1988) *Prison Information Bulletin*. Published by Council of Europe, Directorate of Legal Affairs. Strasbourg: June 1986, June 1987, June 1988.

Dittenhoffer, Tony and Ericson, Richard V. (1983) 'The victim offender reconciliation program: a message to correctional reformers', *University of Toronto Law Journal*, 33: 315–47.

Eckhoff, Torstein (1971) *Rettferdighet ved utveksling og fordeling av verdier*. Oslo: Universitetsforlaget. Eng. ed., *Justice – Its Determinants in Social Interaction*. Rotterdam: Rotterdam University Press, 1974.

Ellingsen, Dag (1987) *Kan vi stole på rettspsykiatrien? Kritisk søkelys på rettspsykiatrien* (Can We Trust Forensic Psychiatry? Critical Searchlight on Forensic Psychiatry). Oslo: Universitetsforlaget.

Falck, Sturla (1987) 'Den problematiske kriminalitetsutviklingen' (The problematical development of crime), in B. Stordrange (ed.), *Forbrytelse og straff*. Oslo: Universitetsforlaget, pp. 26–40.

Feest, Johannes (1988) 'Reducing the prison population. Lessons from the West German experience?', address at the Annual General Meeting of the National Association for Care and Resettlement of Offenders (NACRO).

Fiske, John (1982) *Introduction to Communication Studies*. New York: Methuen.

Folmer Andersen, Tavs and Balvig, Flemming (1984) 'Opvækstvilkår og senere registreret straffelovskriminalitet: En dansk forløbsundersøgelse fra 1948 til 1979 (del 2)' (Conditions during adolescence and later registered crime: a Danish sequential study from 1948 to 1979 (Part 2)). *Nordisk Tidsskrift for Kriminalvidenskab*, 71: 1–15.

Foucault, Michel (1967) *Madness and Civilization*. London: Tavistock.

Foucault, Michel (1977) *Discipline and Punish. The Birth of the Prison*. Harmondsworth: Penguin.

Frank, Jürgen (1986) 'Ökonomische Modelle der Abschreckung' (Economic models of deterrence). Manuscript. Hanover; published in abbreviated form in *Kriminologisches Journal* (1987) No. 1: 55–65.

From, Christina (1976) *Antonsensaken til salgs* (The Antonsen Case for Sale). Oslo: Institutt for rettssosiologi, Universitetet i Oslo, Institute Series No. 14.

Fängelsestraffkommittén (1986) *Påföljd för brott. Hovudbetänkande* (Reactions to Crime. Main Report). Stockholm: Liber (SOU 1986, No. 13–15.)

Galtung, Johan (1959) *Fengselssamfunnet: Et forsøk på analyse* (The Prison Society. An Attempt at an Analysis). Oslo: Universitetsforlaget.

Glaser, Daniel (1964) *The Effectiveness of a Prison and Parole System*. New York: Bobbs-Merrill.

Glueck, Sheldon and Glueck, Eleanor (1937) *Later Criminal Careers*. New York: The Commonwealth Fund.

Goffman, Erving (1961) *Asylums. Essays on the Social Situation of Mental Patients and Other Inmates*. New York: Doubleday.

Graver, Hans Petter (1986) *Den juristskapte virkelighet* (The Legal Construction of Reality). Oslo: Tano.

Greenberg, David F. (1977) 'The correctional effects of corrections. A survey of evaluations', in D. F. Greenberg (ed.), *Corrections and Punishment*. Beverly Hills, London: Sage Publications, pp. 111–48.

Greenwood, Peter W. (1987) 'Sentencing', in F. N. Dutile and C. H. Foust (eds), *The Prediction of Criminal Violence*. Springfield: Charles C. Thomas, pp. 123–36.

Greenwood, Peter W. with Abrahamse, Allan (1982) *Selective Incapacitation*. Santa Monica: Rand Corporation.

de Haan, Willem (1986) 'Explaining expansion: the Dutch case', in B. Rolston and M. Tomlinson (eds), *The Expansion of European Prison Systems*. Working Papers in European Criminology No. 7, Belfast: The European Group for the Study of Deviance and Social Control, pp. 1–15.

Hall, Stuart, Critcher, Chas, Jefferson, Tony, Clarke, John and Roberts, Brian (1978) *Policing the Crisis. Mugging, the State, and Law and Order*. London: Macmillan.

Hart, Hornell (1923) 'Predicting parole success', *Journal of Criminal Law and Criminology*, 14 (1923–4): 405–13.

Hauge, Ragnar (1982) 'Narkotika – landeplage eller syndebukk?' (Drugs – pestilence or scapegoat?), *Nordisk Tidsskrift for Kriminalvidenskab*, 69: 49–59.

Hedlund, Mary Ann (1982), *Politianmeldt momskriminalitet. En undersøkelse av de anmeldelsene som ble ferdig etterforsket i 1977*. (VAT Offences Reported to the Police. A Study of the Reports Investigated by the Police in 1977). Oslo: Universitetsforlaget.

Hellevik, Ottar (1977) *Forskningsmetode i sosiologi og statsvitenskap* (Research Method in Sociology and Political Science). (3rd ed.) Oslo: Universitetsforlaget.

Henningsen, Gustav (1981) *Heksenes advokat* (The Witches' Advocate). Copenhagen: Delta. Rev. ed. of Gustav Henningsen (1980) *The Witches' Advocate. Basque Witchcraft and the Spanish Inquisition (1609–1614)*. Reno: University of Nevada Press.

Henningsen, Gustav (1984) *Fra heksejagt til heksekult 1484–1984* (From Witch Craft to Witch Cult 1484–1984). Copenhagen: Gyldendal.

Hernes, Gudmund (1984) 'Media – Struktur, vridning, drama' (Media – structure, twisting, drama), *Nytt Norsk Tidskrift*, No. 1: 38–58.

von Hirsch, Andrew (1976) *Doing Justice. The Choice of Punishments*. Report of the Committee for the Study of Incarceration. New York: Hill & Wang.

von Hirsch, Andrew (1986) *Past or Future Crimes: Deservedness and Dangerousness in the Sentencing of Criminals*. Manchester: Manchester University Press.

Hjemdal, Ole Kristian (1987) 'Kriminalreportasjen – Myter til salgs, prosjektbeskrivelse' (Write-ups about crime – myths for sale, project description). Oslo: Institutt for rettssosiologi, Universitetet i Oslo.

Hjemdal, Ole Kristian and Risan, Leidulv (1985) *Infromasjonsvirksomhet* (Informational Activity). Report. Oslo: Kommunal og arbeidsdepartementet.

Hopson, Dan (1987) 'How well can we predict for juveniles? A review of the literature', in F. N. Dutile and C. H. Foust (eds), *The Prediction of Criminal Violence*. Springfield: Charles C. Thomas, pp. 161–8.

Hulsman, Louk (1986) 'Critical criminology and the concept of crime', *Contemporary Crises*, 10: 63–80.

Høigård, Cecilie and Balvig, Flemming (1988) *Kriminalitet og straff i tall og tekst* (Crime and Punishment in Figures and Text). Oslo: Universitetsforlaget.

'Innstilling om den sentrale politiadministrasjon' (1970) (The Aulie Report) From a committee appointed 9 September 1966 with Andreas Aulie as chairman. Printed in *Innstillinger og betenkninger*, Oslo, 1970, Part 2.

Johnsen, Jon T. (1979) 'Materialitetstenkningen i rettssosiologien' (Materialist thinking in the sociology of law). *Lov og Rett*: 257–74.

Kinsey, Richard, Lea, John and Young, Jock (1986) *Losing the Fight against Crime*. Oxford: Basil Blackwell.

Klapper, Joseph (1960) *The Effects of Mass Communication*. New York: Free Press.

Klein, Malcolm W. (1979) 'Deinstitutionalization and diversion of juvenile offenders: a litany of impediments', in N. Morris and M. H. Tonry (eds), *Crime and Justice. An Annual Review of Research*, Vol 1. Chicago: University of Chicago Press, pp. 145–201.

Klette, Hans (1982) 'Drinking and driving in Scandinavia – with an emphasis on the law and its effects'. Manuscript. Cologne.

Kohn, Melvin L. (1969) *Class and Conformity – A Study in Values*. Chicago: Dorsey.

Komitéen til å utrede spørsmålet om reformer i fengselsvesenet (1956) Innstilling (Prison Reform Commission 1956). Printed in *Innstillinger og betenkninger*, Oslo 1956, Part 1.

Kommittébetänkande (1976) No. 72 *Straffrättskommittéens betänkande* (The Report of the Penal Commission). Helsinki.

Kongshavn, Halvor (1987) *Rettspsykiatrien – slik fanger ser den* (Forensic Psychiatry – As Prisoners See It). Oslo: Universitetsforlaget.

Kristoffersen, Ragnar (1986) *Bagatellenes tyranni – samhandlingsstrukturen i et norsk fengsel* (The Tyranny of Trifles – the Interaction Structure in a Norwegian Prison). Oslo: Arbeidspsykologisk institutt.

Kuhn, Thomas (1962) *The Structure of Scientific Revolutions*. Chicago: University of Chicago Press. 2nd enl. ed., 1970.

Kutchinsky, Berl (1972) 'Aspects sociologiques de la perception de la déviance et de la criminalité' (Sociological aspects of the perception of deviance and crime). Report in *La perception de la déviance et de la criminalité. Rapports presentés a la neuvieme conférence de directeurs d'Instituts de recherches criminologiques (1971)*. Strasbourg: Council of Europe. (Études relatives à la recherche criminologique, No. 9.)

Kutchinsky, Berl (1973) '"The legal consciousness." A survey of research on knowledge and opinion about law', in A. Podgorecki, W. Kaupen, J. van Houtte, P. Vinke and B. Kutchinsky (eds), *Knowledge and Opinion about Law*. Law in Society Series. London: Martin Robertson, pp. 101–38.

Kühlhorn, Eckhart (1986) 'Allmänprevention och individualprevention' (General prevention and individual prevention), in Fängelsestraffkommittén, *Påföljd för brott. Hovudbetänkande*, Vol. 3, Stockholm: Liber (SOU 1986, No. 15), pp. 27–54.

Langelid, Torfinn (1986) 'Skole i fengslet – støtte for fangene eller fengselssystemet?' (School in prison – support to the prisoners or the prison system?), *Tidsskrift for kriminalomsorg*, No. 1: 4–11.

Lea, Henry Charles (1906) *A History of the Inquisition of Spain*. New York: AMS Press, Inc., Vol. IV. 2nd ed., 1966.

Lea, John (1987) 'In defence of realism', *Contemporary Crises*, 11: 357–70.

Lea, John and Young, Jock (1984) *What is to be Done about Law and Order?* Harmondsworth: Penguin.

Leer-Salvesen, Paul (1988) *Etter drapet. Samtaler om skyld og soning* (After the Murder. Conversations about Guilt and Atonement). Oslo: Universitetsforlaget.

Lorentzen, Håkon (1977) 'Politiopprustning – aktører, interesser og strategier', *Rætferd*, No. 5: 7–26.

McCorckle, Lloyd W. and Korn, Richard R. (1954) 'Resocialization within walls', *Annals of American Academy of Political and Social Science*, 293: 88–98.

McMahon, Maeve W. (1988a) '*Confronting Crime*: review essay' (review of Matthews and Young, 1986), *Critical Criminology*, 15: 111–21.

McMahon, Maeve W. (1988b) 'Changing penal trends. Imprisonment and Alternatives in Ontario 1951–1984.' PhD dissertation. Toronto: University of Toronto.

Martinson, Robert (1974) 'What works? Questions and answers about prison reform', *The Public Interest*: 22–54.

Mathiesen, Thomas (1965a) *The Defences of the Weak. A Sociological Study of a Norwegian Correctional Institution*. London: Tavistock.

Mathiesen, Thomas (1965b) *Tiltak mot ungdomskriminalitet. En opininionsundersøkelse* (Measures towards Juvenile Delinquency. An Opinion Study). Oslo: Universitetsforlaget. (With a summary in English).

Mathiesen, Thomas (1966) 'Konformisme og sosial klasse', (Conformism and social class), *Tidsskrift for samfunnsforskning*, 7: 19–36.

Mathiesen, Thomas (1974) *The Politics of Abolition. Essays in Political Action Theory*. Oxford: Martin Robertson.

Mathiesen, Thomas (1975) *Løsgjengerkrigen* (The Vagrancy War). Oslo: Sosionomen forlag.

Mathiesen, Thomas (1977) *Rett og samfunn* (Law and Society). (2nd rev. ed.). Oslo: Pax.

Mathiesen, Thomas (1980) *Law, Society and Political Action. Towards a Strategy under Late Capitalism*. London: Academic Press.

Mathiesen, Thomas (1982) *Kriminalitet, straff og samfunn* (Crime, Punishment and Society). (3rd rev. ed.). Oslo: Aschehoug.

Mathiesen, Thomas (1984) *Seersamfunnet. Tre essays om offentlighet* (The Viewer Society. Three Essays on the Public Sphere). Oslo: Universitetsforlaget.

Mathiesen, Thomas (1985) 'The arguments against building more prisons', in N. Bishop (ed.), *Scandinavian Criminal Policy and Criminology 1980–1985*, Copenhagen: Scandinavian Research Council for Criminology, pp. 89–98; presented on the occasion of the VIIIth UN Congress on the Prevention of Crime and the Treatment of Offenders.

Mathiesen, Thomas (1986) *Makt og medier. En innføring i mediesosiologi* (Power and Media. An Introduction to Media Sociology). Oslo: Pax.

Mathiesen, Thomas (1987) *Kan fengsel forsvares?* (Prison: Does it Have a Defence?). Oslo: Pax.

Mathiesen, Thomas and Hjemdal, Ole Kristian (1986) *Treholt-saken i offentligheten – et grunnlag for forhåndsdømming* (The Treholt Case in the Public Sphere – A Basis for Prejudgement). Oslo: Universitetsforlaget.

Matthews, Roger (1987) 'Taking realist criminology seriously', *Contemporary Crises*, 11: 371–401.

Matthews, Roger and Young, Jock (eds) (1986) *Confronting Crime*. London: Sage Publications.

Melossi, Dario and Pavarini, Massimo (1981) *The Prison and the Factory*. London: Macmillan.

Messinger, Sheldon L. and Berk, Richard A. (1987) 'Review essay: dangerous people' (review of Blumstein et al., 1986), *Criminology*, 25: 767–81.

Milgram, Stanley (1965) 'Some conditions of obedience and disobedience to authority', *Human Relations*, 18: 57–75.

Moerings, Martin (1986) 'Prison overcrowding in the United States', in B. Rolston and M. Tomlinson (eds), *The Expansion of European Prison Systems*. Working Papers in European Criminology No. 7, Belfast: The European Group for the Study of Deviance and Social Control, pp. 76–92.

Monahan, John (1981) *Predicting Violent Behaviour: An Assesment of Clinical Techniques*. London: Sage Publications.

Morris, Norval and Miller, Marc (1983) 'Prediction of dangerousness', in M. H. Tonry and N. Morris (eds), *Crime and Justice. An Annual Review of Research*,

Vol. 6. Chicago: University of Chicago Press, pp. 1–50.

Murray, Charles A. and Cox, Louis A. (1979) *Beyond Probation*. London: Sage Publications.

Olaussen, Leif Petter (1976) 'Avspeiler fengselsstraffen arbeidsmarkedssituasjonen?' (Does the use of imprisonment mirror the labour market situation?), *Sosiologi i dag*, No. 4: 32–9.

Palmer, Ted (1975) 'Martinson revisited', *Journal of Research in Crime and Delinquency*: 133–52.

Pease, K., Billingham, S. and Earnshaw, I. (1977) *Community Service Assessed in 1976*. London: HMSO. (Home Office Research Study, No. 39.)

Persson, Leif G.W. (1987) *Bostadsinnbrott, Bilstölder samt tillgrep ur och från Motorfordon* (Housebreaking, Auto Theft and Theft from Motor Cars). Stockholm: Trygg Hansa.

Regeringens proposition (1982/83, No. 85)) *Villkorlig frigivning och kriminalvård i frihet m.m.* (Government Bill (1982/83, No. 85) Conditional Release and Offender Care in the Community etc.). Stockholm.

Robison, James and Smith, Gerald (1971) 'The effectiveness of correctional programs', *Crime and Delinquency*, 17: 67–80.

Ross, Laurence H., Klette, Hans and McCleary, Richard (1984) 'Liberalization and rationalization of drunk-driving laws in Scandinavia', *Accident Analysis and Prevention*, 16: 471–87.

Rusche, Georg and Kirchheimer, Otto (1939) *Punishment and Social Structure*. New York: Columbia University Press.

Rutherford, Andrew (1974) *The Dissolution of the Training Schools in Massachusetts*. Columbus: Academy for Contemporary Problems.

Rutherford, Andrew (1986) *Prisons and the Process of Justice*. Oxford: Oxford University Press.

Scheerer, Sebastian (1986) 'Towards abolitionism', *Contemporary Crises*, 10: 5–20.

Schumann, Karl F., Berlitz, Claus, Guth, Hans W. and Kaulitzki, Rainer (1987) *Jugendkriminalität und die Grenzen der Generalprävention* (Juvenile Delinquency and the Limits of General Prevention). Cologne: Luchterhand.

Scraton, Phil (ed.) (1987) *Law, Order and the Authoritarian State*. Milton Keynes: Open University Press.

Sechrest, Lee (ed.) (1979) *The Rehabilitation of Criminal Offenders*. Washington DC: National Academy of Science.

Sellin, Thorsten (1944) *Pioneering in Penology. The Amsterdam Houses of Correction in the Sixteenth and Seventeenth Centuries*. Philadelphia: University of Pennsylvania Press.

Shinnar, Reuel and Shinnar, Shlomo (1975) 'The effects of criminal justice on the control of crime: a quantitative approach', *Law and Society Review*, 9 (1974–5): 581–611.

Sim, Joe (1986) 'Working for the clampdown. Prison and politics in England and Wales', in B. Rolston and M. Tomlinson (eds), *The Expansion of European Prison Systems*. Working Papers in European Criminology No. 7, Belfast: The European Group for the Study of Deviance and Social Control, pp. 41–62.

Simonsen, Gunnar (1976) *Pressen og virkeligheten* (The Press and Reality). Oslo: Institutt for rettssosiologi, Universitetet i Oslo, Institute Series No. 14.

Skaalvik, Einar M. and Stenby, Hans K. (1981) *Skole bak murene* (School Behind the Walls). Trondheim: Tapir.

Stangeland, Per and Hauge, Ragnar (1974) *Nyanser i grått. En undersøkelse av selvrapportert kriminalitet blant norsk ungdom* (Nuances in Grey. A Study of

Self-reported Crime among Norwegian Youth). Oslo: Universitetsforlaget.

Steadman, Henry J. (1987) 'How well can we predict violence for adults? A review of the literature and some commentary', in F. N. Dutile and C. H. Foust (eds), *The Prediction of Criminal Violence*. Springfield: Charles C. Thomas, pp. 5–17.

Stortingsmelding *Om kriminalpolitikken*, 1977–8, No. 104 (Government White Paper On the Criminal Policy, 1977–8, No. 104). Oslo: Justisdepartementet.

Straffelovrådet (1974) *Strafferettslig utilregnelighet og strafferettslige særreaksjoner* (Criminal Unaccountability and Special Penal Measures). Oslo: Universitetsforlaget (Penal Council Report NOU 1974, No. 17.)

Sykes, Gresham M. (1958) *The Society of Captives. A Study of a Maximum Security Prison*. Princeton: Princeton University Press.

Sykes, Gresham M. and Messinger, Sheldon L. (1960) 'The inmate social system', in *Theoretical Studies in Social Organization of the Prison*. New York: Social Science Research Council, pp. 5–19.

Taylor, Ian (1981) *Law and Order. Arguments for Socialism*. London: Macmillan.

Taylor, Ian (1982) 'Against crime and for socialism', *Crime and Social Justice*: 4–15.

Trasler, Gordon (1976) 'Reflections upon the use of custody', *Howard Journal*: 6–15.

Visher, Christy A. (1986) 'The Rand inmate survey. A reanalysis', in A. Blumstein, J. Cohen, J. A. Roth and C. A. Visher (eds), *Criminal Careers and 'Career Criminals'*. Washington DC: National Academy Press, Vol. 2, pp. 161–211.

Ward, David (1972) 'Myten om behandlingsfengslet' (The mythical treatment prison), in A. Syse (ed), *Kan fengsel forsvares?* Oslo: Pax, pp. 63–73.

Warner, Sam B. (1923) 'Factors determining parole from the Massachusetts reformatory', *Journal of Criminal Law and Criminology*, 14 (1923–4): 172–207.

Weber, Max (1948) *The Protestant Ethic and the Spirit of Capitalism*. London: George Allen & Unwin.

Wheeler, Stanton (1961) 'Socialization in correctional communities', *American Sociological Review*, 26: 697–712.

Wilson, Charles (1969) 'The other face of mercantilism', in D. C. Coleman (ed), *Revisions in Mercantilism*. London: Methuen, pp. 18–139.

Wilson, James Q. (1975) *Thinking about Crime*. New York: Basic Books. Rev. ed., Basic Books, 1983.

Wolf, Preben (1967) 'Innlegg i diskusjon om politieffektivitet og allmennprevensjon' (Statement in discussion on police efficiency and general prevention), in *Nordisk kontakt-seminar om politiet og kriminologien*, Brabrand, Denmark, p. 94. Stockholm: Nordisk Samarbeidsråd for Kriminologi.

Wright, Martin (1982) *Making Good. Prisons, Punishment and Beyond*. London: Burnett Books.

Young, Jock (1987) 'The tasks of a realist criminology', *Contemporary Crises*, 11: 337–56.

Young, Jock (1988) 'Radical criminology in Britain: the emergence of a competing paradigm', *British Journal of Criminology*, 28: 159–83.

Index